Political Philosophy Comes to Rick's

Political Philosophy Comes to Rick's

Casablanca *and American Civic Culture*

Edited by
James F. Pontuso

LEXINGTON BOOKS

A Division of
ROWMAN & LITTLEFIELD PUBLISHERS, INC.
Lanham • Boulder • New York • Toronto • Oxford

LEXINGTON BOOKS

A division of Rowman & Littlefield Publishers, Inc.
A wholly owned subsidiary of The Rowman & Littlefield Publishing Group, Inc.
4501 Forbes Boulevard, Suite 200
Lanham, MD 20706

PO Box 317
Oxford
OX2 9RU, UK

British Library Cataloguing in Publication Information Available

Library of Congress Cataloging-in-Publication Data

Political philosophy comes to Rick's : Casablanca and American civic culture /
edited by James F. Pontuso.
   p. cm.
   ISBN 0-7391-0832-8 (hardcover : alk. paper)—ISBN 0-7391-1113-2 (pbk. : alk.
paper)
   Includes bibliographical references and index.
   1. Casablanca (Motion picture) I. Pontuso, James F.
PN1997.C352 P65 2005
791.43/72 22   2005011738

Printed in the United States of America

⊗™ The paper used in this publication meets the minimum requirements of American
National Standard for Information Sciences—Permanence of Paper for Printed Library
Materials, ANSI/NISO Z39.48–1992.

CONTENTS

ACKNOWLEDGMENTS

I was inspired to undertake editing this book by a lecture Paul A. Cantor gave at Hampden-Sydney College in 1988. Entitled "The Closing of the America Ring: How André the Giant Has Failed Democracy," Cantor's presentation showed that much could be learned from the serious, but not too serious, study of popular culture. The Politics and Literature section of the American Political Science Association sponsored a panel with the same title as this book at the 2004 annual meeting in Chicago. I would like to thank the Committee for Professional Development at Hampden-Sydney College for financially supporting this volume. Rosalind Warfield-Brown did her typically excellent job of editing my contribution to the book, trying her best to make it better than it turned out. Serena Leigh Krombach at Lexington Books accepted this project almost as soon as I proposed it, and her editorial staff has wonderfully supported it throughout. Special thanks to Audrey Babkirk and Debbie Justice.

A revised version of Michael Palmer's chapter in this book appeared as an article in *The Maine Scholar* 16 (Winter 2004): 155-68. It is reprinted with permission.

James F. Pontuso
Charlottesville, Virginia

INTRODUCTION

JAMES F. PONTUSO

I

Casablanca began preproduction on May 25, 1942. Born under the sign of Gemini, it has two rather distinct personalities. On the one hand it is the realistic, even hard-nosed, depiction of its main character, Rick Blaine, who, though tough, can be undone by the loss of a beautiful woman. *Casablanca* is a poignant tale about love lost, regained, and lost again. It is a movie about virtue and vice, good and evil, duty and treachery, courage and weakness, friendship and hate. It is a story that ends well, but only because the main characters make a heartbreaking choice.

On the other hand the film has serious plot weaknesses. Why, for example, is the final scene at the airport shrouded in fog? Casablanca is in desert and rarely fogged in. Why are Ilsa Lund and Victor Laszlo so elegantly dressed and looking so marvelous when they reach Casablanca? Wasn't Victor recently tortured in a Nazi concentration camp? Wasn't the couple on the run from the Gestapo for a year, living in the underground network, one step ahead of arrest?

The most glaring problem with the plot has to do with the letters of transit that allow the bearer to leave Casablanca. Guillermo Ugarte says that everyone wants the letters because they are signed by General de Gaulle and "cannot be rescinded, not even questioned." Yet anyone found in possession of the documents can be arrested for the murder of the German couriers from whom they were stolen. Those who hold the letters of transit are *both* absolutely free to leave and legally constrained from escaping. Murray Burnett and Joan Alison, the authors of *Everybody Goes to Rick's* (1940), the initial title of the play on which *Casablanca* is based, expected someone to challenge them about "the absurdity of the exist visas that couldn't be canceled, but no one ever did."[1]

As Ralph S. Hattox makes clear (Chapter 2), it is unclear why General de Gaulle has any power in Casablanca at all, and, even if he has some influence, it is doubtful that the rule of law is firmly established. Ugarte has to hide the letters of transit with Rick so that he will not be arrested. When Ugarte is apprehended and dies on the first night of his captivity, Captain Renault, the prefect of police, cannot decide whether he killed himself or died trying to escape. If

Ugarte can be dispatched with such alacrity, would Major Stasser really have legal qualms about his treatment of Victor Laszlo; would he hesitate to eliminate the most dangerous enemy of the Third Reich?

Despite these failings, *Casablanca* is a great movie. But, what makes a great movie? Movies are primarily a form of entertainment, so it could be argued that the best movies are the most entertaining. Entertainment is a kind of diversion that allows us to escape from our ordinary lives. To be different than the commonplace, movies must have originality and novelty. But what is new today is passé tomorrow. The freshness of a movie plot or concept disappears almost immediately after we watch it and is certainly lost if we watch it more than once. Movies are somewhat like styles of clothing. What seems cutting edge soon looks stale and, over time, even ridiculously out of fashion.

It seems then that a great movie must be more than entertainment. It must have a lasting quality, something that keeps it from becoming outdated or appreciated only as nostalgia. *Casablanca* is perhaps the most widely viewed motion picture ever made. It is aired on television at least twice a year in nearly every television market. There is little nostalgia in *Casablanca's* continuing popularity since most of its original audience are now deceased. Critics always rank *Casablanca* among the greatest American films, often just behind *Citizen Kane*. *Casablanca* has become part of our popular culture: "Round up the usual suspects" and "Here's looking at you, kid," have become part of our popular lexicon. *Casablanca* has been imitated and parodied. Woody Allen's *Play It Again, Sam* is perhaps the best known of the *Casablanca* tributes. Although *Casablanca* has never gone out of fashion, the "*Casablanca* formula" did not work in other movies of the era, even when the same director and many of the same actors were used in such films as *Action in the North Atlantic* (1943) and *Passage to Marseille* (1944). Attempts to make *Casablanca* into a television series have proved a complete failure.

What accounts for *Casablanca's* continuing popularity? What chord does it strike with audiences? What lesson does *Casablanca* teach Americans about themselves? What influence does popular culture have on public mores? The contributors to *Political Philosophy Comes to Rick's* take up these questions. They find that *Casablanca* presents many of the most important issues of political philosophy. Perhaps *Casablanca* has an enduring quality because it is about things that interest people most. Like political philosophy, it raises many of the most enduring questions of human life, such as the nature of love, friendship, courage, honor, responsibility, and justice.

II

At what was perhaps the first panel dedicated solely to popular culture at the American Political Science Association Convention, Harvard professor Harvey C. Mansfield commented that scholars influenced by Leo Strauss—which would include many of the contributors to this book—are often accused of reading texts so closely that they make a great deal out of a very little. He noted that when they turn their attention to analyzing popular culture, they could be charged with making a big deal out of absolutely nothing. Yet Paul A. Cantor, whose thought-provoking, if occasionally tongue-in-cheek, studies of popular culture are the inspiration for this volume, maintains that popular culture should not be underestimated or overlooked. He argues that it is difficult to draw a distinction between "high culture" and "popular culture," for what is now taken to be high culture was, in its day, quite popular.

Cantor sees *Casablanca's* Rick Blaine as a romantic hero—an outsider with a noble streak—similar to those depicted in the poetry of Lord (George Gordon) Byron. Cantor does not argue that the screenwriters of *Casablanca* set out to create a Byronic hero. Rather, the themes of romantic literature permeated the popular understanding and ultimately found expression in the screenplay of *Casablanca*. It is even more evident that *Casablanca's* writers did not view their creation as a work of art, one worthy of scholarly study. They were primarily interested in entertaining their audience, making money for their studio—Warner Brothers—and, perhaps most importantly, given their bosses—Michael Curtiz, Hal Wallis, and Jack Warner—meeting their deadlines. Yet, in spite of the pressure and confusion involved in the writing of *Casablanca*, the creative team did produce something of lasting worth. Cantor argues that, although there was no single authorial genius whose intentions must be closely studied at work in *Casablanca*, the movie is worthy of serious analysis nonetheless, exactly because the writers attempted to please their audience. If there are permanent passions, interests, duties, and questions inherent to the human condition, then it is possible that in trying to please viewers, the writers also touched upon these persistent themes.

Perhaps the greatness of *Casablanca* is due to pure chance; but that does not deny its greatness. Many works of art take on a meaning beyond the intentions of their creators. The playwright Václav Havel explains the nature of intentionality as follows:

> I like it when a work can be interpreted in different ways, when it is something of an enigma and when its meaning, though it may transcend the work itself, does so by radiating in all directions, when it cannot be reduced to a straightforward conceptual formula. Art in general is a little like playing with fire; the artist deals with something without knowing precisely what it is; he creates something without knowing precisely what it "means." The work, it seems to me, should always be "cleverer" than its author, and he should ultimately be able to stand before it filled with the same sense of awe and with the same questions in his mind as someone seeing or reading it for the first time.[2]

Most of the contributors to this book attempt to understand *Casablanca* as if it were a work of political philosophy; they endeavor to explicate its deeper meaning and to grasp its significance in relation to the human condition. However, the authors do not agree on what the significance of *Casablanca* is. As Havel suggests, the movie is open to different interpretations. The diversity of opinion should not surprise us, however; for whatever unity exists in political philosophy has more to do with the questions that are raised than the answers that are provided.

The subject matter of political philosophy is the general conduct of human beings, including normative questions of action. Yet insofar as it is political, political philosophy must also consider the context in which action and thought take place. Ralph S. Hattox employs his training as a historian to provide the actual background in which the real-life people in Casablanca and therefore the fictional characters in *Casablanca* would have found themselves.

Michael Palmer not only gives an analysis of the film, he indicates that *Casablanca* epitomizes typically American principles; belief that natural rights are morally authoritative and universally applicable. He compares the cruelty and decadence of the German Major Strasser and the French Captain Renault to the uprightness of the American Rick in order to show how the ideas of relativism and nihilism—concepts introduced by German philosophers and spread to the world by French academics—have eroded belief in the moral superiority of natural rights.

Mary P. Nichols explores the relationship between love, beauty, virtue, and honor in *Casablanca* and *The English Patient* (1996). She finds that love unconnected to virtue can have destructive consequences since it neglects the responsibilities that true love—as opposed to passion—engenders between partners. She argues that duties may also extend to one's community and nation. Yet we would not have particularly satisfying lives if we sacrificed our personal happiness for the public good. *Casablanca* resolves the tension between the public and the private because its main character chooses noble action. Although Rick does not "get the girl," he can at least be gratified that his self-sacrifice earns honorable respect from his beloved, his friends, and his countrymen.

It is ironic that *The English Patient's* leading character, Count Laszlo Almásy, who proposes that people should forget their national identity and live "without maps," as unencumbered individuals, is Hungarian. Hungary is located at the very center of Europe, yet Hungarians do not speak an Indo-European language. Nomadic Hungarian tribes first arrived in Europe around 889 A.D., but no one is certain where they came from. Hungarians are even misnamed, for Europeans mistakenly believed that the Magyars—as the Hungarians call themselves—were related to the Huns who had invaded central Europe 500 years earlier under the leadership of Attila. In order to become European, Hungarians had to forget their nomadic pagan past. Their first great king, Stephen, foreseeing the difficulty of living in Europe as perpetual outsiders, forced his reluctant people to adopt Christianity. So fully did the Hungarians lose their non-European identity, that they came to live in one of the most complex multicultural societies in history—the Austro-Hungarian Empire. Ruled over by Hapsburg monarchs, Austro-Hungary included Austrians, Hungarians, Slovenes, Romanians, Czechs, Slovaks, Croats, Germans, Poles, Serbs, Roma (Gypsies), Moslems, Jews, and many other small groups too numerous to mention. Is it any wonder that Count Almásy, a man whose nation had to forget and/or moderate its national identity in order to survive, would argue in favor of abandoning national identity as a means of defining the self?

What is even more ironic about Mary Nichols' comparison of *Casablanca* with a picture whose leading character hails from Austro-Hungary is that many of the creative forces behind *Casablanca* also had connections to Austro-Hungary, including Murray Burnett, Michael Curtiz, Paul Henreid, Peter Lorre, and S. Z. "Cuddles" Sakall.

Peter Augustine Lawler argues that *Casablanca* presents an image of nobility and public spiritedness, but that it does so without expecting too much of the characters. True, Rick loses Ilsa, and Renault quits his job, but no one but the reprehensible Ugarte and the evil—but not particularly menacing—Strasser lose their lives. Rick is not expected to make the ultimate sacrifice for his country. Lawler argues that the movie does little more than reinforces the current ethos of America's leading class, bourgeois bohemians, who are eager to espouse high principles so long as few duties, and only those voluntarily acknowledged, are required.

My essay for this volume deals with a little-discussed aspect of *Casablanca*, its un-politically correct reliance on stereotypes. I argue that although stereotypes may lead us to prejudicially judge people from other cultures, we cannot ignore the power of cultures to shape individual behavior. If we dismiss every generalization about cultural traits as chauvinism, we may miss important elements of the diversity and complexity of the human condition.

My treatment of the typically American character differs from Lawler's on one important point. I argue that while Americans are more dedicated to their own interests than to those of the country most of the time, they can be roused to *real* noble action during times of crisis. As evidence of this national commitment to higher principles, I offer the many enemies of liberal democracy—America's political ideal—that have found themselves, with America's help, on the trash heap of history.

Nivedita N. Bagchi's essay on Ilsa Lund examines the sacrifices that at least one of the main characters has to make in order to sustain noble action. In the extreme circumstances created by war, Ilsa must choose between love and duty, between passion and commitment, and between self-indulgence and virtue. Bagchi argues that Ilsa is required to make the most difficult choice in the movie because her future is the most tragic. She will gain none of Rick's honor, and she will play only a supporting role in her husband's cause. Her commitment to virtue demands that she stay in a passionless marriage, always out of reach of the man she passionately loves. Bagchi maintains that Ilsa's choice has a wider meaning, for it reveals the tension that often exists between responsibility and longing.

David K. Nichols uses the career of Humphrey Bogart to open a wider discussion of nature of heroism. Bogart, of course, became a Hollywood star. His audience expected him to be a leading man. Thus, his choice of parts can provide a glimpse into what Americans thought, and perhaps still think, was "leading" or important in its archetypical heroes. Nichols traces the multifarious

American understanding of heroism through Bogart's various film roles. Americans seem to value toughness and independence, so Bogart's early gangster parts struck a chord with moviegoers. As the result of the social upheaval of the 1930s, Americans began to lose confidence in their social institutions and to question their traditional conceptions of good and evil. Bogart again captured the spirit of the times with his depiction of Sam Spade, the not-so-respectable, not-so-law-abiding private detective who always ends up doing the right thing. Nichols argues that Bogart's Rick Blaine in *Casablanca* personifies America's view of honor during the crisis of war, while Bogart's postwar films, such as *Sabrina* and *The Harder They Fall*, explore the proper balance between ambition and personal happiness in times of peace and prosperity. According to Nichols, not only did America's idea of the hero undergo change during the years of depression, war, and a return to relative peace, but Bogart's art grew and attuned iself to those changes, such that it became a good barometer of American ideals.

If Bogart represents what Americans idealize, the career of Michael Curtiz shows that the American success story is not just a myth. Curtiz had been an important director in Europe before the rise of fascism, but his Jewish heritage obliged him to emigrate to the United States. In his adopted homeland, Curtiz's talents fully bloomed; he directed more than one hundred films, including *Captain Blood*, *Kid Galahad*, *The Adventures of Robin Hood*, *Angels with Dirty Faces*, *The Third Degree*, *White Christmas*, *Yankee Doodle Dandy*, *Life with Father*, *Mildred Pierce*, *Jim Thorpe—All-American*, and *King Creole*. Paul Peterson examines Curtiz's extraordinary range and command of filmmaking. He shows that although there was some confusion during the production of *Casablanca*, an artist with clear vision and great mastery guided its creation.

Kenneth De Luca returns to the relationship between Rick's character and the American regime. He sees Rick as an exemplar of the Jeffersonian individual, someone who wants to be free, but who also wants freedom to be moral and even beautiful. Rick sacrifices his love of Ilsa for the sake of a personal autonomy; he would not really be free if he were haunted by doing the wrong thing. Like most Americans, Rick is able to combine what seems irreconcilable: freedom aimed at gratifying self-interest and freedom directed to some higher moral purpose.

Leon Harold Craig takes our discussion back to where it began; can popular culture in general and *Casablanca* in particular truly teach us anything beyond what we already know and conventionally accept? Craig says no, for a film such as *Casablanca* is meant to entertain, not elevate. Craig takes the side of Plato against the poets, insisting that it is possible for artists to create beautiful images without fully comprehending the nature of the phenomena they are presenting. For instance, although Rick may embody a kind of noble action, none of the writers of *Casablanca* had a clear notion—other than the most conventional views—of the quality of true nobility. Craig agrees with Mansfield's assessment of the study of popular culture—the contributors to this book have brought more to the film than is warranted. Political philosophy has come to Rick's, but perhaps as an uninvited guest.

NOTES

1. Aljean Harmetz, *Round Up The Usual Suspects: The Making of Casablanca—Bogart, Bergman and World War II* (New York: Hyperion, 1992), 55.
2. Václav Havel, *Letters to Olga: June 1979-September 1982*, trans. and intro. Paul Wilson (New York: Knopf, 1988), 170-71.

CHAPTER 1

"AS TIME GOES BY": *CASABLANCA*
AND
THE EVOLUTION OF A POP-CULTURE CLASSIC

PAUL A. CANTOR

I

Casablanca is a tribute to the vitality of popular culture. At the time of its release in 1942, it was both a commercial and a critical success. Audiences flocked to theaters to see it, the initial reviews were generally favorable, and it went on in 1943 to win three Oscars, for Best Picture, Best Director, and Best Screenplay. The popularity and critical reputation of *Casablanca* have only grown over the years. New genera- tions of movie viewers have continued to enjoy the film in big screen revivals, tele- vision broadcasts, and VCR and DVD reissues. In the sixty or so years since its de- but, the film has become one of the most beloved of all American movies, on the level of *The Wizard of Oz*, *It's a Wonderful Life*, and *Gone with the Wind*. At the same time, *Casablanca* has been embraced by the academy; scholars have studied the film from every angle and proclaimed it a masterpiece of the cinematic art. In rec- ognition of both the popularity and artistic reputation of *Casablanca*, the American Film Institute ranked it second in its 1998 list of the greatest American movies of all time (behind only Orson Welles's *Citizen Kane*). If one were trying to prove the viability of commercial culture, *Casablanca* could be exhibit A. The reception of the film shows that it is possible to please a mass audience and still come up with a work of artistic merit that can stand up to the most rigorous critical analysis.

Many elements had to come together to make *Casablanca* an artistic and com- mercial triumph. Of course the film's appeal to audiences rests fundamentally on the star power of Humphrey Bogart (Rick Blaine) and Ingrid Bergman (Ilsa Lund); they both light up the screen whenever they appear, and their chemistry together is of Astaire/Rogers or Tracy/Hepburn caliber. But the film is filled with marvelous performances, turned in by some of the most accomplished actors in Hollywood at the time, their ranks swelled—ironically in view of the movie's theme—by refugees from Europe, such as Conrad Veidt (Major Heinrich Strasser) and Peter Lorre (Ugarte). Just think that the stars of *The Cabinet of Dr. Caligari* and *M* have supporting roles in *Casablanca*. The Englishmen Claude Rains (Captain Louis Renault) and Sydney Greenstreet (Signor Ferrari) are key to the film's success, and Dooley Wilson is perfect as Sam the piano player. *Casablanca* was a product of the much derided studio system of Hollywood; it in fact demonstrates how effective that system could be when it came to casting. A studio's stable of actors often had the cohesion of a theatrical repertory company, and, although not all the cast members of *Casablanca* had the benefit of having worked together before, there are many scenes in which the familiarity of the actors with each other gives a natural quality to their interaction on the screen.

But as memorable as the characters of *Casablanca* are—as well as the performances of the actors who created the roles—someone had to integrate those performances into the movie as a whole; and for that task director Michael Curtiz proved well suited. A veteran of action films, such as *Captain Blood* and *The Adventures of Robin Hood*, both starring Errol Flynn, Curtiz kept the plot of *Casablanca* moving, and its effective pacing is one of the movie's great virtues. In its cinematic aspects, *Casablanca* was neither groundbreaking in the way that *Citizen Kane* was nor even particularly innovative; but the film is well shot and well edited—a typically professional Hollywood job of the 1940s. Of the many ingredients that combine to make a successful film, the contribution of the music of *Casablanca* should not be underrated. As one of the great Hollywood composers, Max Steiner drew upon the leitmotif technique of Richard Wagner's operas and achieved many subtle effects of mood painting and psychological commentary in his score. In fact, for a movie that is not a musical, *Casablanca* relies to a surprising extent on music to advance the drama. When people remember the film, they inevitably think of the song "As Time Goes By," so integral is the tune to the unfolding of the love story of Rick and Ilsa.

Thus *Casablanca* scores well in all the categories that typically contribute to a movie's success—star power, colorful characters, remarkable acting performances, effective direction, skilled cinematography, a good score, and even a hit tune.[1] But what really elevates *Casablanca* into a movie classic and a genuine work of art is the strength of its screenplay, which is also what makes the film worthy of sustained scholarly attention. Thanks to the contribution of Julius and Philip Epstein, the script of *Casablanca* sparkles with wit and pointed repartee. The screenplay is so well written that an extraordinary number of its lines have stuck with viewers; phrases like "the usual suspects" have become part of our language. But even more remarkable than the sharpness of the dialogue in *Casablanca* is the seriousness of the subject matter the film explores. To be sure, the film is Hollywood entertainment and was marketed for its escapist value as an adventure story.[2] But *Casablanca* violates our expectations for an escapist Hollywood production. The world looked like a grim place in 1942, and American audiences were going to movies to leave their troubles behind them. But far from ignoring the troubled state of the world in 1942, *Casablanca* made its original audience look right in its face.

It is remarkable how many of the problems that confronted the world in 1942 come up in *Casablanca*. The movie opens with a powerful evocation of the massive refugee problem that German conquests in Europe had created, and the film in fact centers on the plight of political refugees trying to escape Nazi persecution. It even refers frequently to Nazi concentration camps at a time when most Americans were unaware of the problem, or at least not focused on it. *Casablanca* intervenes specifically in some of the most heated political controversies of its day. For example, the film unequivocally condemns the collaborationist policies of the Vichy government in France, most pointedly in the moment early in the film when one of the usual suspects is brutally shot down right in front of a poster of Marshal Pétain (the leader of the Vichy puppet regime).[3] As if to remind the French of how they are betraying their own cherished ideals, the camera pans to a sign on the Palace of Justice proclaiming the French Revolution slogan that translates as "liberty, equality, fraternity."

Above all, *Casablanca* sought to intervene in the debate over whether America should remain neutral in World War II. Of course by the time the film came out, this debate had been rendered moot by the Japanese attack on Pearl Harbor[4]—indeed, the film was given a publicity boost when Churchill and Roosevelt chose to hold a war conference in Casablanca. But still, the script of *Casablanca* clearly refers to the neutrality debate, in a retrospective effort to show why those who had argued for America staying out of the war were wrong. As an American thrust in the middle of the Old World's troubles in Casablanca, Rick Blaine tries very hard to avoid becoming involved in them. When quizzed by Captain Renault about whether he will intervene on behalf of one of the suspicious characters in Casablanca, Rick says: "I stick my neck out for nobody."[5] When Renault calls this "a wise foreign policy," he directs us from Rick's personal attitude to the more general issue of U.S. involvement in European affairs. As if to highlight the issue, shortly thereafter a conversation among Rick, Renault, and Major Strasser keeps returning to the word *neutral*; the Frenchman says: "Rick is completely neutral about everything," but the German corrects him, telling Rick: "You weren't always so carefully neutral." Strasser is referring to facts about Rick's background that frequently come up in the film. As Renault reminds him at one point: "In 1935 you ran guns to Ethiopia; in 1936 you fought in Spain on the loyalist side." *Casablanca* keeps raising the issue of American neutrality and clearly argues against it. The film shows that Rick was right when he took an active and heroic part in European affairs and he is wrong when he subsequently tries to steer clear of them.[6] The plot of *Casablanca* culminates in Rick's decision to suppress his personal concerns and do something for the cause of humanity by saving the life of the anti-Nazi freedom fighter Victor Laszlo (Paul Henreid). For all its sheer entertainment value, *Casablanca* was one of the most effective pro war, anti-Nazi propaganda films Hollywood turned out in the 1940s.

As the representative American in the film, Rick Blaine is a very interesting figure and more complex than most Hollywood heroes of the 1940s. In a wartime propaganda film, one might have expected a more straightforward heroic type, eager to sacrifice himself from the beginning for truth, justice, and the American way. But *Casablanca* makes its point all the more effectively with a character like Rick. It shows that even an American expatriot—for some mysterious reason Rick cannot return to the United States—must learn to act patriotically, with the clear implication that "If Rick can do it, any American can." But the complexity of Rick's character, the mixture of cynicism and idealism, seems calculated to make a larger point, a prediction about the outcome of World War II. We must remember that 1942 was a dark time in the war, and with German and Japanese troops doing well on all fronts, an Allied victory was by no means assured. The Nazis in *Casablanca* exude confidence, and their ability to project themselves as winners attracts many fence sitters to their side.

The film wants to show that if Americans will cast their lot against the Nazis, Germany will be defeated; but it must make this outcome seem plausible. And here *Casablanca* is very canny in suggesting, contrary to standard Hollywood mythology, that if America is to prevail in World War II, it will not simply be due to the superiority of its democratic ideals, but will somehow involve beating the enemy at its own game. And that will be a tough business, requiring tough guys like Rick Blaine. Under the leadership of Woodrow Wilson, America had characterized its intervention in World War I as idealistic, and the label had largely stuck to describe Americans throughout the 1920s and '30s. But the problem with idealism is that it passes over easily into naïveté, and, by comparison with worldly-wise Europeans, Americans often looked too unsophisticated to deal with the complexities of world politics. Thus it is very important that Rick Blaine not be the typical American hero of Hollywood—young, fresh faced, idealistic, uncorrupted by the world. Given the enemies he is going to have to face, he must be experienced in the ways of the world, to the point of world weariness, and capable of cunning and deception. *Casablanca* seems intent on showing how the overconfident Nazis are prone to underestimate Americans. In one scene between Rick and the Nazis, they brag about their takeover of Paris and suggest that London will soon fall under their control. When Strasser taunts Rick with the prospect that New York might be next on the Nazi agenda, the American calmly threatens him back: "There are certain sections of New York, Major, that I wouldn't advise you to try to invade." Here *Casablanca* brilliantly exploits the casting of Humphrey Bogart as Rick Blaine. Bogart was well known for playing tough gangsters in movies in the 1930s, and he in effect invokes his cinematic past at this moment to remind viewers that not all Americans are childlike and naïve.[7] Rick's association with American gangsterism, far from undermining his heroic status, actually points to his ultimate triumph over the Nazis. His gangster-like background—he is after all a saloon keeper and runs an illegal, and crooked, gambling operation—gives him the skills necessary to outwit Major Strasser and save Victor Laszlo. The subliminal message of *Casablanca* held out hope for the Allied cause: "Americans are not the naïve idealists Europeans and especially the Nazis think they are; Americans are tough guys, and they will fight fire with fire."

II

This brief discussion of the character of Rick Blaine suggests that *Casablanca* does repay close analysis, and the other essays in this volume take up the challenge of exploring what the movie can teach us about a whole range of political, philosophical, and other questions. And yet many might still balk at the idea of taking a Hollywood movie this seriously. Can we really learn something about a subject as important and complex as American character by talking about a film whose primary purpose was to please an audience and earn money at the box office? Should we analyze a work of popular culture with the same care we would apply to a work of high culture? Here *Casablanca* can be particularly helpful in opening up the serious study of popular culture, because this example can show us how artificial and arbitrary our conventional efforts to distinguish high culture from popular culture turn out to be.

 Casablanca seems to be situated squarely in the realm of popular culture, and yet in at least one respect the film reaches back into the realm of what we think of today as high culture. Rick Blaine is a late avatar of one of the central cultural icons of nineteenth-century Europe—the Byronic hero.[8] This claim may seem at first hard to believe—Rick, as we have seen, appears to be a distinctively American figure and as played by Bogart became a cultural icon of the twentieth century. How could this hero of American pop-culture have his roots in European high culture? And yet, as we shall see by a brief review of Byron's career, Rick Blaine fits the archetype of the Byronic hero very well. This ceases to be surprising once one recalls that Byron was the most popular poet in Europe in the nineteenth century. Thus the Byronic hero entered the world of nineteenth-century popular culture and gradually suffused it, penetrating into the most popular artistic media of the day, the opera and the novel. Having saturated popular culture in the nineteenth century, the archetype of the Byronic hero was available for a similar role in the twentieth century. The figure keeps reappearing in movies and television shows, in part because they often remake and rework nineteenth-century novels that featured Byronic heroes, like Emily Brontë's *Wuthering Heights* or Charlotte Brontë's *Jane Eyre*. The story of Rick Blaine as Byronic hero is worth examining, because it reveals the subterranean circulation between popular culture and high culture, often obscured by academic efforts to keep the two realms separate.

 Byron's poetry, as well as the nineteenth-century novels and operas derived from it, was in fact the popular culture of its day and has only been retroactively baptized as high culture by twentieth-century critics. In short, the very distinction between high culture and popular culture is largely an optical illusion—a trick of temporal perspective. Today's high culture is often simply yesterday's popular culture, elevated by academics and other cultural gatekeepers out of its original context to be enshrined on a kind of museum pedestal. No art form seems more highbrow to contemporary Americans than opera, and yet in the nineteenth century it was routinely scorned by cultural critics as vulgar and what we would call lowbrow. What opera was to the nineteenth century, the motion picture was to the twentieth, and thus we should not be surprised to see the Byronic hero migrate from the opera to the motion picture.[9] Examining Rick Blaine as a Byronic hero will help us break out of our tendency to view high culture and pop culture as two entirely distinct realms.

Byron introduced the figure that grew into what we know as the Byronic hero in the poem that made him famous, *Childe Harold's Pilgrimage*, the first portions of which were published in 1812. He went on to develop the archetype in a series of so-called "Oriental" tales: *The Giaour* (1813), *The Bride of Abydos* (1813), *The Corsair* (1814), and *Lara* (1814). These poems were amazingly popular, selling thousands of copies and establishing new records for the circulation of poetry. As Peter Thorslev points out:

> Each romance was immediately and astonishingly successful. *The Giaour* . . . by December [of its first year of publication] had gone through seven editions. *The Bride* sold six thousand copies in a month. *The Corsair*, the most successful, . . . sold ten thousand copies on the day of publication ("a thing perfectly unprecedented," as [Byron's publisher John] Murray remarked), and in just over a month it had gone through seven editions totaling twenty-five thousand copies. *Lara*, even after the first enthusiasm for these works had waned, sold six thousand copies in five days.[10]

The Byronic hero is featured in most of the narrative poems and plays Byron wrote for the rest of his life, and he was able to ring an extraordinary series of changes on this one motif. Typically, the Byronic hero leads an outlaw existence, living on the fringes of society and often engaged in some kind of illegal, or at least morally questionable, activity. He may be a bandit, a pirate, a black magician, a rebel leader, or even the first murderer, Cain. His past is almost always mysterious, and we do not know exactly what drove him to a life of crime or why he cannot fit into conventional society. He may be some kind of alien—for example, a Christian in a Muslim world. He often seems to be in a state of exile, unable to return home, because of some nameless crime or transgression. He has a cruel streak and usually has blood on his hands, but he also has a tender side and broods over his crimes. He may be wracked with guilt or remorse for something he did in the past. As criminal as he may have become in the present, we usually get a sense that he once was noble and acted out of admirable motives. If he now seems bitter and cynical, we feel that it is a result of his youthful idealistic impulses having been thwarted. For example, in a late version of the Byronic hero in *Don Juan*, Byron portrays a pirate named Lambro who has become a vicious slave trader, but who in his youth fought worthily in the name of Greek independence from the Ottoman Empire; as Byron writes: "His country's wrong and his despair to save her / Had stung him from a slave to an enslaver."[11] Because the Byronic hero retains elements of his original nobility even in his degradation—above all, his courage, his force of character, and, one might add, his good looks—he remains attractive to women, often fatally so. Indeed, he worries that he might cause the death of anyone he loves. He sometimes gets involved with more than one woman at once, and he also has a knack for ending up in love triangles, competing with a rival male for a woman's affections.

One only has to give this kind of thumbnail sketch of the Byronic hero to realize that with a few twists Rick Blaine is a modern cinematic version of the type. Indeed, a line Ilsa speaks to Rick—"One woman has hurt you and you take your revenge on the rest of the world"—could be the motto for a whole series of Byron's poems. Ilsa almost seems to be aware that she is dealing with the Byronic archetype when she tells Rick: "Strange: I know so very little about you"—a sentiment that a long line of Byron's heroines might echo. But for me the clincher in the identification of Rick as a Byronic hero comes in one of Renault's most famous speeches to his American friend: "I have often speculated on why you don't return to America. Did you abscond with the church funds? Did you run off with a senator's wife? I like to think that you killed a man—it's the romantic in me." When Rick replies: "It was a combination of all three," he could be defining the Byronic hero. Indeed Renault has run through the whole gamut of the Byronic hero's typical transgressions, and although he is almost certainly talking about being a romantic with a small *r*, one might detect a covert tribute to Byron's Romanticism in this speech. Renault sounds as if he has been reading Byron when he tells Rick: "Under that cynical shell, you're at heart a sentimentalist." Finally, the orientalism of *Casablanca* is a particularly Byronic touch, recognizing the value of an exotic setting to a heroic tale.

I am not claiming that the writers of *Casablanca* were scholars of the Romantic period or even necessarily familiar with Byron's poetry. As I have suggested, the Byronic hero quickly moved from Byron's already popular poetry into the most popular forms of nineteenth-century culture, and countless novels and operas wove the figure into the fabric of European and American consciousness. Melville's Captain Ahab is a variant of the Byronic hero, and some of Hemingway's heroes fit the mold as well. Thus when the writers of *Casablanca* sat down to develop the character of Rick Blaine, even as Americans they had the archetype of the Byronic hero at their disposal. Moreover, as originally conceived, the figure of the Byronic hero answered to a cultural need remarkably similar to what the creators of *Casablanca* experienced. To use a twentieth-century term, Byron and the Byronic hero were products of a lost generation. Byron grew up in an era of disenchantment and disillusion, as he witnessed first the failure of the French Revolution to live up to its professed ideals and then the horrors of the Napoleonic Wars. He saw Napoleon originally present himself as the champion of the French Revolution and the liberator of Europe, only to have to watch him turn into a despot himself, indeed to have himself crowned Emperor in the image of the old regime he had at first challenged. As a rebel who turned into a tyrant, Napoleon provided one of the models for the Byronic hero and his twisting of initially idealistic impulses into cynical cruelty.

One reason for the immense popularity of Byron's poetry is that it managed to capture the mood of his generation, embittered by two decades of revolutionary and counterrevolutionary violence. One cannot draw exact parallels between the experiences of Byron's generation and that of the famous Lost Generation that developed in the aftermath of World War I. And yet the two generations do have much in common in their experience of senseless warfare and failed revolutions. Given the idealistic hopes raised by World War I as the war to end all wars, Europeans and Americans in the 1920s and '30s had much to be disillusioned about, especially as the portents of World War II began to multiply. Although the details are only hinted at in *Casablanca*, this is the experience that Rick Blaine is presented as having gone through; he has even participated in the great lost cause of the American Left in the 1930s—he fought on the republican side in the Spanish Civil War. It is no accident, then, that Rick Blaine should resemble the Byronic hero. He is cut out of the same cloth and has undergone the same kind of experience. This is precisely the value of cultural archetypes and explains why they persist over long periods of time, and especially why the Byronic hero migrated from high to popular culture. Created to come to terms with the embittering experience of the first two decades of the nineteenth century, the Byronic hero was available to capture once again the disillusionment of revolutionary idealism when similar circumstances recurred in the twentieth century.

III

I have tried to make a case for taking *Casablanca* seriously as a work of art by showing how a category from what we usually think of as high culture—the Byronic hero—is applicable to this pop-cultural phenomenon. But my invocation of Byron might provoke another form of objection to any serious attempt at analyzing *Casablanca*. Whatever we might say about the popularity of Byron's poetry and the way it spoke to his generation, the fact remains that Byron wrote it, and we can feel comfortable using all the sophisticated techniques of literary analysis in trying to understand Byron's works. But who wrote *Casablanca*? I have spoken about two of the credited screenplay writers, the Epstein brothers, but they were by no means solely responsible for the script of the movie. Like almost every product of Hollywood, *Casablanca* was a corporate effort, and many different people had a hand in determining the shape the movie took. Indeed the history of the genesis of *Casablanca* may seem unusually complicated, but in fact it is fairly typical of how a film gets made in Hollywood.

First of all, *Casablanca* was derived from a work originally intended for another medium, a stage-play called *Everybody Comes to Rick's*, written by Murray Burnett and Joan Alison. When the Warner Brothers studio bought the rights to this play, the job of adapting it to the screen was given to Julius and Philip Epstein. But when the Epstein brothers were summoned to work on Frank Capra's *Why We Fight*, the screenplay was turned over to another Hollywood writer named Howard Koch. Roughly, the Epstein brothers were responsible for the first half of the story and Koch for the second half. But another studio writer, Casey Robinson (who did not get a screenplay credit), was asked to integrate the two halves. In the process, he came up with the idea for the Paris flashback; thus he was responsible for many of the most romantic scenes in *Casablanca*. Later the Epstein brothers returned to the project and in particular worked on the end of the movie. To make matters even more complicated, throughout the filming of *Casablanca*, both the director, Michael Curtiz, and the producer, Hal Wallis, felt entitled and indeed compelled to make alterations in the script. These are the principal figures who had a say in shaping the plot and dialogue of *Casablanca*; no doubt others were involved.[12] But even the eight names I have mentioned are enough to start people thinking: "too many cooks spoil the broth." If so many people worked on the script of *Casablanca*—and the record shows that they were often at odds with each other, even over basic matters of plot—how could the film end up a unified work of art? The idea of taking *Casablanca* seriously as an aesthetic object seems to fly in the face of all our notions of what constitutes art.

Our basic model of artistic creation is derived from the Romantic poets. A poem, and by extension any work of art, becomes a perfectly unified organic whole because it is created by an artistic genius who has a vision of that whole and can suit every part of the work to his vision of the whole. We have thus come to associate the idea of artistic perfection with the idea of a single creator, the solitary genius of the Romantic tradition.[13] We have been taught to regard any interference with the autonomy of the creative genius as a corruption of art. Only when artists are left to go their own way will they be able to remain true to their aesthetic visions and produce genuinely unified works of art. In particular, in this understanding of art, nothing is more antithetical to the true aesthetic spirit than the demands of commerce. Any attempt by artists to please the paying public will lead them to compromise their visions and debase their art to the low level of the marketplace. The idea of the autonomy of art was developed at just the time when the characteristic forms of modern commercial culture were beginning to emerge (the late eighteenth and early nineteenth centuries), and the notion of the artist as necessarily creating in isolation was promoted precisely as a way of shielding artists from these new commercial pressures.[14]

It is this Romantic conception of art as the product of the solitary genius that interferes with our understanding and appreciation of popular culture. People look at the typical production process in the motion picture industry and conclude that no genuine work of art could result from such conditions. With so many people involved in a typical Hollywood production, any form of artistic integrity is said to be impossible, and commercial considerations are assumed to trump aesthetic considerations. A film takes the shape it does, not in accord with a single artist's vision, but with the corporate goal of making money by pleasing the public. This view of the Hollywood culture industry led to the development in the 1950s of the auteur theory of film in France—the idea that a motion picture can be a genuine work of art only when a single artistic genius bucks the studio system, usually a director who writes his own screenplay and oversees every aspect of the film making, like a Charlie Chaplin, an Orson Welles, a Federico Fellini, or an Ingmar Bergman.[15] But *Casablanca* is not the work of an auteur-director; rather it is, as we have seen, a product of the Hollywood studio system. If the Romantic theory of art in general, and the auteur theory of film making in particular, are true, then *Casablanca* cannot be a genuine work of art, and to devote serious analysis to the film would seem to be a waste of time.

The idea that the conditions of production in Hollywood are antithetical to the true spirit of art has a certain plausibility. We have a hard time imagining how a genuine work of art could be produced by a committee. And the American film industry has certainly turned out many movies over the years that lack any artistic merit and were clearly designed only to make money. Many of the people involved in film making, and especially directors and screenwriters, have often complained about how producers and studio executives forced them to compromise their integrity as artists. But even if the studio system was heavily stacked against the achievement of artistic quality, that does not mean that it simply precluded any form of artistic achievement in Hollywood. There may well be more than one viable model of artistic creation. The evidence shows that many great works of art have been produced by more or less solitary geniuses. But perhaps it is also possible for art to be a cooperative enterprise. One can imagine ways in which several people collaborating on a work of art might not cancel out each other's efforts but instead produce a form of synergy.

That is evidently what happened in the case of *Casablanca*, or else the film could not be so good. One might conclude on various theoretical grounds that it cannot be a work of art, but the evidence of watching it tells a different story. Anyone who views the film, as most people do, with no knowledge of the history of its genesis, would never guess how many troubles beset the production and in particular how much its creators quarreled over the script. In fact to most viewers *Casablanca* appears to be a seamless work of art, with all its elements fitting together beautifully. Many critics have analyzed the film as if it were a Romantic poem, with each part having a carefully defined place in the whole. Here is a sample critical encomium: "Every gesture, every turn of the head is important. *Casablanca* is that rare movie miracle, a film with not one inconsequential frame, not one insignificant line of dialogue. . . . Don't even consider blinking during this film, in which every moment is inextricable from the whole."[16] What all this tells us is that we must expand our understanding of the preconditions of art. Artistic perfection may often be the result of a single genius carefully planning out his creation in advance. But *Casablanca* was the product of a process, involving many people working together over a long period of time, and the film only gradually took shape, with many false starts and midstream corrections. It was not the product of a single moment of perfect artistic conception, but that does not mean that the film could not be perfected over time. To borrow terminology from another field, the best way to understand the genesis of *Casablanca* is not using a creationist model, but an evolutionary one. In order to understand how some commercial movies can be as artistically successful as they are, we need to study how the conditions of production in Hollywood allow for feedback processes that actually improve the final product, instead of corrupting it, as the auteur theory would suggest. *Casablanca* is a good place to begin this investigation.

All accounts of the making of *Casablanca* stress the mood of uncertainty that surrounded the production. The conditions on the set were chaotic, with the script changing from day to day and production falling behind schedule. Up until almost the last moment, no one was even sure how the film was going to end, above all whether Ilsa was going to leave with Victor or Rick in the final scene. This uncertainty unnerved Ingrid Bergman; her daughter, Pia Lindstrom, reports that her mother complained that the film makers "didn't seem to know what they had in mind." Feeling that she needed to know how the film would end in order to play the part of Ilsa properly, Bergman finally confronted the Epstein brothers: "Who do I go off with at the end, Henreid or Bogart?" As Julius reports, all they could reply was: "As soon as we know, we'll let you know." That line seems to capture the spirit of the production of *Casablanca*. Like many of the best Hollywood movies, the film was basically a product of improvisation, rather than of elaborate preplanning. The movie took shape only as people worked on it. The production team kept bouncing ideas off each other and looked at what did or did not work on the screen. The success of the production depended on a variety of feedback mechanisms, which allowed the creators of the film to test their ideas and correct them as they went along. And here is the real surprise for partisans of the Romantic theory of art—in the end it was commercial pressures that had a disciplining effect on the creation of *Casablanca* and in effect forced the film into shape. The fact that everybody working on *Casablanca* wanted it to be a financial success (and had a stake in that success) compelled them to resolve their differences and work out the proper structure of the film. In this case, commercial and artistic demands turned out to be in harmony.[17]

In order to document this claim, I will look at one scene of *Casablanca* where we have an unusually full account of how it came into being. Fortunately, it is the final scene, one of the most celebrated moments in the history of motion pictures. The airport scene of *Casablanca* has been paid the ultimate compliment in Hollywood—it has been endlessly copied and parodied, culminating in its brilliant recreation in Woody Allen's tribute to Humphrey Bogart, *Play It Again, Sam.* If there is one moment in *Casablanca* that is responsible for the film's lasting fame, it is the airport scene. According to conventional aesthetic theory, one would have thought that this scene was carefully preplanned, that indeed the makers of the film had it in mind from the very beginning and designed the whole film to build up to it. But, as we have seen, nothing could be further from the truth. During much of the production process, *Casablanca* did not have an ending, much to the consternation of all the participants. The pressure kept building until the Epstein brothers felt that they had to come up with something.

As Julius Epstein tells the story,[18] the breakthrough came one day when he was driving to the studio with his brother, and they suddenly turned to each other and said simultaneously: "Round up the usual suspects." Contrary to what we might have thought, this famous line did not follow from the logic of the action in the final scene, but just the opposite—the Epstein brothers began with the line and worked up the plot to make it appropriate. They decided that the scene would have to feature a murder to justify the key line. As Epstein reconstructs their thought process, they asked themselves: "Who does the audience want to see murdered?" Their answer was: "Major Strasser." Their next question was: "Who do they want to see kill Major Strasser?" Their answer was: "Humphrey Bogart." Epstein reports their final question: "And who do they want to see round out the whole thing?" And the Epstein brothers concluded: "Claude Rains with the line 'Round up the usual suspects.'" Such was the genesis of perhaps the most famous concluding scene in any movie. It is regarded as a perfect moment of cinematic art, and yet the Epstein brothers thought it up at the spur of the moment.

What is even more interesting about this account is the fact that the Epstein brothers were led to their conception of the final scene of *Casablanca* by following, not the inner voice of artistic conscience, but the lead of their audience. At each stage, they imagined what the movie viewers wanted and made sure that as screenwriters they delivered. According to the Romantic theory of art, this was a betrayal of artistic integrity and a sellout to commercialism, and it should have resulted in an aesthetically unsatisfying ending to the film. But in fact no one can imagine *Casablanca* ending any differently than it does; every touch in the final scene seems perfectly calculated to bring the movie to the proper close. The Epstein brothers have shown that the customer is not always wrong, and setting out to please an audience may result in the correct artistic decisions. This may come as a shock to certain aestheticians, but there really is a logic to the Epstein brothers' procedure. Audience expectations are to a great extent generic expectations. People come to expect a certain ending because they have seen many films, have subliminally learned how a given genre of film works, and thus know instinctively how a plot should be properly resolved. As the Epstein brothers viewed it, they were merely articulating what their hypothetical audience wanted, thereby discovering what the genre they were working in demanded. The Epstein brothers were not thinking of themselves as Romantic magicians pulling an ending to *Casablanca* out of thin air. On the contrary, they thought of themselves as humble craftsmen, shaping a film to order, and their goal was to find the end to the film that was in some sense already there—implicit in the material. Imagining what their audience wanted was as a good a way as any to find that ending. This is not the Romantic way of thinking about art, but it is just as valid a model, and in this case the end truly justified the means.

But the story of the ending of *Casablanca* was not yet over. After the final scene was shot, the Epstein brothers were dismayed to be approached on the studio lot by both Michael Curtiz and Hal Wallis, with the ominous words: "Your ending does not work." They viewed the footage and immediately diagnosed the problem; the director had cut too quickly to "Round up the usual suspects." Julius Epstein explained to Curtiz his error: "You can't do that. You've got to show a shot of Bogart waiting, a shot of Rains looking, and then back and forth, and then he says" the famous line. And that is how the scene is cut in the version with which we are all familiar; sometimes a director has to listen to his writers.[19] But the producer of a movie in those days had the final say, and Hal Wallis was not yet through with *Casablanca*. A few weeks after production closed, he decided the film needed one more concluding line. The rest is motion picture history. Wallis brought Bogart back to overdub the very final words: "Louis, I think this is the beginning of a beautiful friendship."[20] Look at the scene the next time you view the movie: Bogart's back is to the camera as he delivers the immortal line, and dubbing it in was a cinematic piece of cake. But, as we all know, it was also the frosting on the cake, and *Casablanca* would not be *Casablanca* without those words. They seem completely integral to the scene, indeed the perfect ending, and yet we now know that they were an afterthought, and from the producer, not the writers or the director. According to the auteur theory, producers are supposed to ruin films, not improve them.[21] But Hal Wallis knew a thing or two about movies, and his instinct about how to end *Casablanca* turned out to be correct.

Casablanca may be a pretty picture, but the story of its production is not. If one merely heard the tale of how the ending was cobbled together, one would expect it to have been botched. Under pressure to finish the film on time, the writers, the director, and the producer all fiddled with the ending, sometimes working at cross purposes, and usually with an eye to audience reaction and, hence, box office results. According to the Romantic aesthetic, this is not supposed to be the way to produce genuine art. But the proof of the picture is in the viewing, and of course the end of *Casablanca* works very well indeed, as does the whole movie. The production history of *Casablanca* is an object lesson in aesthetics, in how we need to broaden our conception of the artistic process. Production in Hollywood may be different from the creation of Romantic poetry, but that does not mean that commercial movies cannot in their own way be works of art. The conditions of production in Hollywood may normally work against genuine artistic achievement, but when everything fell into place, the studio system could function in positive ways. The producer, the director, and the writers of *Casablanca* worked together as a team, united by commercial motives, and they kept experimenting with the elements of the movie until they got things right. Ultimately all that matters is the final product—if the movie coheres artistically, how it came into being should not trouble us. Obviously a great deal of artistic talent went into the making of *Casablanca*, even if it was deployed in ways that depart from norms familiar to us in certain forms of high culture.

Thus we are justified in taking *Casablanca* seriously as a work of art and analyzing it with the care we would devote to a novel or a poem, even if it was produced differently. Different media in fact require different modes of production. And the people who worked on the film certainly approached their task in all seriousness; they knew very well that they were dealing with a grave subject. As we have seen, from the beginning they were determined to take up some of the most important and disturbing issues of their day. Exploring the implications and full ramifications of the ways *Casablanca* deals with these issues is the task of the essays in this book. Together they are the best evidence of the way that *Casablanca* managed to combine artistic depth with commercial success.

NOTES

1. "As Time Goes By" was not in fact written for *Casablanca*, but originally came out in 1931; it was not especially successful at that time. The fame of the song clearly rests on its use in *Casablanca*.

2. The adventure aspects of the film were stressed in the original theatrical trailer; it in fact begins: "If you are looking for adventure, you will find it in *Casablanca*." The escapist angle in the marketing of the film is evident in producer Hal Wallis's decision to name it *Casablanca*, an attempt to capitalize on the success of the 1938 film *Algiers*, starring Hedy Lamarr and Charles Boyer and featuring the famous Casbah.

3. This aspect of the film was not lost on contemporary reviewers. *The New York Times* reviewer, Bosley Crowther, wrote of *Casablanca*: "It certainly won't make Vichy happy—but that's just another point for it," as quoted in Gail Kinn and Jim Piazza, *Four-Star Movies: The 101 Greatest Films of All Times* (New York: Black Dog & Lewenthal, 2003), 19. Incidentally, *Casablanca* also comes in second in this list, this time behind Coppola's *Godfather* films.

4. The action of *Casablanca* takes place in December 1941, a fact revealed by an offhand remark Rick makes to Sam; Rick's subsequent comment—"I bet they're asleep all over America"—takes on a larger meaning in this context, pointing to the initial blindness of many Americans to the threat the new world war represented to their country.

5. I have transcribed all my quotations from *Casablanca: Two-Disc Special Edition*, (Warner Home Video, 2003). This DVD set is invaluable to the study of *Casablanca*, with a beautifully restored print of the film and bonus material that illuminates it from many angles. The documentary "You Must Remember This: A Tribute to *Casablanca*" is especially helpful in analyzing the film, and all uncredited quotations in this essay, especially the reminiscences of Julius Epstein, are taken from this documentary. The DVD also includes a section called "Production Research," which contains an academic treasure trove of documents, chiefly the surviving studio correspondence concerning *Casablanca*, as well as contemporary publicity material.

6. In another exchange that draws upon the language of foreign policy debate in a personal situation, Signor Ferrari tells Blaine: "My dear Rick, when will you realize that in this world to-day isolationism is no longer a practical policy?"

7. Among the highlights of Bogart's career as a movie gangster are *The Petrified Forest* (1936), *Dead End* (1937), *The Roaring Twenties* (1939), and *High Sierra* (1941). In a studio press release dated September 1942, written by Ezra Goodman and titled "Exit the 'Bogey'-Man," Bogart is quoted as saying: "This gangster stuff is old hat to me. I've been playing mobsters and gunmen for eight years now in more than thirty pictures. . . . All of a sudden I'm a hero."

8. For a general overview of this subject, see Peter L. Thorslev Jr., *The Byronic Hero: Types and Prototypes* (Minneapolis: University of Minnesota Press, 1962).

9. Probably the two most famous operatic incarnations of the Byronic hero based directly on Byron are Giuseppe Verdi's *Il Corsaro* (from *The Corsair*) and *I Due Foscari* (from *The Two Foscari*).

10. Thorslev, *Byronic Hero*, 146.

11. Byron, *Don Juan*, canto iii, stanza 53, lines 423-24; text taken from Jerome J. McGann, ed., *The Oxford Authors: Byron* (Oxford: Oxford University Press, 1986), 501.

12. This account of the writing of *Casablanca* is based on the DVD documentary. A similar account, with some variation in the details, is given in Jack Stillinger, *Multiple Authorship and the Myth of Solitary Genius* (Oxford: Oxford University Press, 1991), 175. Stillinger mentions another contributing writer, Aeneas McKenzie, and also discusses the effect censorship by the infamous Breen Office had in shaping the script of *Casablanca* (a matter also discussed in the DVD documentary).

13. For a useful discussion of the development of this idea, and a cogent critique of it, see Stillinger, *Multiple Authorship*, especially Chapter 9.

14. For a penetrating analysis of these intellectual developments, see Martha Woodmansee, *The Author, Art, and the Market: Rereading the History of Aesthetics* (New York: Columbia University Press, 1994).

15. The auteur theory is associated with the director François Truffaut and the journal *Cahiers du cinéma*. See Stillinger, *Multiple Authorship*, 178-81.

16. Kinn and Piazza, *Four-Star Movies*, 17. In *Adaptation*, the Spike Jonze/Charlie Kaufman movie about the writing of a screenplay, when they wanted a standard to aspire to, they chose *Casablanca*, referred to in the film as "one of the greatest screenplays ever written" and "the finest screenplay ever written."

17. For a forceful defense of commercial art, see Tyler Cowen, *In Praise of Commercial Culture* (Cambridge, MA: Harvard University Press, 1998).

18. This account is taken from the DVD documentary. Many different accounts have been given of the way the ending of *Casablanca* was written, and I cannot be sure that Epstein's is entirely accurate. His memory of the events may have been faulty, and he certainly emphasizes the role that he and his brother played. But Epstein's version of the story is at least as good as any and has some claim to being authoritative.

19. The variety of cutting possible in the final scene is illustrated by the theatrical trailer. It contains a line that is not in the final cut of the movie; in the trailer, when Rick shoots Strasser, he says: "Alright, major, you asked for it." This Hollywood cliché was wisely struck from the film or perhaps simply added to the trailer to attract fans of Bogart's gangster movies.

20. This story is confirmed by two studio memoranda (dated August 7 and 21, 1942) reproduced in the "Production Research" section of the Special Edition DVD, in which Wallis formulates the famous concluding line (he knew his movies, but not his spelling; he writes "Luis" both

times instead of "Louis"). Wallis wrote out a more extended dialogue between Rick and Renault, but evidently efforts to bring back Claude Rains for reshooting failed, and he had to settle for the single concluding line from Bogart. That was probably for the best and illustrates how sometimes mere accidents (in this case Rains's scheduling difficulties) can positively affect a movie's final shape.

21. The *Casablanca* archive offered on the Special Edition DVD does contain evidence of the remarkable extent to which studio executives intervened in the day-to-day production of the movie. For example, in a memo dated June 4, 1942, Wallis wrote to Curtiz: "I don't like your choice of the Bartender. I don't think he is at all funny, and I want to give him as little to do in the picture as possible." One example of Wallis's detailed notes for the cutting of *Casablanca* has survived; dated August 21, 1942, it goes on for several pages, at this level of detail: "In the opening shot of the café, lose the silent cut of the woman crying. Cut before the pan." Occasionally even the studio head, Jack Warner, got involved; a memo dated July 15, 1942, shows the big boss invoking the infamous bottom line in a note to Curtiz: "Dear Mike: I can't understand why a fifty-four second take must be started seven times. You must cut down on the amount of negative and positive film. Jack." How one interprets this kind of evidence depends on one's theory of film. If one accepts the auteur theory, these are all examples of the studio tyrannically meddling in artistic matters. But these memos might just as well be taken as evidence of the incredible care with which the studio heads oversaw production—which may have been in part responsible for the artistic success of *Casablanca* and certainly played a role in the film being successfully completed within a reasonable amount of time and a reasonable budget. From all the evidence, I conclude that there are good and bad producers, just as there are good and bad directors, and even good and bad auteur*s*. *Citizen Kane* is widely regarded as the greatest motion picture ever made, and it was created by the model auteur, Orson Welles. But the movie widely regarded as the worst ever made is *Plan 9 from Outer Space*, and it too was created by an auteur, Ed Wood. Tim Burton's brilliant film *Ed Wood* forces us to contemplate the implications of the fact that Wood modeled himself on Welles; indeed the film builds up to an astounding scene in which Burton contrives a meeting between Welles and Wood and suggests how much the good and bad auteurs had in common (in the scene Welles complains about a studio casting decision, the choice of Charlton Heston to play a Mexican in *Touch of Evil*).

CHAPTER 2

THE HISTORICAL CONTEXT OF *CASABLANCA*

RALPH S. HATTOX

Never go to the movies with a historian, at least not if you wish to enjoy the film. They carp, they criticize, they comment on every mistake made by the script writers, costume designers, actors and director. In short, they miss the point. And so, before launching into a discussion of the events leading up to those evenings at Rick's, I give a piece of advice to young men who are aspiring historians. Never, while Rick, Victor, and Ilsa are on the tarmac and your date is dabbing her eyes, *never* point out all the subtle points wrong with the scene. It isn't appreciated. Trust me.

It is trite, but nonetheless accurate, to assert that World War II was spawned directly by the Great War of 1914-1918; it may even seem a mere continuation of that conflict, after a lull to get one's breath back and adjust alliances. Certainly the world of *Casablanca* is very much created by World War I, and the lives of the characters that come together at Rick's were all products either of that war or of the ludicrously inept attempt by the victors to fashion a peace in its aftermath. But if characters in *Casablanca* were forged by the Great War, then Casablanca, and Morocco as a whole, had its role in bringing that war about.

In 1905 Wilhelm II of Germany insisted upon making an international ruckus over tentative steps by France to exert control over Morocco. From the distance of a century the picture of the kaiser in popular imagination has, I suspect, become rather distorted, owing to images from Anglo-American wartime propaganda and to a later, half-conscious, half-accidental tendency to conflate the kaiser and Germany's leader in World War II. What was wrong with Wilhelm was not that he was an evil genius—since that would presuppose that he was any kind of genius—but rather that he was a bungler. From his father and grandfather he inherited as chancellor Otto von Bismarck, arguably one of the most skillful statesmen of the nineteenth century, who had crafted a brilliant but complicated system of alliances all working to Germany's advantage. Within two years of taking the throne Wilhelm sacked Bismarck; within six years he scared Russia into forging an alliance with Germany's one implacable enemy,

France; within twelve years he had so alarmed the British with his naval policies that they were well on the road to forgetting their traditional distaste for the French and abhorrence for the Russians and settling their colonial and other differences with each. By 1900 Germany had only one reliable ally, Austria-Hungary, and one other friend, Ottoman Turkey. The latter was crumbling, while the former, though still a major power, had such grave problems with neighboring Slavic nationalists and their Russian backers that the alliance with her could serve only to drag Germany into a war that it didn't really need. After Britain and France concluded their Entente Cordiale in 1904, Wilhelm cast about desperately for some wedge by which he could drive the two former rivals apart once again. Morocco, he thought, provided the answer.

FRENCH MOROCCO

France had, as was indeed the very definition of a great European power at the end of the 1800s, for centuries been vigorously acquiring colonies abroad. Although thwarted regularly by the British, the French were still to be found in Asia, in Africa, in the Caribbean, and in the South Pacific. But western North Africa, tantalizingly near and vulnerable, they marked early on for their particular attention. By 1830 Algeria was colonized, and in 1881 Tunisia became a protectorate. But Morocco held out.

The far western stretches of North Africa had a long record of maintaining separation from outside interference, if not always actual independence. Less than a hundred years after conquest by Arab Muslims, Morocco drifted out of the control of the Abbasid central government at Baghdad. Centuries of going their own way under independent dynasties followed. Even when the Ottomans established suzerainty over Algeria and Tunis, the Moroccans, under the rule of sultans who could claim descent from the Prophet Muhammad himself, remained free from direct control of the Turkish sultan thousands of miles away at Istanbul. But Morocco was too close to Europe, and too strategically important, to escape the attention of her acquisitive neighbors in the nineteenth century. The sultan offended the French in the mid-1840s by giving refuge to a fugitive Algerian prince, and his forces were badly mauled in consequence. Several years later had to contend with Spanish insistence on maintaining a base at Ceuta in the north, and again the war went badly: not only did the Spanish remain, but their enclave was larger, and Morocco had to pay reparations. What most likely kept Morocco from being swallowed up by one European power or the other was rivalry among those powers themselves. Colonies were a major source, perhaps *the* major source, of friction in Europe in the last half of the nineteenth century, and Morocco, ripe for the picking and a land where every power believed it had a political, strategic, or economic interest, had the potential to be a prize over which war could easily start. To keep this from happening, in 1880 an agreement among European powers was concluded to the effect that all had to be consulted if any of them wished to take control of Morocco.

And that, in 1904, was just what France sought to do. When the sultan's government proved increasingly unable to protect European interests in Morocco from anti-Western rebels, France saw the need, and the opportunity, to extend her control westward from Algeria. By the Entente she had recognized Britain's protectorate over Egypt, and now, in early 1905, she would take steps to establish a similar arrangement of her own over Morocco. The sultan, seeking some recourse, appealed to Berlin, furnishing Wilhelm with the ammunition he needed, or so he thought, to blow apart the new Anglo-French understanding. But he was rebuffed at the international conference on Morocco at Algerciras in Spain in 1906, receiving support only from Austria. The British, far from being estranged from the French, saw the Moroccan crisis as just further evidence of the kaiser's aggression. The Second Moroccan Crisis in 1911 further drove Europe toward war. Wilhelm sent the warship *Panther* into Agadir not so much to challenge the impending establishment of the French protectorate as to extort concessions from the French. The matter ended peaceably enough, but again Paris and particularly London viewed the kaiser with even greater mistrust. For the Moroccans it all made little difference: in 1912 the sultanate officially passed to French control as a protectorate.

It seems almost obscene to pass in silence over the conduct of the bloodiest conflict that the world had known up to that time. Certainly horrors of the war, the millions of dead, played as a deep bass note in the background of the frantic 1920s and depressed 1930s. But while the conditions by which the war ended and the subsequent peace negotiations had a material effect on those at Rick's Café twenty-two years later, few of them likely experienced things firsthand. Perhaps Karl served in the kaiser's army; perhaps Strasser was a young officer. But the one direct allusion to the conflict, Louis Renault's reference to stumbling into Berlin with the Americans in 1918, while a great line, draws on a memory of something that did not actually happen. When the armistice came into effect on November 11, Germany was certainly gripped by chaos (the kaiser had abdicated on the ninth and gone into exile in the Netherlands, and the sailors of the fleet were in a state of mutiny), but Berlin saw no foreign troops. The front, in point of fact, was still in France. But the German commanders had decided that defeat was merely a matter of time and opted to cut their nation's losses. One of the reasons that is often cited for the bitterness that led to World War II was that while the high command could see that defeat was certain, most Germans, though weary of the war, did not realize that they had lost and were consequently shocked when the Allies imposed crushing terms as a condition of peace.

VERSAILLES

When the victors met in Paris early in 1919 to begin discussions on how to settle the affairs of Europe, and indeed the world, they were by no means in complete agreement. Woodrow Wilson, always the idealist, saw tremendous promise of a new world order with mechanisms to make the repetition of such a horror unlikely or even impossible. His British and particularly French allies, with ample memory of the frightful losses their nations had suffered and short on Yankee optimism, saw the only hope of peace in rendering Germany utterly impotent. To this end her military was completely dismantled, her warships turned over for destruction, and she was banned from having tanks, submarines, warships over a certain tonnage, military aircraft, or even heavy artillery. In short, her army was reduced to the firepower of a well-armed police force.

Territory was bound to change hands, and the Germans certainly had to expect that Alsace and Lorraine, stripped away from France in 1871, would have to be returned. Germany actually suffered little more territorial loss, with one important exception. Poland was being reconstituted for the first time since the eighteenth century, and while most of her land was what had been taken from the Russians (having briefly passed through German hands), the new state was given a strip out of what had been German territory to give her access to the sea. This Polish corridor also split Germany into two parts, with the great bulk to the west separated from East Prussia. As long as Germany remained weak (and the Allies believed that they had seen to that) she would have to accept the new arrangement; but should she ever regain her strength, Poland would be in trouble.

The reestablishment of a Polish state was part of a larger policy of the victors that the frontiers of Europe should be redrawn to suit the aspirations of national groups to have their own states. Austria-Hungary and the Ottoman Turks saw their holdings carved up in a way that supposedly accommodated all national aspirations. The process, while perhaps rational and theoretically practical for western Europe, created chaos in the east, where boundaries between ethnolinguistic groups were hardly neat. In the early twenty-first century we are still dealing with the mess created in the Balkans by the Allies in Paris.

Two exceptions existed to the general policy of accommodating ethnolinguistic national aspirations. Neither Britain nor France were ready to recognize the aspirations of subject peoples from Morocco to India to Guiana. Furthermore, by the terms of the treaty, confirmed by the League of Nations, they were put in charge of large tracts of land, inhabited by Arabs, stripped from the Ottomans in the Levant and Mesopotamia. Again we live daily with the consequences of the conference.

The other exception concerned the national aspirations of those who had been defeated. The logic that guided the new frontiers, that a people whose boundaries encompassed their entire national group were less likely to engage in irredentist wars against their neighbors, stopped short when it came to Germans. On the one hand, steps were taken to ensure that there would be no single state for Germans, as there was for Poles or south Slavs or Romanians. The Germans in Austria, no longer the nucleus of a multinational empire but rather stripped down to a German-speaking core, were specifically forbidden from forming a national union with Germany. At the same time, many Germans found themselves on the wrong side of the frontier in states created for specific non-German nationalities. If the economic or political interests of one of the new non-German national states were best served by splicing on land inhabited by ethnic

Germans, it would be done, and the Germans would simply have to like it. So it was with the Polish corridor, and so it was that when Czechoslovakia was formed from former Austro-Hungarian territory, a decidedly German-speaking area, the Sudetenland, was given to the new state. As was the case with Poland, this made Czechoslovakia a natural target if the military fortunes of Germany were ever revived.

HITLER AND THE COMING OF WORLD WAR II

By forcing the newly created demo cratic government of Germany to acquiesce to such terms, the Allies virtually assured that that government would from the start be discredited in the eyes of its own people, many of whom still believed that Germany had been betrayed rather than defeated. Foremost among these, of course, were the political extremists, right and left, who had tried to exploit the chaos that attended defeat for their own ends. In spite of all this the Weimar government maintained some semblance of order until 1923 when, under the weight of reparations payments, the economy collapsed in breathtaking fashion. Overnight the currency was utterly worthless. The time seemed appropriate for revolution, and in November of that year Adolf Hitler came for the first time to the attention of those outside his little circle in Munich.

So vast is the literature concerning this one man, and so obsessed are both academic publishers and the popular press with him to this day, that most readers are familiar with the outline of his career. The son of an Austrian customs officer whom he disliked and a mother whom he adored, Hitler was a bright but indifferent student. Moving to Vienna in 1908 he failed to gain admission to the academy to study art and slowly drifted into vagrancy. By 1913 he scraped together enough to move to Munich, where he was in 1914 when the war broke out. Though never rising above the rank of corporal, he served with distinction and clearly loved the life of a soldier. He was recuperating from a gassing when he learned of Germany's surrender and thought, like so many Germans, that treachery and cowardice rather than actual defeat had brought Germany down. Returning to civilian life, he hooked up with a small ultranationalist political group and quickly became, not their chief philosopher, but their chief speechmaker. In November 1923 Hitler and the National Socialists failed miserably in an attempt to foment a revolt in Munich, and Hitler wound up in prison for a short time. He emerged no less contemptuous of democracy and just as determined to rid Germany of its effects, but with an understanding that it could best be done from the inside. By 1933 Germany, her promising recovery cut short by the worldwide depression, was ready to turn to somebody who could promise both economic recovery and national salvation. The National Socialists—the Nazis—were not the largest political party, but they were perhaps the strongest, and certainly the most strident. On January 30 old President Hindenburg, much against his better judgment, made Hitler chancellor. Within two months Hitler managed to have the Reichstag vote him virtual dictatorial powers.

There is little doubt that much of the economic recovery that Hitler managed to effect came through massive governmental expenditure on pet projects, but in this his approach can be seen as little different than that of Roosevelt. But if economic recovery was necessary for him to enjoy continued popularity, so was a recovery of national dignity. To this end he launched a systematic attack on the Versailles Treaties, generally loathed even by the most moderate of Germans. To Hitler, of course, the most annoying aspect of the agreement was the military limitation placed on Germany, and in the mid-1930s he violated the provisions one by one—rebuilding a powerful *Wehrmacht*, developing of an air force, acquiring armaments that had specifically been forbidden, and sending troops into the Rhineland, that part of Germany adjoining France that was supposed to remain demilitarized. Each time he was ready to back away at any sign of resistance, and each time the former victors, now preoccupied with their own problems, let him proceed. In March 1938 came the first real adventure using his new military strength. Hitler, the German Austrian now chancellor of Germany, would give his former compatriots the chance to be part of greater Germany. Troops were sent in, and Austria formally annexed. Film images die hard, but *The Sound of Music* notwithstanding, the *Anschluss* was widely, if not universally, popular among Austrians.

Next came the Czechs' turn. As was implicit in Hitler's policies from the beginning, and perhaps inevitable from the moment the Versailles conference was concluded, the fate of the Sudeten Germans now had to be considered. While there is no doubt that much of the agitation and claims of mistreatment on their part were deliberately planned in Germany and carried out by Nazis within the Sudetenland, it is equally clear that a good many Germans on the wrong side of the border did indeed look upon Germany, not Czechoslovakia, as their natural homeland. The crisis came to a head in September 1938, when Hitler, threatening war on behalf of the Sudeten Germans, allowed himself to be satisfied by the offer made by Chamberlain and Deladier, without the agreement of Prague, to hand the disputed territory over to Germany. This of course was not the end. In March 1939 Hitler finished the job by occupying the rest of Czechoslovakia. Britain and France were mortified and determined to make no further concessions. And Victor Laszlo, wherever he was, now had a cause.

Spain, in the meantime, was being ravaged by a vicious civil war between Franco's Fascist forces and the republicans. Making the conflict bloodier yet was the participation by foreign governments, as well as foreign individuals, in the conflict, with Stalin backing the republicans and Germany backing Franco. Aside from the political advantages to be gained from a Fascist victory, by throwing their forces behind Franco the Germans could also test the quality of their new armaments and the skill of their fighters. Franco, of course, emerged victorious.

It is in the context of this Spanish Civil War that we get the one and only solid fact that we have about Rick's past. Everything earlier is fuzzy, but he shows up in Spain on the republican side—running guns, mind you, and for cash at that, but still contributing to the ultimately lost cause. This was a symbol that everybody in the movie audience was bound to recognize: in the late 1930s there was nothing more effective a person could do to earn his credentials as a romantic champion of liberal democracy. Indeed, being a gun runner is perhaps more romantic, because it is a trifle shady, than actually fighting; not as heroic, perhaps, but this is Bogart we are talking about, not Gary Cooper.

By late summer 1939 it was clear that a German assault on Poland was imminent. This time the French and the British were determined not to back down, although Hitler perhaps didn't really believe that they were willing to go to war over Poland. It mattered little, for on August 23 Germany signed a non-aggression treaty with the one person Hitler was worried about, Stalin. Included were secret provisions for carving up a conquered Poland. The attack came on September 1, and on September 4, their ultimatums having been ignored, France and Britain declared war on Germany.

"... THE GERMANS WORE GRAY"

It was the beginning of months of "Phony War," with little happening on the front and neither side seeming to be inclined to change that state of affairs. In April 1940 the British and Germans clashed over Norway, which the Germans occupied. But the crushing blow came in May 1940, as the German forces rolling through the Ardennes crushed the allied forces and forced hundreds of thousands of them back on the North Sea port of Dunkerque, whence they were rescued. France was, however, doomed. In June German forces closed in on Paris.

There, of course, the great prologue to events at Rick's takes place. As the Germans get closer, Rick and Ilsa, helping the *patron* of the Belle Aurore polish off his champagne lest the filthy *Boches* get a sip, plan to meet at the station. Rick's romantic credentials are still intact, for he is clearly on the Germans' list of people to round up. But at the station Ilsa doesn't show (we find out later that she has had word from Victor), Rick, drenched to the skin, gets her kiss-off letter, and Sam has to drag him onto the train. Exit the romantic, enter the cynic.

A year and a half later we're at Rick's, and so are the collection of specimens created by the interwar years and the first year of the war. There are refugees and people on the make from all parts of Europe—the Norwegian Resistance man, the innocent Bulgarian couple, the Russian barkeep, the German waiter, the French floozy, and the like. There is Ugarte, the weasel-like dealer in useful papers (probably a Spaniard who learned to profiteer during the Civil War); Louis, the corrupt prefect of police serving the Vichy government as readily (and just as disloyally) as he served the Third Republic; Victor Laszlo, Czech patriot and Resistance hero; Ilsa, his wife, who, perhaps because she's in her early twenties seems to have little past to speak of before she met Victor, and of course Rick, whom we find a cold and bitter man. From the audience's point of view, he has two redeeming features: he has a brooding air of mystery and romance, and, except for Karl the waiter, he still dislikes Germans. Particularly Major Strasser. But what authority exactly does Major Strasser have in Casablanca? What is his relationship to the authorities in Morocco? And why does Louis seem so eager to accommodate him?

The status of colonies of a mother country that has itself been conquered and occupied is bound to be equivocal. A conquering power might not, after all, have the reach to scoop in all of its victims' overseas possessions, and Germany, for all its military capability, lacked the surface fleet necessary to enforce its will across oceans. Nor did the fact that the government at Vichy was cooperative ensure that the colonies would fall into line: a lot depended on the inclinations of those on the ground, administrator and civilian alike. Of course, without the protection of the home government, such colonies are easy prey for ambitious and resourceful powers in their own vicinity. French Indochina, for instance, with the acquiescence of Vichy witnessed the establishment of Japanese military bases, but even if Vichy had not cooperated Japanese occupation was certain.

The choice was more often up to those who ran the administrations in the individual colonies. When the movie was released in 1942 it was a given that any Frenchman who was a real Frenchman had nothing but contempt for the collaborationist regime of Vichy, and indeed there is very little good one can say for the likes of Pierre Laval. From a distance, however, perhaps our take might be a bit different. The choice between continuing to respect what *was* the only French government remaining, led by Pétain, the hero of Verdun, and transferring one's allegiance to exiles that claimed to represent the real France, was a serious and doubtless painful one. Those who followed Vichy were not all mere Fascist stooges. In July 1940 the British cornered a French fleet in the Algerian port of Merz al-Kebir. Admiral Gensoul, cordially inclined toward the British and hardly one to have welcomed the fall of France, nonetheless had orders from what he clearly believed to be the legitimate French government not to surrender. He did not, and some thirteen hundred French sailors perished in the exchange. Surrender of the fleet contrary to the orders of his government was to Gensoul's mind no more in keeping with the dignity of France than to collaborate with the Germans. Men of good conscience, like him, doubtless found themselves in a bind.

Of course Louis Renault's conscience hardly seems to enter into the matter, and the administration at French Morocco, which he served, did indeed recognize Vichy until the Allies arrived with Operation Torch in November 1942. We may pause to compare the urbane, ironic and charming Louis Renault with Captain Renard, the detestable Vichy prefect of police on Martinique confronting another Bogart expatriate in *To Have and Have Not*. He was played with soft-spoken menace by Dan Seymour, whose bloodhound jowls seemed perpetually to sport a five o'clock shadow. Sadly, we must assume that the Renards were more common than the Renaults.

But what then of Major Strasser, the real source of menace in the film? It may have been judicious for the Vichy administration to accommodate representatives of the German and Italian governments, to cooperate in those who murder their nationals, and even to allow their military attachés to lead the boys in a few choruses of "Die Wacht am Rhein." But those representatives actually had no authority whatsoever. Vichy was not synonymous with Germany. Captain Renault himself would have been justified in shooting a foreigner who took it upon himself to stop the takeoff of the Lisbon plane. But then he would not have gotten to utter what is easily the most memorable, and most anticipated, line in film history.

CHAPTER 3

HISTORICISM, RELATIVISM, AND NIHILISM VERSUS AMERICAN NATURAL RIGHT IN *CASABLANCA*

MICHAEL PALMER

In the recent, highly acclaimed film *Adaptation*, the teacher of screenwriting (Brian Cox) tells the film's protagonist (Nicolas Cage), a screenwriter, that *Casablanca* is the finest screenplay ever written. *Casablanca* is, indeed, a film that has achieved classic status more than sixty years after its initial release in theaters. In 1977, the American Film Institute judged it to be the third-best *American* film ever made, while the British Film Institute, in 1983, judged it to be the best film ever made, period.[1] Speaking more than thirty years after he worked on it, Howard Koch, one of the four main writers, among several others who worked on the screenplay, asserts that, "More articles have been written about it than any other picture with the possible exception of *Citizen Kane*."[2] As for interpretations of the film that have emerged from this plethora of secondary literature, they are multitudinous and multifarious: Freudians, Jungians, and Lacanians have attempted a number of psychoanalytic interpretations; sociologists, deconstructionists, and feminists have also examined the film in excruciating detail; beginning with Umberto Eco in 1987, semiologists entered the fray. They are all in agreement, however, on one thing: the film "has meaning far beyond what was in the conscious minds" of those who made it.[3]

This is one of the rare cases of a text (I say "rare," because this is not the hermeneutical theory to which I usually adhere) where the question of authorial intention must simply be thrown out the window. The script went through so many revisions, written by several authors who were not always even in contact with one another; memos came from the studio, calling for last-minute changes in dialogue or the shooting of key scenes; some lines appeared in the film, but appeared *only* in the final screenplay that was produced *after* the film had been shot; the studio added the first scene after the film was thought finished, and all the main actors had gone on to other projects; Humphrey Bogart was called back, several months later, to record the famous last line of the film, "Louis, I think this is the beginning of a beautiful friendship"; and the only reason "As

Time Goes By" was not replaced as the theme song, which is what the film's composer, Max Steiner, who hated the song, wanted, was that Ingrid Bergman had already cut off most of her hair for her next picture and could not return to reshoot the necessary scenes. How impossible it would be to determine what the writers, director, producers, or actors intended when they made the film.[4] Andrew Sarris calls *Casablanca* "the happiest of happy accidents, and the most decisive exception to the *auteur* theory" of filmmaking.[5] It's almost as if the film had a mind and intention of its own and refused to defer to the meddling of mere mortals! All we can do, really, is view the film as it appears on the screen, the perfectly crafted and successful piece of filmmaking that it is—whether by happy accident; divine providence; or possibly the significant, intentional crafting of one or more of the participants in the making of it, whose story, however, has been lost in the mists of time—and discover what we find in the film that might offer a coherent interpretation. This is what I attempt in this chapter.

I offer a political-philosophical interpretation of the film: *Casablanca* (one needs very little Spanish to translate the film's title: "White House"[6]) is a political allegory justifying the United States' involvement in World War II; more deeply, it is a defense of the doctrine of modern natural right upon which the political principles of the American democratic republic are based. What is the American political credo defended in this film? It is the classic liberal doctrine that emerged in modern political theory in writers such as Hobbes, Locke, and Montesquieu. According to modern natural-right theory, human beings have a nature, a nature that does not and cannot change. If one understands human nature correctly, it is "self-evident," as the Declaration of Independence puts it (using a word coined by John Locke in his *Essay Concerning Human Understanding*, according to the complete *Oxford English Dictionary*), that human beings are endowed by their creator with certain "unalienable rights." "Not all rights are alienable," says Hobbes (before Locke) in the famous chapter 14 of part one of *Leviathan*, "Of the First and Second Laws of Nature, and of Contracts." Among these "unalienable rights," according to the American Declaration, are "Life, Liberty, and the Pursuit of Happiness."

This modern natural right theory is antihistoricist. Historicism holds that Truth is historically mutable by History. Developed in Germany in the nineteenth century in the philosophies of thinkers such as Kant, Hegel, and Marx, it ultimately leads to the view that the doctrine of natural rights to things such as life and liberty is merely the product of a liberal society, which is inevitably an ephemeral historical worldview. In its radical form (found in Marx, Nietzsche, and Heidegger), it despises these rights of liberal, bourgeois societies.

Modern natural right theory is antirelativist. Relativism is the view that all values are relative; therefore, no values can claim to be superior to any other values, leaving room for the logical conclusion that intolerance henceforth shall be *my* value, and I shall impose it on others, by my will, depriving them of their lives, their liberty, and their pursuit of happiness. The softer version of value relativism, preferred by most contemporary Americans, is the more pleasant, but unfortunately illogical and sophomoric conclusion that if all values are relative, all value systems are obligated to be tolerant of all others, which really means, of course, that values are *not* relative, that tolerance is universally and transhistorically more valuable than intolerance. As usual, contemporary Americans typically want to have their cake and eat it, too; this is why *Casablanca* can be such an instructive film for them. The doctrine of value-relativism is also grounded in a nineteenth-century German insight, which became the foundation of the twentieth-century social sciences: the alleged insight that there is a fundamental distinction between a question of fact and a question of value. If this is true, then modern natural-right theory and the founding principles of the American democratic republic are false.

Finally, modern natural right theory is antinihilist. Nihilism is more difficult to encapsulate than the two aforementioned philosophical enemies of the modern doctrine of natural right. Among other things, it expressed itself differently in different countries, especially in Russia as compared with the European nations. Let us say that nihilism holds that the ground of Being is nothing, the *Nihil*. In Germany, via thinkers such as Nietzsche and Heidegger (however much their thinking may have been vulgarized), the view transformed itself into the position that only by commitment to a freely chosen project, a project radical enough to destroy Western civilization, which was irretrievably decadent, could an authentic German nation be purged of bourgeois liberalism, the Jews, and other despicable things. This view came to power in Germany with Hitler's national socialism.

The modern natural-right doctrine, on the contrary, maintains that Being and all the beings in Being have a given meaning; it is not true that nothing exists that is eternal and loveable; Man is not, as Nietzsche's Zarathustra puts it, "a rope over an abyss."[7] The principles and practices—the ideologies, especially Nazism—of the nations against which America fought in World War II were grounded in the antiliberal philosophical doctrines outlined above. I maintain that the main characters in *Casablanca* are representatives of these political-philosophical positions. Moreover, I assert that the political-philosophical teaching of the film supports adherence to the doctrine of modern natural right, the foundation of the American democratic republic and its political credo, and opposes historicism, relativism, and nihilism. I hope to support these contentions with a selective outline and commentary upon the film.

ANALYSIS OF THE FILM

> With the coming of the Second World War, many eyes in imprisoned Europe turned hopefully, or desperately, toward the freedom of the Americas. Lisbon became the great embarkation point. But not everybody could get to Lisbon directly, and so a tortuous, roundabout refugee trail sprang up: Paris to Marseilles, across the Mediterranean to Oran, then by train or auto or foot across the rim of Africa to Casablanca in French Morocco. Here the fortunate ones, through money or influence or luck, might obtain exit visas and scurry to Lisbon, and from Lisbon to the new world. But the others wait in Casablanca, and wait, and wait, and wait.

After this narration, with Moroccan music and the "Marseillaise" playing in the background, as we view a spinning world globe that then focuses in on maps of Europe and North Africa, the film opens with a series of scenes that culminates in the shooting of a French Resistance fighter. First we see a Nazi relaying a message that two German couriers carrying important official documents have been murdered on the train from Oran to Casablanca: "Round up all suspicious characters, and search them for stolen documents: Important." The scene shifts to the marketplace in the center of the city, where the most notorious pickpocket in Casablanca informs us—while warning a naive old English couple to beware, that "the scum of Europe has gravitated to Casablanca," that it is "full of vultures, vultures everywhere, everywhere," as he robs them—that the customary roundup of suspicious characters always includes beautiful young girls for Captain Renault, prefect of police. The scene culminates in the shooting of a man who is discovered, after he is shot, to be a Free French Resistance fighter. He is shot, ironically, in front of a sign on the front of the city's Palais de Justice, a sign upon which is a large picture of General Pétain—the head of the Vichy French regime, scarcely more than a puppet of the Nazi's—along with a sentence that appears in bold capitals, "JE TIENS MES PROMESSES, MÊME CELLES DES AUTRES." ("I KEEP MY OWN PROMISES AND EVEN THOSE OF OTHERS.") The camera then pans up to three words engraved above on the historic building, the three words that were the rallying cry of the French Revolution—"LIBERTÉ, ÉGALITÉ, FRATERNITÉ"—putting the lie immediately to Pétain's "promesses."

Next, we see a plane from Lisbon coming in for a landing; it flies past a sign—Rick's Café Américain—over an unseen building. In the marketplace, all heads turn toward the plane, and a young woman named Annina (who will later figure in an important scene in the film that reveals Richard "Rick" Blaine's true character) remarks hopefully to the young man beside her, her husband, Jan, "Perhaps tomorrow we'll be on the plane."

The plane lands, and from it emerges Major Heinrich Strasser, apparently the most important senior representative of the Third Reich ever to visit the city, and, later, Rick's Café Américain. Officials of unoccupied France, Nazi Germany, Vichy France, and Fascist Italy greet him. (Strasser contemptuously ignores the Italian Fascist, as he does in all scenes in which he appears.)

"Unoccupied France welcomes you to Casablanca," says Captain Renault and wonders whether Strasser might find the climate of Casablanca too uncomfortably hot.

"We Germans must become accustomed to *all* climates," Strasser replies.

Renault then informs Strasser that he has rounded up "twice the usual number of suspects," due to the importance of the case of the two German couriers, and that later that evening, at Rick's Café, Strasser will witness the arrest of their very murderer.[8] Strasser expected no less of Renault, and has already heard about this café, and about Mr. Rick himself. Strasser informs Renault that a man has arrived in Casablanca who is never to be allowed to leave: Victor Laszlo, who is presented in the film as the most important Resistance leader in Europe.

Enter Rick, proprietor, of course, of the Café Américain. But first, the café: As the camera follows patrons through the entrance, under the sign "Rick's Café Américain" (the sign is focused upon several times in the film), we find it chock full of interesting characters—refugees fleeing Nazi Germany or the Nazi occupation of their homelands; British, Russian, and other expatriates; Nazi, Free French, and Vichy agents; smugglers, thieves, and cutthroats—and at every table or seat at the bar, conspiracies are being hatched. Rick, himself (although we have yet to meet him), is presented as an American expatriate, who is apparently a strict isolationist who maintains a scrupulous neutrality (these are terms used to describe him throughout the film) in the face of the dire events that engulf the world in which he lives and pervade the microcosm of that world, his café. "I stick my neck out for nobody," he says (twice in the film), and more than a few times we are informed that he never drinks with customers, no matter what their nationality or political persuasion. But, as we shall see, Rick's apparent isolationism and neutrality are suspect; indeed, they will ultimately prove illusory.

Strictly speaking, our introduction to Rick is a view of his hand: we watch it sign what we might call an executive order brought to him by an employee. We then see that he has been interrupted from a game of chess, which he is playing alone. (Chess was invented as a game of war; it also came to represent philosophy, as, for example, in Shakespeare's *The Tempest*.)

This first scene in the café is crucial, for it displays evidence both for and against Rick's isolationism and neutrality on all political questions. For example, in response to the request of a high official of the Deutsches Bank for entrance to the café and its casino, Rick rips in half the man's business card but then relents in part; he still will not grant him credit in the casino, but, "Your cash is good at the bar."

"What, do you know who I am?" demands the German.

"I do," says Rick. "You're lucky the bar's open to you." Later in the scene, presented with a German check by his bartender and asked to endorse it, Rick tears it in half, too, and lets the pieces drop to the floor (to be swept—dare I say it?—into the dustbin of history?).

In the midst of this confrontation, a Signor Ugarte squeezes by the German with a casual, "Excuse me, please. Hello, Rick." A conversation between Ugarte and Rick ensues. Ugarte remarks, "You know, Rick, watching you just now with the Deutsches Bank, one would think you'd been doing this all your life."

"Well, what makes you think I haven't?" Rick snaps back.

"Too bad about those two German couriers, wasn't it?" Ugarte observes.

"They got a lucky break," Rick retorts. "Yesterday, they were just two German clerks. Today they're the 'Honored Dead.'"

"You are a very cynical person, Rick, if you'll forgive me for saying so." Ugarte offers.

"I'll forgive you." Rick says.

"Thank you. Will you have a drink with me?" (Ugarte has forgotten Rick's isolationist policy).

"No!" Rick snaps again, emphatically. Then comes my favorite exchange in the movie, simply for its arid wit.

"You despise me, don't you?" queries Ugarte.

"Well," Rick dryly responds, "if I gave you any thought, I probably would."

Ugarte then reveals that *he* has the letters of transit that were in the hands of the dead German couriers. He asks Rick if he will hold onto them for him, just until that evening, when he has arranged to sell them for a king's ransom. He trusts Rick with them, he says, "somehow just because you despise me." It soon becomes clear that Ugarte is the killer of the German couriers.

The scene ends with Ugarte's remark, "Rick, I hope you are more impressed with me now."

Rick responds, slowly and deliberately, "Yes. . . . I *am* a little more *impressed* with you."

Later that evening, just before Ugarte is arrested at the café, Captain Renault warns Rick not to try to help Ugarte.

"I stick my neck out for nobody," Rick asserts.

"A wise foreign policy," Renault responds, significantly.

Rick repeats his statement, verbatim, moments later to a café patron.

Enter Signor Ferrari, the owner of Rick's Café's competition, The Blue Parrot. Ferrari wants Rick to sell him the Café Américain, but it's not for sale at any price. Ferrari then asks about Sam, the black piano player who has been Rick's companion at least as far back as Paris before the German invasion: What would it cost Ferrari to buy Sam's services from Rick? Ferrari will have to ask Sam, himself. Why?

"I don't buy or sell human beings," Rick curtly replies.

Ferrari implies that Rick is naïve, that human beings are "Casablanca's leading commodity." He wants to know when Rick will wise up; if they became partners they "could make a fortune. . . through the black market."

"Suppose you run your business and let me run mine," Rick responds.

"In this world today, isolationism is no longer a practical policy," Ferrari informs him.

In any event, Sam is no more interested in Ferrari's offer, at any price, than Rick is in selling his café: Sam knows the difference between Rick's principles and Ferrari's, and his own human freedom and dignity are more important to him than any amount of money. (In a later scene, this time at The Blue Parrot, Ferrari boasts, "As leader of all illegal activities in Casablanca, I am an influential and respected man.")

In the next important scene, Renault speaks with Rick outside the café. "I have often speculated on why you don't return to America. Did you abscond with the church funds? Did you run off with a senator's wife? I like to think that you killed a man: it's the romantic in me."

No, Rick came to Casablanca for his health, "for the waters."

"Waters? What waters? We're in the desert."

"I was misinformed," is the famous, ironic reply.

They then move up to Rick's office over the café. This is when Renault tells

Rick that Victor Laszlo has arrived in Casablanca. For a moment, Rick's cynical affect cracks. This is the first time that Renault has seen Rick impressed by anybody or anything. Renault, for *some* reason, suspects that Rick would like to assist Laszlo, "Because," he remarks, "under that cynical shell you're at heart a sentimentalist."

Rick recovers; he evinces only a sporting interest in whether or not Laszlo will escape Casablanca: he makes a wager with Renault. More importantly, in this scene Renault confirms the rumors about Rick's past. He *did* runs guns to Ethiopia in 1935, and he *did* fight against the Fascists in 1936 in the Spanish Civil War.

"I got well paid for it on both occasions," Rick submits.

"The winning side would have paid you much better," Renault astutely responds. (Later in the film, in the lengthy flashback scenes to Paris, we learn that Rick must flee before the arrival of the Nazis because he is, he admits, "on their blacklist already, their roll of honor.")

Major Strasser now arrives at the café. He has been given the best table, says Rick's employee, Carl, because "He is German, and would take it anyway." Strasser's presence in Casablanca has one goal: to ensure that Victor Laszlo never escapes Casablanca to Lisbon and freedom.

Captain Renault joins Strasser's table to observe the arrest of Ugarte; Rick soon follows suit. When Strasser complains that Renault refers to the "'*Third* Reich' as though you expect there to be others," Renault casually responds, "Personally, Major, I will take what comes." When Rick is asked his nationality—a rhetorical question to which Strasser already knows the answer—Rick's reply is "a drunkard." According to Renault, this makes him "a citizen of the world." Strasser's aide asks Rick if he is one of those who cannot imagine the Germans in their beloved Paris. Rick demurs.

"Can you imagine us in London?"

"When you get there, ask me," Rick replies sardonically.

"Ho, diplomatist," remarks Renault.

"Who do you think will win the war?" Strasser next queries.

"I haven't the slightest idea," avers Rick. Renault adds, "Rick is completely neutral about everything."

But Strasser, too, has a file on Rick. Like Renault, he knows about Rick's prewar activities in Ethiopia and Spain. (Note, by the way, that later, in the flashback scenes to Paris, which focus on the love story, Rick can tell what kind of guns the Germans are firing by the sounds of them, the distance from which they are being fired, and that they are "getting closer every minute.")

Rick excuses himself from the table with the comment, "Your business is politics. Mine is running a saloon." (Later, when a fight breaks out between a German soldier and a French patriot, Rick breaks it up, sternly warning them to "lay off politics or get out.") Before he leaves the table, Rick does, however, advise Strasser that there are certain parts of New York City that he would suggest the Nazis not even attempt to invade.

Enter Victor Laszlo. He is at the café to find Ugarte and the letters of transit, which he was to purchase that evening from him. In Laszlo's company is Ilsa Lund, the true love of Rick's life, by whom he feels deeply betrayed. As her story unfolds, we learn why she abandoned Rick. Ilsa thought Laszlo, her husband, was dead when she fell in love with Rick, just before the German occupation of Paris. Learning only at the last minute that he was alive, that he had escaped a concentration camp and was holed up in a freight car somewhere in the outskirts of the city, she had no choice but to go to him, thus abandoning Rick. (Ilsa will later ask Rick for the letters of transit that will allow Laszlo and her to escape Casablanca on the plane for Lisbon, but Rick does not then know the truth of her story, so he refuses her, although he is clearly disturbed about the moral dilemma involved.)

Captain Renault cordially welcomes Laszlo, remarking that it is not often that Casablanca has had so distinguished a visitor, and Laszlo cordially responds. When Strasser joins them, he orders Laszlo to report to Renault's office the next morning, but Laszlo will not recognize Strassser's authority in unoccupied France: Laszlo insists he is a Czechoslovakian; he has never accepted the "privilege" of being a subject of the German Reich. Captain Renault diplomatically changes the order to a "request . . . a much more pleasant word."

Laszlo subsequently leaves Ilsa alone at the table, and the famous scene in the love story ensues: Ilsa invites Sam to her table and persuades him to play and then sing, "As Time Goes By," the theme song of the film, which has a special place in the hearts of both Rick and Ilsa, but which Rick has forbidden Sam to play since the day they left Paris. Sam is only partway through the song when Rick races to the table to stop him and discovers that Ilsa Lund has appeared again in his life. Laszlo returns, and Renault joins them. Rick compliments Laszlo on his work.

"I try," says Laszlo.

"We *all* try," Rick submits, which means that he must include himself among those who try; "you succeed."

Renault is startled that two precedents are then broken: Rick joins these customers for a drink, and he picks up the check; Renault closes the scene remarking that it has been a "very interesting evening."

The film now builds to its climax. Rick is in crisis; he is torn; furthermore, it is the middle of the night, and he is drunk. He demands that Sam play "As Time Goes By." In his drunken stupor, he looks at Sam, and asks as oddly worded a question as one could imagine: "If it's December 1941 in Casablanca, what time is it in New York?"

Sam doesn't know: "My watch stopped," he says. (Indeed, at this moment, with the sempiternal question of natural right or natural justice looming, we might say that time itself has stopped.)

"I bet," says Rick, "they're asleep in New York"; then he adds, "I'll bet they're asleep all over America."

What are the implications of this intriguing question at the heart of the film and Rick's own response to it? America is not yet involved in World War II; it is the first week of December 1941; in fact, it is the first weekend of December.

What are we to surmise? While Rick undergoes his moral crisis in Casablanca, which results in his re-entry into the fight for freedom, America is asleep, and Japanese planes are in the air, on their way to attack Pearl Harbor. Rick and the United States enter the war at the same moment. Henceforth, in the film, Rick begins again to act overtly and swiftly on the side of freedom.

But first, in the café, in his drunken stupor, Rick's mind drifts off to his time with Ilsa in Paris, and the film engages in a long series of flashback scenes. The only things I wish to observe are these: First, as I just noted, the flashbacks take place in Rick's head, so the scenes are reminiscences, not true flashbacks. Second, the reminiscences contain the only scene in the film in which we hear the third verse of "As Time Goes By"; "It's still the same old story/ A fight for love and glory/ A case of do or die." These are the among "The fundamental things [that] apply/ As time goes by."

Once Rick learns the truth the next day about Laszlo and Ilsa and what happened to him on his last day in Paris, he consistently acts, seriously endangering himself—indeed, risking his life—for the common good and the cause of freedom. He essentially gives away thousands of francs to a young couple from Bulgaria, Annina and Jan, so that Annina won't have to prostitute herself to Renault in order to get two exit visas. He completely drops his neutrality and isolationist foreign policy, which have always been, I submit, facades, or at least were never the foundation of Rick's personal ethics. He helps Laszlo with his wound after the latter's narrow escape from the police, who broke up a resistance meeting. Laszlo remarks in the scene that Rick's cynicism is the stance of a man trying to convince himself of something that he doesn't really believe (Laszlo does not really understand Rick, or his motives). Ilsa, who subsequently tries, but cannot bring herself to shoot Rick in order to get the exit visas from him, tells him that from now on he must do the thinking for both of them.

"For all of us," she says. "I will," Rick responds. And he does.

From that point to the end of the film Rick betrays everyone, in a sense, including, ironically, Laszlo and even Ilsa, who does not really understand Rick any better than does Laszlo. But it is all to effect Rick's plan to arrange the successful escape of Laszlo to freedom, which requires that Ilsa, too, must leave. He betrays Renault, getting him to believe that he will help the captain get a really big charge against Laszlo that will put him away in a concentration camp for good.

"Germany [Renault slips], uh, Vichy, [quickly recovering] would be very grateful." He adds, laughingly, "Ricky, I'm going to miss you; apparently you're the only man in Casablanca with even less scruples than I." (No one around him, it seems, really understands Rick!)

Ironically, in Laszlo's ensuing arrest scene, Renault asserts "Love, it seems, has triumphed over virtue," when, unbeknownst to him, exactly the opposite happened; Rick pulls a gun on him, beginning the sequence of events that leads to Laszlo and Ilsa escaping on the plane to Lisbon and Rick's killing of Major Strasser. (As Strasser drops to the floor, "Die Wacht Am Rhein" melds into the "Marseillaise" in the musical score.) Laszlo's final words to Rick are, "Welcome back to the fight; this time, I know our side will win." Ilsa's are, "Good-bye, Rick. God bless you."

After the killing of Strasser and the escape of Laszlo and Ilsa, Renault's police squad arrives, and it is his turn to make a final moral decision: he looks at Strasser's body, the police squad, and Rick, and pauses; then comes the classic punch line: "Round up the usual suspects."

"You're not only are you a sentimentalist, but you've become a patriot," Renault half-mockingly admonishes Rick.

"It seemed like a good time to start," Rick responds.

"I think perhaps you're right," Renault concurs, as he throws a bottle of Vichy water into the trashcan and kicks it over. This initiates their "beautiful friendship," as they, too, plan their departure from Casablanca to join the war effort openly.

CONCLUSION

Rick's Café Américain is not merely the gathering place for all these refugees who dream of escaping *to* the United States; it *is*, in a sense, the United States, which must enter the war if the enemies of freedom are to be defeated. It is the United States in another sense, too: America has always been a land of immigrants.[9] To be an American does not mean to belong to a particular race, creed, or color; it means to be an adherent of the political credo of the American democratic republic—that people are endowed by nature and nature's God with certain inalienable rights and that the purpose of government is to secure these rights.

The Nazi's are Nietzschean nihilists, and the ineffectual Italian Fascists are a watered-down version of the same. The Vichy regime's principles are a kind of corruption of French values as they came increasingly under the domination of German philosophy (especially of Nietzsche and Heidegger) between the two great wars, just as France herself is now dominated by Nazi occupation.[10] (In an earlier scene in the film, Strasser asks Renault if he's entirely certain which side he's on, and Renault replies, "I have no conviction, if that's what you mean. I blow with the wind, and the prevailing wind happens to be from Vichy"—he is a relativist whose values are subjective, at least until Rick's example better instructs him.) The principles of the Free French, on the other hand, are those of the "Marseillaise"—Liberty, Equality, and Fraternity—which is played at the beginning of the film, and featured in a key scene in the film, drowning out the Nazi's refrain "Die Vaterland, Die Vaterland," and leading to cries of "Vive la France!"—even from Yvonne, the barfly who has "collaborated" with the enemy, arriving at the café with a German soldier. (Note, by the way, that while Laszlo orders the orchestra to play the "Marseillaise," and gets credit for it afterward, it is not until the orchestra gets an approving nod from Rick that they play it.)

Despite his attempt to pose as an isolationist on foreign policy, strictly neutral on all political questions, Rick in fact retains a belief in the credo of the

American democratic republic and its founders—"Life, Liberty, and the Pursuit of Happiness"—and he finally acts upon it at the climax of the film. (Signor Ferrari, and Italian expatriate, represents a corruption of those values of freedom in a commercial republic. One might say that he is the capitalist as Marx describes him: human beings are, to Ferrari, commodities to be bought and sold on the free market.) The American credo, which grounds Rick's personal ethics, is based on the doctrine of modern natural right, which is antihistoricist, antirelativist, and, above all, antinihilist. In the words of the theme song of the film, played throughout as background music, along with the "Marseillaise," and in the foreground, along with the "Marseillaise," in key scenes in the film, it *is* "still the same old story"; it *is* "A case of do or die"; and it is *true* that "The fundamental things apply/ As time goes by." This is true, of course, even today, as Americans face the threats and perils of the twenty-first century.

"When Howard Koch," Aljean Harmetz writes, "speaks of people today returning to *Casablanca* as to 'political church,' he calls it a hunger 'for political, social, and human values that are missing today.'"[12] The "political church" of *Casablanca* is one, I submit, to which we should all consider returning.[11]

NOTES

Earlier versions of this essay were presented at the Annual Meeting of the Association of Core Texts and Courses, held in Montreal, Canada, in April 2002; before the director and fellows of the Institute for United States Studies, University of London, United Kingdom, in July 2002; and at the Biennial Conference of the International Society for the Study of European Ideas, held in Aberystwyth, Wales, United Kingdom, in July 2002. I thank my wife, Rachel Palmer, for her invaluable assistance during the process of the several expansions and revisions that this essay has undergone.

1. See Aljean Harmetz, *Round Up the Usual Suspects: The Making of Casablanca—Bogart, Bergman, and World War II* (New York: Hyperion, 1992), 346. This is the best book I have found for information detailing the making of *Casablanca* in all its aspects: the Warner Brothers studio that produced it, the convoluted story of the "writing" of the screenplay, the actors in the film and their relevant life histories, the effects that the outbreak of the war had on the production of the film, the history of its popularity, et cetera. All quotes from *Casablanca* can found at: http://www.geocities.com/classicmoviescripts/script/casablanca.pdf.

2. Howard Koch, *Casablanca: Script and Legend* (Woodstock, New York: Overlook Press, 1973), 17. This book, too, is immensely useful. It is actually an edited volume of the work of several authors, although not presented as such, bibliographically. There is a preface; an essay entitled, "The Making of *Casablanca*: Conceived in Sin and Born in Travail"; and a conclusion, "What Happened to Story in the Contemporary Film?" These were all copyrighted in 1973 by Howard Koch. There is an introductory note, written by Ralph J. Gleason, copyrighted 1971. The book also contains the entire script of the film, by Julius and Philip Epstein and Koch, copyrighted 1943, although the film was produced at Warner Brothers from early December 1941 until early August 1942. There are the original reviews from Bosley Crowther and Howard Barnes, which appeared in 1942 in the *New York Times* and the *New York Tribune*, respectively. Finally, there is a 1973 essay "Analysis of the Film," by Richard Corliss. It follows the script and precedes the reviews from 1942.

3. Harmetz, *Making of Casablanca*, 347. For brief outlines of what I have called the "multitudinous and multifarious" interpretations of the film, and full citations, see pages 347-54. Koch, himself, admits that others have "discovered overtones and reverberations in the

film of which [he], at least, was not conscious," but are undoubtedly there; see Koch, *Casablanca*, 26.

4. See Harmetz, *Making of Casablanca*, which chronicles all this information.

5. Quoted in Harmetz, *Making of Casablanca*, 75.

6. Richard Corliss, "Analysis of the Film," in Koch, *Casablanca*, 186-87, briefly discusses the possible legitimacy of a political reading of the film that was current sometime before 1973, although he does not attribute it to anyone. (He even hints at a philosophical one: he refers to Rick's "vigorous stoicism.") He mentions that *casa blanca* is Spanish for "white house" and that Rick is like President Roosevelt, "a man who gambles on the odds of going to war until circumstances and his own submerged nobility force him to lose his casino (read: partisan politics) and commit himself—first by financing the Side of Right and then by fighting for it. The time of the film's action (December 1941) adds credence to this view, as does the irrelevant fact that, two months after *Casablanca* opened, Roosevelt (Rick) and Prime Minister Winston Churchill (Laszlo) met for a war conference in Casablanca." How Corliss correlates Winston Churchill with Victor Laszlo is puzzling, although not incomprehensible.

7. Friedrich Nietzsche, *Thus Spoke Zarathustra*, in *The Portable Nietzsche*, trans. Walter Kaufmann (New York: Penguin Books, 1976), 126.

8. The screenplay in Koch, *Casablanca*, 36, says that in this scene Renault speaks to Strasser "courteously, but with just a suggestion of mockery beneath his words." The Epsteins' stage directions indicate that "It is very hard to tell whether [Renault] is being servile or mocking"; consider Renault's introduction of Major Strasser to Rick: "Major Strasser is one of the reasons the Third Reich enjoys the reputation it has today" (Harmetz, *Making of Casablanca*, 47).

9. There is a story I have heard of President Franklin Roosevelt's giving an address to a national gathering of the Daughters of the American Revolution with the shocking (to them) salutation: "Fellow Immigrants!" I do not know whether or not the story is apocryphal.

10. Virtually everything one finds in the most fashionable twentieth-century French philosophers, such as Jean-Paul Sartre, Maurice Merleau-Ponty, Georges Bataille, Maurice Blanchot, Jean-Francois Lyotard, and Jacques Derrida—in a word, postmodernism—has its roots in Nietzsche's and Heidegger's thinking.

11. Harmetz, *Making of Casablanca*, 238.

12. The story of the making of *Casablanca* really does border on the miraculous. The rights to the film, based on the play, "Everybody Goes to Rick's" (in some ways similar, in other ways decisively different from the screenplay "Everybody Comes to Rick's" and certainly from the final film) were purchased before the outbreak of the war (for the United States, that is; a point that I, a Canadian, feel compelled to make). The film began production on December 8, 1941, the day after the bombing of Pearl Harbor. It was completed in August 1942, but its general theater release in January 1943 corresponded with the announcement of the Casablanca conference between President Roosevelt and Winston Churchill. It won an Academy Award for Best Picture in the spring of 1944, as the allies were preparing for their imminent invasion of Europe (Harmetz, *Making of Casablanca*, 14).

CHAPTER 4

SEDUCTIVE BEAUTY AND NOBLE DEEDS: POLITICS IN *THE ENGLISH PATIENT* AND *CASABLANCA*

MARY P. NICHOLS

Casablanca and *The English Patient* have similar settings—northern Africa during World War II—and involve similar themes—how passionate love threatens friendships, national loyalties, and all human obligations. By exploring *The English Patient's* treatment of these themes in the 1990s, we can better appreciate the achievement of *Casablanca*, a film made over fifty years earlier. Count Laszlo Almásy (Ralph Fiennes), in the more recent film, lets nothing stand in the way of his love of Katharine Clifton (Kristin Scott Thomas), even turning over British documents to the Germans so that he can return to her. *Casablanca's* Rick, in contrast, tells his beloved Ilsa Lund that she should remain with her husband Victor Laszlo, for he needs her support in his fight for the Resistance. Thus *The English Patient* is generally understood as locating individual fulfillment in love regardless of political costs, whereas *Casablanca* appears to valorize personal sacrifice for the sake of a noble cause. The one privileges love over politics, the other politics over love.

I argue that this dichotomy between love and politics is too simple to shed light on the differences between these films. In the first place, *The English Patient* does not romanticize love to the extent that is often thought. Although the film depicts the beauty and seductiveness of passion free from all political loyalties, it also shows the dangers of such an infinite love. *The English Patient* leaves us with the tragic conflict between the limits that seem necessary for human life and humanity's unbounded desire for transcendence. *Casablanca* is no less complex because of its patriotic fervor. It answers *The English Patient* by demonstrating that passionate love need not lie beyond political loyalty as it does for the English patient, but can preserve itself by deriving strength from a noble political cause. The protagonists' political choices are inseparable from their love for each other. Only because Rick and Ilsa leave each other to serve the fight against Hitler will they "always have Paris." Beauty, when experienced as nobility of soul and expressed in noble deeds, mediates between individual happiness and moral and political obligations. *Casablanca* thus offers the middle ground that *The English Patient* lacks.

LOVE IN THE DESERT

Anthony Minghella's screen adaptation of Michael Ondaatje's *The English Patient* opens with slow brush strokes drawing lines in the sand. The music is foreign, unfamiliar, yet haunting and compelling. We learn later that it is a Hungarian folk song, one sung to the film's protagonist Count Laszlo Almásy when he was a child in Budapest. From the outset we are drawn into a strange, exotic, mysterious world. Only slowly do we recognize that the brush might be forming human figures: when the arms appear extended, and then the head, we see the original line as a body. We understand only in time, as parts are revealed from which we can infer a whole. But what are the figures doing? And who is painting them? They seem suspended. Later, Almásy and his international team of explorers find similar figures on the wall of a cave in the desert. The drawings prove the existence of an ancient oasis, for the figures are swimmers. Water in the desert indicates relief in two senses. It is both necessary for survival, and makes swimming possible, a playfulness and joy not immediately connected to survival, a superfluity or abundance perhaps in its own way equally necessary, if not to life, at least to human life.

When Almásy's expedition is disbanded due to the oncoming war, his British friend Madox (Julian Wadham) comments about their exploration of the desert: "We didn't care about countries, did we? Brits, Arabs, Hungarians, Germans. None of that mattered, did it? It was something finer than that."[1] War suspends their work, and it is countries that lead to war. At their farewell dinner, they toast "The International Sand Club," using the name with which Geoffrey Clifton (Colin Firth) has jokingly christened them. A rather drunk Almásy accuses the world in which nations demand allegiance: "Mustn't say 'international;' Dirty word. Filthy word. His Majesty! Die Führer! Il Duce!" To him, all nations seem equal, and equally culpable.

That "something finer"—beyond nationalities—to which the explorers devote themselves is represented by ancient drawings in the cave of the swimmers. The film shows their joy—and awe—at the discovery of the drawings. The beauty they experience transcends their national differences and can be owned by no one, even if powerful men leave their names on maps as a result of such discoveries. Such freedom from nations is what the dying Katharine Clifton longs for—to be with Almásy, "with friends, an earth without maps," in other words, a world with friends but no enemies. Katharine and Almásy's love for each other, an English woman whose husband works for British intelligence and a Hungarian count who seems to have no political loyalties of any sort, also transcends the lines drawn on maps. Almásy's exploring is connected with his love, just as his love of the desert is connected with his love of Katharine.[2] Soon after they discover the cave figures they acknowledge their love.

Katharine has read Almásy's monograph on the desert and is impressed, she admits, by such "a long paper with so few adjectives." "A thing is still a thing, no matter what you place in front of it," Almásy tells her, offering examples of a big car, a slow car, and a chauffeur-driven car, which are still cars. Even a broken car is a car, Almásy claims when Geoffrey offers it as a possible exception. Still dubious, Geoffrey points out that a broken car is "not much use." Katharine appears to take the side of her husband, offering examples of love—romantic, platonic, filial—"quite different things, surely?" Yet she has read Almásy's monograph and wants to meet the man who has written it. She is British and longs for familiar rainy climates and her garden and home by the sea yet is fascinated by the desert, as she will soon become by Almásy himself.

Geoffrey's example of "uxoriousness" or "excessive love of his wife," as his "favorite kind of love" is ominous. So too is Almásy's immediate conversation with Madox as to whether Clifton might be a useful member of their team. He is recommended by the Royal Geographic Society, according to Madox, and "a ruddy good pilot," who can make "aerial maps of the entire area." If one could explore from the air, Almásy observes, "life would be very simple." Geoffrey's aerial vision, at least the low-flying one useful for photographs, gives him the distance to see the differences between things and thus to distinguish between better and worse examples of their kind. Almásy seeks a greater immediacy that he supposes will allow him to bypass what is unessential. When his nurse Hana (Juliette Binoche) later comforts the dying Almásy by placing a ripe plum in his mouth, he expresses his appreciation by calling it simply "a plum plum." His adjective adds nothing to what it is.[3]

So too nothing qualifies for Almásy his love of Katharine—not her husband, for example, or her Britishness or her wartime loyalties. It is his own perspective, ironically, not Clifton's, that "makes life very simple." And when the men at the camp toast their wives—their absent wives (which applies to most of them), their present wives (which applies to Clifton), and their future wives (which is meant to apply to Almásy, who alone of the group is unmarried), all their different adjectives not withstanding—they toast the only woman present. Given her developing love for Almásy, Katharine is becoming Clifton's past wife and Almásy's future "wife." Their love makes past and future a timeless present for them. And it is Katharine's forgetting of time—her and Geoffrey's first anniversary—that leads to her husband's discovery of her affair with Almásy.

Soon after the Cliftons arrive at the desert camp, Katharine entertains the group around a campfire by reading a story from Herodotus's history, a story of the ancient king Candaules, whose wife is the most beautiful of women. Not content to enjoy her beauty alone, Candaules insists that his servant Gyges spy on his wife naked.[4] The queen becomes aware of her husband's transgression, summons Gyges, and threatens him with death "for gazing on that which [he] should not," unless he kills her husband and takes his place. Gyges accepts her offer. "Let that be a lesson to you," Madox warns Geoffrey. Madox does not see that he should warn Almásy as well, at least, not until it is too late.[5] Almásy gazes on Katharine as he should not, and she becomes aware of it. When Geoffrey agrees to go to Cairo to take pictures for the British army and decides to leave his wife at camp, Almásy questions whether it is appropriate, "for the desert is tough on women." But like Candaules, Geoffrey does not understand what he is doing, its effect on his wife, or the implications for his future.

It is when Clifton is absent that the scouting team locates what they call the Cave of Swimmers. When a car accident necessitates that part of the group remain behind while others go for help as a devastating sandstorm approaches, Almásy and Katharine take cover in one of the cars. A broken car, it turns out, Geoffrey to the contrary, can be of use, even if it does not serve the use that cars were built to serve. When the couple are practically buried in sand, their survival at issue, Almásy passes the time by relating stories of terrifying winds, such as whirlwinds in southern Morocco that inhabitants defend themselves against with knives, or the red wind that carries red sand so dense that it produces showers mistaken for blood. When Katharine claims Almásy's stories are mere fiction, he appeals to her friend Herodotus as witness.

It is not clear, however, that Herodotus is their friend in the same way or that he is their friend at all. Through the story of Candaules, Herodotus teaches the dangers of transgressing limits, of looking, for example, at another man's wife. Katharine does not heed such lessons, however, and even uses Herodotus's story, as we see in her glances at Almásy during her recounting it, as a means of seduction rather than warning. By comparing Katharine's telling of the tale with the original, we see that she leaves out Gyges' initial rebuke to Candaules when he proposes that Gyges look upon his wife that "we must look only on our own." And Katharine adds a line not found in Herodotus's text: when Candaules' wife stood naked before Gyges, she was "more lovely than he could have imagined."[6] Whether consciously or not, Katharine modifies Herodotus's text to fit her situation, converting the warning of the story into enticement.

Almásy's Herodotean stories of the winds, in contrast to Katharine's story of Candaules, involve the wonders and terrors of nonhuman nature rather than of human passion.[7] Like Herodotus, Almásy travels and looks, but, unlike Herodotus, he does not understand the possibility of transgression and the need to resist not only natural terrors such as the winds but human terrors that arise from unbounded passions, such as Candaules'. Commentators who see a postmodern perspective in *The English Patient* refer to Almásy's ragged copy of Herodotus, which he "employs as a physical and emotional scrapbook," filled with "primary text, marginalia, and pasted-in cuttings" to exemplify "the textual and subjective nature of history."[8] But it is at least as plausible that the materials that Almásy has added to Herodotus's text indicate that he has made it is his own in such a way as to simplify its complexity and to neglect those aspects that might serve as a warning or a reproach to his own desires.[9] Herodotus is not merely what we make of him, but rather lurks in the background as the explorer who knows both the attraction of beauty and its dangers.

We see those dangers when the explorer becomes lover. He tells Katharine that he most hates ownership, and being owned, and that when she leaves she should forget him. But Almásy is no more able to forget Katharine than

Katharine is able to forget him. They become consumed by their love: "I can't work. I can't sleep," Almásy admits. Although he hates ownership, he "claims this shoulder blade," as he looks at and touches Katharine's naked body. He changes his mind when he turns her over and sees the hollow under her throat, "This place, I love this place,"—"this is mine!" Becoming like those explorers who give their name to things, he will ask the king's permission to call the hollow under Katharine's throat the Almásy Bosphorus.

Later, when the war is about to break out and the work of the "International Sand Club" is suspended, Madox is concerned about the whereabouts of the explorers' expedition maps, which belong to "His Majesty's Government," and "shouldn't be left around for any Tom, Dick, and Harry to have sight of." Madox knows in a war that "if you own the desert, you own North Africa." But Almásy does not grasp what Madox is talking about, for he thinks that no one "owns the desert." He is concerned only with whether Madox can tell him the name of that hollow under a woman's throat—the very place he claims as his own. Indeed, he claims Katharine as his own, for after she leaves him, he returns for "the things that are mine. Which belong to me." His love alone seems to give him title and even to confer innocence, an innocence highlighted by the corruptions of war: "Betrayals in war," he writes, "are childlike compared with our betrayals during peace. . . . The heart is an organ of fire."

Katharine, in contrast to Almásy, is torn by their love. Whereas Almásy quickly betrays his hatred of ownership, Katharine cannot bear to live with the lies and deceptions she hates.[10] She is not just a woman, but a married woman. She worries that her affair will devastate her husband. She yields to her passion for Almásy at the embassy Christmas party, while Geoffrey entertains dressed as Santa Claus. Afterwards, she pleads with her husband to take her home, to England, where "green, anything green, or rain" offers an alternative to the heat, and the passion, of North Africa. But for Geoffrey, the war (or its threat) complicates his loyalties. They can't go home, he tells her, for war may be coming. And Geoffrey works for the British government under the cover of working for the Royal Geographic. "You do so love a disguise," she tells him. "I do so love you," he corrects her. Geoffrey's lies or disguises are more benign than Katharine's, for he knows who he is and who and what he loves. And he would not betray them. In fact, it is his betrayal by others that drives him to his last desperate act. His playing Santa Claus is the disguise that reveals the man he is or, at least, the man he would like to be.

Geoffrey and Katharine fly to pick up Almásy after he packs the camp at the Cave of the Swimmers. The maddened Geoffrey, long aware of wife's affair, finally tries to crash his plane into Almásy. Perhaps he intends to kill all three of them. Instead, he kills himself and badly injures his wife. Even for Geoffrey, as for Almásy, loves triumphs over all else. Almásy has no choice but to leave the injured Katharine in the cave, promising to return for her. She has just enough water and food for the three days it will take him to walk to El Taj and the three hours to return in a car. "Although, given all the traffic in the desert these days," he muses, he is "bound to bump into one army or another." Obviously, either army will do, when it comes to saving Katharine's life.

Arriving at El Taj, exhausted and frantic, Almásy insists on being given a car, a doctor, and morphine. He attacks a British soldier who insists on seeing "some form of identification" and finding out his "nationality" and is imprisoned. It is a world of only friends and enemies, not neutrals. It never occurs to Almásy to explain that it is an Englishwoman whose life he is trying to save, the wife of a British intelligence agent. Instead he refers to Katharine as his wife. She has become his own, just when he is losing her, when her being "Mrs. Clifton" might have saved her.[11] He is in need of Geoffrey's aerial view.

Almásy eventually escapes from the British and sells the Royal Geographic's maps of the desert to the Germans in exchange for the fuel to fly Madox's old plane back to the desert to rescue what is now Katharine's corpse. When flying away with her body, his plane is shot down by the Germans, for he neglects to replace the British markings on Madox's plane.[12] Who you are matters, the side to which you give or refuse your loyalties matters, and at last burned beyond recognition he attains for a moment the anonymity he once held as his ideal. Lest we be so attracted by the beauty and power of Almásy and Katharine's love as to blame their tragic end on a world with limits and boundaries that allows no place for their infinite love, Minghella shows us that Almásy escapes from the British only by brutally murdering a young private, who at the time is showing Almásy a kindness.[13] And, prior to his murder, the camera reveals that the young man is reading a book while guarding the prisoners. Those who read Minghella's published screenplay know that the book is Swift's *Gulliver's Travels*. Like Almásy himself, the youth carries with him a book of travels and adventures to strange lands, even one by an Irishman that is critical of British politics, and yet the young man is a soldier, a patriot.

LOVE IN THE ITALIAN MONASTERY

The foregoing account of Almásy and Katharine's love is one pieced together from Almásy's memories, from his flashbacks, as he lies dying. Rescued after the plane crash, cared for by bedouin tribesmen and then handed over to Allied forces in southern Italy, Almásy at first cannot remember who he is. He doesn't know his nationality, although he can speak German. He "remember[s] a garden, plunging down to the sea," and "a cottage . . . right on the shore, nothing between you and France," perhaps his or his wife's. He thinks he was married. His memories indicate only his desires—he was never married, and as far as we know never in England—the home "on the South coast of England" that he remembers as his own recalls the one where Katharine told him she wanted to be buried ("in the garden, where I grew up, with a view of the sea"). Presumably he was heading there with her body when his plane crashed. As he nears death, he yearns not for the desert, but for the sea—and for rain: "I'm dying for rain—of course I'm dying anyway—but I long to feel rain on my face." His longings are a reproach to his past. The examining officer records him as an "English patient."

The dying man is cared for by a Canadian nurse and member of the Allied forces, Hana, who insists on staying behind with him, because he is too feeble to be moved. They stay in an Italian monastery, abandoned and ruined by bombing. There they are joined by Caravaggio (Willem Dafoe), a Canadian and spy for the Allies, who has been hunting for Almásy, a man whom he believes to be a German spy, whose maps led the Germans through the deserts to Cairo. Finally, assigned to remove bombs planted by retreating Germans, the Indian Kip (Naveen Andrews), a Sikh lieutenant in the British army, and his English friend Sergeant Hardy (Kevin Whately) set up their tents on the grounds of the monastery. As Almásy jokes when Hana tells him about the visitors who have moved in, "we should charge." The film's present constitutes another international society.[14]

It is not at first obvious that the man who lies dying is the same Hungarian count whom we meet in his memories. But he does come to remember his past before he dies—with the help of his copy of Herodotus, of Caravaggio's proddings, and of his conversations with Hana. In spite of Hana's unconditional care for him, who he is does matter. The film is about the identification of the English patient as Almásy.

The English patient does not simply remember who he is, however, but he learns other things from Caravaggio—the way his acts were seen by others and their effects on others' lives. When Caravaggio accuses him of getting Rommel's spy across the desert into British headquarters in Cairo, Almásy does not deny it, but tries to explain—"I had to get back to the desert. I made a promise. The rest meant nothing to me." Caravaggio, however, has the better of the argument, for "it was not just another expedition" that Almásy took with the Germans, for "there was a result to what he did," a result that Caravaggio demonstrates by holding up his maimed hands. Almásy's expeditions had sought knowledge for its own sake, a beauty without consequences, but those expeditions and the maps they made possible were put to other uses—the Germans' drive into Cairo and Almásy's rescue of Katharine's corpse.

When Caravaggio tells him that his turning maps over to the Germans might have led to the deaths of thousands of people, Almásy comments that "thousands of people did die, just different people." Caravaggio again gets the better of the argument by mentioning that Madox was one of those people who died: "he shot himself, your best friend, when he found out you were a spy." Madox is not simply one of thousands of people; he has a name, and he was Almásy's friend. Almásy cannot be indifferent to his death. Almásy may literally speak the truth when he denies that he was ever a spy for the Germans, insofar as that suggests commitment to their cause, but Almásy performed the actions of which Caravaggio accuses him that prompted Madox's suicide. The circumstances of Madox's death is one of the significant changes Minghella made from Ondaatje's story, in which Madox commits suicide simply because of the war. As Ondaatje writes, "Madox returned to Somerset, where he had been born, and a month later heard the sermon in honour of war, pulled out his desert revolver, and shot himself."[15] Minghella thus converts an act of protest against war and against appeals to the honor of war into a protest against betrayal. The betrayals in war are not merely those of love, but of friendship and of the distinction between right and wrong. Minghella's Madox, in contrast to Ondaatje's, dies as a friend and a patriot.[16] As a consequence, his suicide can have a greater effect on Almásy, for Almásy was implicated in it. The betrayals in war are not childlike.

When Caravaggio accuses Almásy of killing the Cliftons, he first denies it, but then as he remembers more of the past he acknowledges that "maybe I did." Having heard his story, Caravaggio no longer desires to kill him. Perhaps he realizes that Almásy died years ago, as the patient sadly observes. Almásy's story seems to have put Caravaggio's anger and bitterness to rest. Almásy's fondness for Hana, Kip, and even Caravaggio, to say nothing of his shock on the hearing of Madox's suicide, all qualify his statement that other than his promise to Katharine "the rest [means] nothing to [him]."

The English patient notices and encourages Hana's growing fondness for Kip: "you like him, don't you?" He observes, "your voice changes." Hana comes to accept her love, in spite of her fears that she will lose Kip in the war, as she has lost both her sweetheart and her best friend, and that she is a curse to anyone who loves her. As a gift to Hana, Kip shows her the paintings in an Italian church. By means of a pulley, he elevates Hana so that she is able to see the Renaissance frescoes up close. A flare Kip gives to her illumines the paintings in the dark church, just as the explorers' flashlights illumine the drawings in the cave. In both instances there is a sense of wonder and beauty, which serves as a precious and elevating moment in the lives of the lovers. Commentators have noted parallels: "When Hana is suspended in the cathedral, she seems to be floating and swimming as a shadowy echo of the figures in the Cave of the Swimmers."[17] In contrast to Almásy and Katharine's love, however, theirs requires no betrayal. The beauty they appreciate together arises in the Renaissance; it is not prehistory, precivilization.

Hana nevertheless loses Kip, not to death, but apparently to his own fear of loving and losing someone—the very fear that Hana has overcome—for he withdraws from her after his friend Hardy is killed by a bomb the Germans left behind. Hana begs Kip to talk to her, but he does not respond. In Minghella's published screenplay, Kip asks Hana to come with him to India. When she hesitates, he understands her reaction to be due to the racial differences that separate them: "I know, here I am always a brown man, there you would always be a white woman." Whereas Almásy would allow no differences, or conventions, to qualify his love for Katharine, Kip allows them to have too much sway. Almásy rejects adjectives, and Kip lets them determine too much.

Hana loves both men. Earlier, when Caravaggio appears at the monastery, a man who lived two blocks from Hana in Montreal, she tells Almásy when "there's a war, where you come from becomes important." But with Kip, she sweeps the racial differences he mentions aside, saying, "I'm thinking about your heart, not your skin, and how to reach it. I don't think I can."[18] If race separates them, it is because such difference and the conflict it brings highlight and intensify the fragility attaching to their temporal lives. And Hana's own love for Kip demonstrates the courage to risk loss in the face of such fragility.

In Ondaatje's novel, a radio announcement of the U.S. bombing of Hiroshima and Nagasaki has a momentous impact on Kip: his visions of "the streets of Asia full of fire," "the tremor of Western wisdom," leads to outrage.[19] The film's omission of all reference to the atomic bomb, and consequently Kip's passionate reaction to it, has been denounced by film critics, who applaud the novel as a criticism of Western imperialism. Elizabeth Kella, for example, argues that the novel criticizes "the ways in which humanism has historically been made to serve imperialist and racist agendas." The changes made by the film, such as the excision of the bombing of Japanese cities, "all shore up the representation of war as a timeless human tragedy rather than to question it."[20]

Moreover, without the atomic bombing of Japan and Kip's dramatic reaction, the climax becomes the narrative closure of Almásy's romance rather than Kip's racial awakening. Thus, the film is personal, the novel is political.[21] Whereas the novel suggests that "there are multiple subjectivities located in myriad and simultaneous loyalties to structures such as family, nation, and race," the film "constructs and fetishes an essential interior self," implying that "the self is located in a person's ability to love and is evidenced by acts inspired by such sentiments" and that the lover is "the true subject," set against other fleeting and mutable identities.[22] Indeed, the novel according to these critics deliberately leaves open the English patient's identity, whereas the film clearly identifies him.[23]

Although Minghella's changes are as significant as critics argue, there is an alternative account of their import. When Minghella replaces the bombing of Japan by the United States with Hardy's death from a German bomb as the catalyst for Kip's leaving Hana, he is not turning from politics to the simply personal. German imperialism, not Western imperialism, is the target, as is the devastating, tragic effect it has on human life. Minghella's omission of an opportunity to condemn American aggression and Western imperialism is therefore not a sign that for him love "overwrite[s] politics" and that, being "timeless and essential," love "possesses the ability to justify almost anything."[24] To the contrary, the film is clearly critical of "a love that knows no bounds."[25] The film accomplishes this by means of Caravaggio's maimed hands and Almásy's murder of the British private, as well as Caravaggio's reference to "thousands of people" who could have died as a consequence of Almásy's attempt to keep his promise to Katharine. In the words of Caravaggio, Almásy's expedition with the Germans "wasn't just another expedition." Nor was Madox's death just another death, not even for Almásy. The film does not show that love justifies any of these events.

Almásy's coming to understand who he is, moreover, does not fix the lover as the true subject, with all other identities mutable and fleeting, but, rather, fixes his responsibility for his actions. That his memories flow from Caravaggio's prodding does not indicate that they question the historically real and are only a product of Caravaggio's investment in Almásy as the object of his hunt.

Rather, Caravaggio prods in order to find out whether the patient is in fact the man responsible for what happened to him. Caravaggio seeks to know the truth before he punishes, even though the truth dissipates his anger and hence his desire to do so. To assign and accept moral responsibility does recover an essential self that bears that responsibility, but it also indicates that that self is constituted by moral obligations flowing from its myriad relations—such as Almásy's obligations to Katharine's husband, to his friends, and, most fundamentally, to the civilized human life that the war defends. Contrary to what most critics purport, the film does echo Ondaatje's critique of human essence in the form of Almásy's humanism, but not in order to demonstrate the underlying despotism of Western ideals. Rather, essence cannot be stripped of all the particulars that constitute character and on the basis of which we can make judgments about things. Almásy's love for Katharine is in a sense a broken love, as broken as the car in the desert in which it was first acknowledged.

Consider the scene in which Kip reads to Almásy from Kipling's *Kim*. Kip confides to Almásy his objection to Kipling's message "that the best destiny for India is to be ruled by the British." When Almásy tells Hana that "we have discovered a shared pleasure, the boy and I," she supposes that it lies in "arguing about books," but Almásy jokingly indicates that it lies in "condensed milk— one of the truly great inventions." The film indicates Kip's fondness—in spite of racial and political differences—for the man he still supposes to be an English patient, by his tender smile and offer to get him another tin of condensed milk. It is when Kip goes on this errand that Almásy encourages Hana to pursue her growing affection for Kip. In other words, the film's allusion to Kipling serves less as a reminder of British imperialism and of Almásy's naive complicity in it[26] than as an indication that differences need not undermine affection and respect. Kip, after all, is British educated and a lieutenant in the British army. He tells Hana that "the Patient, Hardy—they're everything that's good about England. I couldn't even say what that was." Kip sadly couples the English patriot killed by a German bomb with the man who gave British maps to the Germans. Almásy is neither English nor represents everything good about England. Kip is mistaken about the English patient. He nevertheless knows both that everything about England is not good and that there is something about England worth admiring.

At the end of the film, Kip leaves to join his unit, his job in the area completed. When he tells Hana good-bye, their farewell is awkward. "I'll always go back to that church," Hana says, to "look at my painting." But without Kip, Hana will never have the close-up vision Kip's pulley offered her, nor will her vision have anything but a memory of their love to give it meaning. Kip says that he too "will always go back to that church," but we have no reason to think that when and if they do they ever will meet there, as Hana says they will. The beauty of the frescoes that they share and that was Kip's gift to Hana does not sufficiently touch their lives to keep them together. Hana appears to see beyond the frescoes in her love for Kip, and that in fact is why she can imagine returning to the church. But just as Kip cannot articulate just what it is he admires in

Hardy and the English patient, Hana is not able to communicate to Kip why they should stay together. That to which the frescoes in the Italian church points, paradoxically, is more difficult to define or articulate than the freedom or boundlessness represented by the swimmers in the cave.

After all his past has returned to him, Almásy asks Hana to administer a lethal dose of morphine. Because Hana earlier insisted that as a nurse she must keep him alive, the rightness of her compliance is ambiguous. If Almásy is at last assuming responsibility for his acts, all the more ironic is Hana's reading to him Katharine's last words of love as he dies: "We are the real countries, not the boundaries drawn on maps."

After her patient dies, Hana too leaves the monastery to rejoin her unit. Caravaggio is also summoned to service by the Allies, where he is called to interpret at trials, although he is "allergic to courtrooms." The man who suffered when his torturer dismissed the limits imposed by the Geneva convention and who came to the monastery to seek revenge against Almásy will now acknowledge the limits that law imposes and the proper place of law in pursuing justice. The possibility of redemption through politics, hinted at but left ambiguous in *The English Patient*, takes center stage in *Casablanca*, where the "Marseillaise" drowns out the German soldiers and their pro-German song.

LOVE IN CASABLANCA

Whereas *The English Patient* opens with a view of the unbounded desert, *Casablanca* opens with a map of Axis-occupied Europe in December of 1941, distinguishing the Allied powers, the Axis powers, and neutral nations. The latter, a voice over tells us, include French Morocco, where Casablanca serves as a resting station for refugees on their way to freedom, especially to Portugal, where flights from Lisbon bring them to America. A bold line appears on the map, tracing their route from Paris to Marseilles on the French coast, to Casablanca, to Lisbon. Lines between countries are pushed back by military might, while others are drawn by the routes of the refugees to safety. As in *The English Patient*, boundaries between countries are fluid, and the film's characters attempt to slip through them. But the goal of the refugees is America and the freedom it represents. One cannot live free from nations, as Almásy tries to do, for nations make possible freedom and its defense.

In the corrupt city of Casablanca, life is cheap, and the opening scenes tell us of pickpockets, bribery, and murders. A pickpocket warns the couple whom he is about to fleece that "the scum of Europe has gravitated to Casablanca." There are those who are desperate for exit visas and those ready to take advantage of them. The opening shots of Casablanca reveal another international sand club of sorts, peopled by native Arabs, members of the Free French Resistance, German sympathizers, disparate refugees, and criminals preying on whomever they can. French police shoot a fleeing suspect who falls beneath a poster of Marshall Pétain, head of Vichy France, inscribed with his words, "I keep my promises, just as I keep those of others." When "the whole world crumbl[es]," the film thus questions, can a person's word be trusted? While it is Almásy's promise to Katharine to return for her that leads to his collaboration with the Germans, Ilsa's marital promise leads her to leave Rick in Paris and later influences Rick to insist that she leave him in Casablanca. For the protagonist of this film, war does not confer innocence on betrayal. One must do better than Marshall Pétain. It is Rick who keeps his promise to do the thinking for both him and Ilsa and ensures that Ilsa keep hers to her husband as well, for he needs her, Rick believes, in his work against Hitler. Promises are more complex for Rick, because loyalties are more diverse and the good to be achieved broader in scope than for Almásy.

French Captain Louis Renault, who nominally governs the city, reflects the diversity of Casablanca itself—a Frenchman who caters to the Germans, a womanizer not above bribery who is also friendly with Rick. A plane soars over Casablanca at the beginning of the film, as one does over the desert in *The English Patient*. Whereas Almásy is trying to rescue Katharine's body from the cave, in *Casablanca* a European couple imagines the plane is bringing refugees to safety in Lisbon. Their hopes too are disappointed, for the camera reveals the plane's German markings. While the British markings on Almásy's plane ironically conceal his collaboration from the German gunners below, there is nothing misleading about the markings on the plane in *Casablanca*. It is bringing Major Strasser of the Third Reich to Casablanca to ensure that the recent murderer of two Germans carrying transit papers will be apprehended and punished.

At the center of life in Casablanca is Rick's Café Américain. Rick is reputed to be above politics and national loyalties, reminding us of Almásy. Rick claims to be "a drunkard" when Major Strasser inquires of his nationality. Renault interprets this to mean "a citizen of the world" and "completely neutral about everything." Asked by Strasser whether he "cannot imagine the Germans in their beloved Paris," Ricks responds that "it's not particularly my beloved Paris." As to the Germans occupying New York City, Rick helpfully warns that, "there are certain sections of New York, Major, that I wouldn't advise you to try to invade." Among Rick's most characteristic lines in the film are "I stick my neck out for nobody" and "I'm the only cause I'm interested in." His indifference seems to apply to women. Early in the film we see Rick send home a young Frenchwoman, Yvonne, who is apparently smitten by him. Renault observes to Major Strasser that Rick's neutrality extends to women as well as politics.

In our first view of Rick in the film, he is playing chess—alone. He moves the pieces for both sides, overseeing their struggle. We see his hands before we see his face, handsome, bland, aloof. Almásy is also handsome, but his face seldom bland, and he does not long remain aloof. Almásy encounters Katharine shopping in Cairo's bustling marketplace, just as Rick meets Ilsa in Casablanca's. But in the later film's parallel scene, Almásy continues to follow Katharine. His desire not to be obligated, which he expresses when Katharine offers him drawings she made of the figures on the wall of the cave, is short lived. It is not obligation, however, that best expresses Almásy's feelings, except perhaps later toward Hana. Rick, in contrast, recognizes any number of obliga-tions, although they are not distinct from his affection, such as to his piano player Sam (Arthur "Dooley" Wilson)[27] and to his waiter Carl, as we see when he provides for them when he finally sells his café. As the murderer of the Ge r-man couriers discovers, in *Casablanca's* war-torn world one cannot successfully play both sides. But, then, Rick never really tries to do so, except on the chess board, and we see that his obligations to human beings are inseparable from his principles.

Early in the film, there are hints that Rick's indifference is not as great as he claims. Major Strasser is suspicious of the neutrality of a man who "ran guns to Ethiopia" in 1935 after it was invaded by Italy (in violation of Roosevelt's 1935 Neutrality Law) and then fought in Spain against Franco the following year. At the beginning of the film, we see Rick bar a German banker from entering his private game room and lets the banker know that he is lucky that his cash is good at the bar. Rick is characteristically the protector of boundaries, although he allows Ugarte, black market dealer and now apparently the murderer of the German couriers whose letters of transit he now possesses, to slip through the door of the game room. It is precisely because Ugarte knows that Rick despises him, he says, that Rick is the only one to whom he trusts the letters for safekeep-ing. Ugarte may be despicable, but he understands that Rick's indifference to exploiting others is the flip side of his integrity. Rick's integrity, however, eventually demands more than his safekeeping of the letters—their use in the service of a cause. As we saw in the case of Almásy and the British maps of North Africa entrusted to his safekeeping, neutrality is difficult to maintain, whether one uses what one has in one's possession for good or ill.

Rick seems to fit into none of the categories that define the city's teeming population, insofar as he is neutral to both sides in the war and also lacks the desires for safety, women, or money that move others. He cares not even for an honest profit, inasmuch as he continually resists selling his café to black-market king Signor Ferrari. When the frustrated Ferrari proposes instead to buy for his own club Rick's piano player, Sam, Rick insists that he "does not buy or sell human beings." And while he rejects Yvonne's advances, we see him try to make her stop drinking and to get her safely home. That there is more to Rick than Renault's words to Strasser indicates, however, is suggested most poign-antly when he intervenes to thwart Renault's exploitation of a young Bulgarian woman, Annina, who is trying to get exit visas for herself and her husband.

Indeed, Annina is so young that, as Rick observes, she should not be al-lowed in Rick's club. She is there with her husband, Jan, who is trying to win enough at the roulette table for their exit visas, and with Renault, who offers her another way to get them. But is Renault's word to be trusted, she asks Rick, as she contemplates breaking her marital vows. She asks Rick even more: "if someone loved you very much, so that your happiness was the only thing she wanted in the whole world, but she did a bad thing to make certain of it, could you forgive her?" Like *The English Patient, Casablanca* raises the question of the limits to what one should do for love. Whereas Almásy sells British maps—

and therewith thousands of innocent lives—to the Germans, Annina is contemplating selling herself to Renault. She is trying to escape from political oppression (in Bulgaria "a devil has the people by the throat"), not indifferent to it. Because she knows it is "a bad thing" she is considering doing, she is torn.

With Rick's help, Annina's husband wins enough at roulette for the exit visas. Annina tries to thank Rick, but he tells her that her husband is "just a lucky guy." Rick's noble deeds require no thanks, and when disclaiming his obvious intervention in the wheel of fortune, he speaks truly in another sense. Fortune has blessed Jan in his wife. As Rick cynically observed when Annina asked him about the dilemma of a woman who loved someone so much that she would do "a bad thing" for the sake of his happiness, "Nobody ever loved me that much." The waiter, Carl, who keeps his eye on all that goes on in the café and who is later revealed to work for the Resistance, tells Rick that he has done "a beautiful thing." Renault is of course not entirely pleased at the outcome, but concedes to defeat. It is with some begrudging admiration that he reproaches Rick for being after all "a rank sentimentalist."

When Victor Laszlo and his wife Ilsa arrive in Casablanca, and soon thereafter at Rick's Café, we learn even more about Rick. Not only has he fought for freedom, he has been in love. Ilsa's appearance at his café awakens his memories of his past with her, memories he has been trying to forget. Like Katharine Clifton, Ilsa is a beautiful and striking woman. And while both women are fond of their husbands and do not want them hurt, neither is passionately in love with them. Katharine married her childhood sweetheart, whose loyalty to her over the years was steadfast. And Ilsa confides to Rick that Victor Laszlo is a great and courageous man about whom she had heard for years and whom, when she met him, she came to "worship . . . with a feeling she supposed was love." Like Geoffrey Clifton, Laszlo is a patriot, in fact, he is the Czech leader of the Resistance to Hitler, a man whose work will affect "the lives of thousands and thousands of people." And, like Katharine, Ilsa discovers that love takes many forms, which are "quite different things." Like Katharine, she falls passionately in love with someone else.

When Ilsa met Rick in Paris, shortly before the German occupation, she had been told that her husband had died in a concentration camp. Her marriage had to be kept secret for her own safety, given how much she knew of her husband's work; and when she learns that he is indeed alive, ill, and in need of her, she leaves Rick, unable for everyone's safety to tell him the truth. What looks like a failure to keep her promise to him—to leave Paris with him—is actually her keeping her marriage vows. When Rick learns the truth, he also learns of Ilsa's enduring love for him: "I'll never have the strength to leave you again," she tells him, and also that "I don't know what is right anymore; you'll have to think for both of us, for all of us." The camera cuts, leaving them in each other's arms. In the next scene, Victor arrives at the café with Carl, seeking safety from the police who have broken up their Resistance meeting. Just before Renault arrives to arrest him, he appeals to Rick to adopt the cause that was once his and also to use the letters of transit he suspects Rick has to take Ilsa away from Casablanca.

He knows, he says, that his wife is in love with Rick. He is no Geoffrey Clifton, and his intended sacrifice for the sake of the happiness of the woman he loves will be repeated in another form by Rick at the end of the film. Victor Laszlo inspires not only Ilsa but Rick as well.

The stirring ending of the film is well known. Rick sells his café to Signor Ferrari, tells Renault his plan to leave with Ilsa, and gets him to free Laszlo, whom Renault is holding in jail for the opportunity of apprehending in possession of the letters of transit. Renault agrees to help, observing that "love, it seems, triumphs over virtue." At this point, it is not clear to the audience what Rick intends. While it seems inconceivable that the man we have to grown to like would in effect hand Laszlo over to the Germans, is Rick intending to help Laszlo leave alone for Lisbon, as Ilsa believes, or help Laszlo and his wife to leave together, as Laszlo now supposes?[8] We do not know, but the film does show Rick noticing Ilsa's horrified look when Renault suddenly appears to arrest her husband as accessory to the murder of the German couriers and her move to his side. Rick pulls out his own gun on Renault, and they all race to the airport where the plane to Lisbon is waiting. Renault watches Rick put Ilsa on the plane with her husband, telling her that Victor needs her to carry on his work. Besides, if she does not go with him and stays with Rick, she will regret it, "maybe not today, and maybe not tomorrow, but soon, and for the rest of [her] life." As to their love for each other, Rick and Ilsa "will always have Paris," which they had lost but now recovered.

As Laszlo and Ilsa prepare to board the plane, Rick tells him that Ilsa had pretended that she was still in love with him in order to obtain the exit visa for him, but that he knew it was over long ago. Like Annina imagined herself doing, Ilsa in Rick's story is willing to do "a bad thing" for the sake of the man she loves. Rick's story twists the truth, for, while Ilsa is willing to do a bad thing for the sake of the man she loves, the man she loves is Rick, not Laszlo. Rick prevents her too from the deed, and like Annina she also tries to thank him as she leaves with her husband, saying, "Good-bye, Rick. God bless you."

Major Strasser appears, picks up the phone to stop the plane from leaving, and pulls his gun on Rick. The man we saw playing chess for both sides at the beginning of the film draws his gun and kills Major Strasser. He now stands clearly on one side of the struggle. Chess pieces differ only in their color; not so the players in World War II. Renault, also moved by all he has witnessed, makes a choice. "Round up the usual suspects," he tells the police when they arrive. Rick is not only a "sentimentalist," Renault observes, but he has become "a patriot." So too has Renault. The pair walk off together, with plans to leave Casablanca to join the Free French forces, with the music of the "Marseillaise" in the background. Love does not triumph over virtue, as Renault earlier thought, but in fact sustains virtue. It is, after all, when Rick feels betrayed by Ilsa in Paris that he becomes cynical about politics and adopts his "wise foreign policy," in the words of Renault, looking out only for himself. And now when he has recovered his love for her, his political ideals are reawakened. Rick believes that Laszlo's love for Ilsa also supports his work against Hitler: she must leave with her husband, he tells her, for "You're part of his work, the thing that keeps him going."

It is not, however, that virtue triumphs over love in *Casablanca*. In the end Rick acts not simply as patriot but in the only way in which he could be true to his and Ilsa's love. Inasmuch as Ilsa would eventually regret leaving her husband, they would have lost Paris again. Rick's insisting that Ilsa leave with Laszlo preserves Paris for both of them. They love each other for who they are. Love and virtue are inseparable for them. Rick's love for Ilsa is reawakened when he learns the reason she left him in Paris—to return to her husband, and to the cause to which all three of them were devoted. The Ilsa he loves is the woman who made the choice she made in Paris. Ilsa too comes to see that her love for Rick is for a man of a certain sort, as she reveals when she supposes that he is no longer that man: "Last night, I saw what has happened to you. The Rick I knew in Paris, I could tell him [about her marriage to Laszlo] he'd understand. But [not] the one who looked at me with such hatred." The Rick she loves is not a man who would urge the wife of Victor Laszlo to leave him, no more than he is one for whom love could triumph over virtue. Rick has come to see that and shows it to Ilsa as well.

Rick tells Ilsa that "I'm no good at being noble, but it doesn't take much to see that the problems of three little people don't amount to a hill of beans in this crazy world." But the problems of these three people, the film itself testifies, do amount to a hill of beans, and so much more. It is the choices that these three people make, and the ways in which they resolve their problems, that ennobles the cause for which they fight as much as that cause ennobles them. Ilsa and Rick do not sacrifice themselves for a greater cause; they remain true to themselves and to their love.[29]

While Renault's statement that love triumphs over virtue does not apply to Rick, it applies to Almásy. As critics who contrast the two films point out, for Almásy and Katharine "the problems of the world, and the millions of people threatened by Nazism, don't amount to a hill of beans."[30] Although the film does not condone such an attitude but shows its tragic consequences, it lacks that understanding of nobility on the basis of which *Casablanca* suggests a resolution of those conflicts. The difference between the films lies not in the choice of the personal over the political, or the political over the personal, but in the understanding of beauty and its place in human life.

Among the nine Academy Awards received by *The English Patient* was one for best cinematography. Both the physical beauty of the desert and the physical beauty of Katharine are seductive and like the swimmers in the cave suggest the dissolution of conventions and limits.[31] The film shows the conflict between beauty and moral responsibility. In *Casablanca*, in contrast, the desert exerts no similar pull.[32] When Renault asks Rick why he came to Casablanca, he claims that he is there "for the waters." When Renault points out that they are in the midst of a desert, Rick says simply that he was misinformed. The physical character of northern Africa enters the movie only as a jocular subterfuge.

Beauty, in *Casablanca*, in contrast to *The English Patient*, lies in deeds as well as in physical features, in souls as well as bodies, in political ideals as well as works of art. Although Ilsa is remarkably beautiful, her physical beauty is highlighted by her character—her choice in Paris, her standing by Laszlo as he sings the "Marseillaise," her appeal to what is noblest in Rick. Whereas Almásy and Katharine share a love for the desert and its freedom from limits, Rick and Ilsa share a love for the cause of political freedom. Laszlo's resistance to Hitler "was your cause, too," Ilsa reminds Rick. The woman with whom Rick fell in love was one who would look up to Victor Laszlo with a feeling of admiration she could suppose was love. Laszlo was able to call forth in her the sentiments that moved him and that she and Rick then shared. As Ilsa explains to Rick, "Everything I knew or became was because of him." "He opened up for me," she says, "a whole beautiful world of knowledge and thoughts and ideals." Beauty has a larger range of meaning in *Casablanca* than in *The English Patient*.

As we have seen, Rick's waiter, Carl, praises Rick's intervention in the affairs of the young couple seeking exit visas as a "beautiful thing." When beauty appears in actions, the actions can be called noble. Rick claims that he is no good at being noble, just when his nobility shines through in his deeds. The noble is the middle ground between the cause that demands individual sacrifice and the individual who seeks to do the right thing for its own sake. It is where larger cause and individual meet so that neither is sacrificed to the other. *The English Patient* does not valorize love and the individual subject, as some critics maintain, but it does not offer or even explore this middle ground. Thus Almásy's deeds lead his friend to commit suicide, whereas Rick's evoke in Renault what makes possible "the beginning of a beautiful friendship" between them. It is significant that *Casablanca* does not end with Rick walking off alone to join the Resistance but with his doing so with Renault. "Becoming a patriot" goes hand in hand with forming ties of love and affection.

Casablanca suggests that the experience of the nobility of others will inspire others to like nobility, as Laszlo inspired Ilsa and Rick, and Rick inspired Renault. Just as Renault stages for Major Strasser a demonstration of the efficiency of his administration in apprehending Ugarte, *Casablanca* stages for its audience a demonstration of heroism. The art in the Cave of the Swimmers, in contrast, inspires Almásy and Katharine's forbidden love and betrayals, while that of the frescoes in the Italian church is not sufficient inspiration for Hana and Kip to affect their lives. They may always have those paintings, but their farewell suggests that they may not mean very much. *The English Patient* itself leaves us with a tragic conflict between love and beauty, on the one hand, and moral and political action, on the other. *Casablanca* is art of another sort. It exemplifies art's high calling to support regimes of liberty by encouraging virtue and noble deeds. Not only Rick and Ilsa, but the audience of *Casablanca*, as well, will always have Paris.

NOTES

1. All quotations, unless otherwise noted, are from the film *The English Patient*, directed by Anthony Minghella (Miramax Home Entertainment, 1996). All quotes from *Casablanca* can found at: http://www.geocities.com/classicmoviescripts/script/casablanca.pdf.

2. In his novel, Michael Ondaatje weaves Almásy's love of the desert even more clearly with his rejection of the distinctions between nations. "We were German, English, Hungarian, African," Almásy says. "Gradually we became nationless. I came to hate nations. We were deformed by nation-states." And then, "Erase the family name! Erase nations! I was taught such things by the desert. . . . By the time the war arrived, after ten years in the desert, it was easy for me to slip across borders, not to belong to anyone, to any nation"(*The English Patient* [New York: Vintage International, 1993], 138-39). Here Almásy connects the infinite expanse of the desert (where borders become permeable, insignificant) with the essentially human, stripped of all particulars of time and place (family and country). For Almásy, "There is God only in the desert" (Ondaatje, *The English Patient*, 250).

It is a difficult question as to how far one can refer to the novel on which a film is based to interpret a film. In some instances, light is shed on the themes of Minghella's film by their elaboration in Ondaatje's novel. In other instances, Minghella's changes of events and emphases contribute to the integrity of his own work. Awareness of the changes sometimes sheds light on that integrity. Ondaatje, commenting on the film, observes, "What we have now are two stories, [each with] its own organic structure. . . [S]cenes and emotions and values from the book emerged in new ways, were reinvented, were invented with totally new moments, and fit with a dramatic arc that was different from that of the book" (introduction in Anthony Minghella, *The English Patient: A Screenplay* [Hyperion: New York, 1996], xvii-xviii. David Thomson notes the close collaboration between Minghella and Ondaatje during Minghella's work on *The English Patient*, but Minghella "[insisted] that the film was his" ("How They Saved the Patient," *Esquire* 127 no. 1 [January 1997]: 39-53.

3. In an earlier draft of the film script, Almásy simply comments, "The plumness of this plum," when he tastes it (revised draft, August 28, 1995). This script can be found at http://www.dailyscript.com/scripts/englishpatient.html. The change for the film allows Almásy's comment to resonate with his earlier discussion with the Cliftons about adjectives and their avoidance.

4. In Herodotus's story, Gyges is Candaules' bodyguard. In the film, all reference to what his relation is to Candaules is omitted. The omission makes the parallel between Gyges and Almásy easier.

5. Once their affair is consummated, Almásy tells Katharine that Madox keeps talking about Anna Karenina. "I think it's his idea of a man-to-man chat," Almásy says.

6. Herodotus, *The Histories*, I. 8-14. In Ondaatje's novel, neither the omission nor the addition occurs (Ondaatje, *The English Patient*, 232-34).

7. Ondaatje's presentation of Almásy's reading of Herodotus is more complex than in the film. See, for example, Ondaatje, *The English Patient*, 119 and 150. Minghella's presentation of the differences between Almásy's and Katharine's readings of this text is nevertheless suggested by Ondaatje: "I would often open Herodotus for a clue to geography," Almásy tells us in the novel, whereas "Katharine had done that as a window to her life" (Ondaatje, *The English Patient*, 233).

8. Jacqui Sadashige, "Sweeping the Sands: Geographics of Desire in *The English Patient*," *Literature/Film Quarterly* 26 (1998): 242. See also Stephen Scobie, "The Reading Lesson: Michael Ondaatje and the Patients of Desire," *Essays on Canadian Writing* 53 (Summer 1994): 92-106. Scobie argues that the image of Almásy's text of Herodotus, filled with cuttings from other books as well as his own observations, is Ondaatje's dramatization of the concepts of supplementarity and intertextuality. Similarly, D. Mark Simpson sees Almásy's text of Herodotus as "a literal foliation of the very notion of intertextuality. . . . a kind of talis-

man for Ondaatje's distressed text, wrought by all means of conflicting and insurgent knowl-edges" ("Minefield Readings: The Postcolonial English Patient," *Essays in Canadian Writing* 53 [Summer 1994]:216-37).

9. In the novel, Almásy says of the Gyges' story that he "always skim[s] past that story. It is early in the book and has little to do with the places and period I am interested in" (Ondaatje, *The English Patient*, 232). Ondaatje recounts that Almásy glued brown cigarette papers "into sections of *The Histories* that recorded wars that were of no interest to him" (Ondaatje, *The English Patient*, 172). Ondaatje thus suggests not only that we can see in texts what we want to see in them, but that we distort the text when we do so.

10. In the film, before saying what she most hates, Katharine catalogues for Almásy what she loves (water, the fish in it, hedgehogs, baths, islands, your handwriting, and "could go on all day") whereas Almásy reveals only what he most hates. The difference follows that re-vealed in their discussion of his monogram. Almásy could not go on all day about what he loves; he can capture it only in a moment.

11. In Ondaatje's novel, when recounting the story, Almásy recognizes this (Ondaatje, *The English Patient*, 251).

12. In Ondaatje's novel, the plane crashes when Almásy hits a tree and the fuel tank ex-plodes (Ondaatje, *The English Patient*, 175). Whereas Ondaatje emphasizes the role of acci-dent in our lives, Minghella uses the crash as an opportunity to highlight the effect of national identity and of Almásy's neglect of it.

13. In fact, the private is honoring Almásy's request to use the lavatory, which is a ruse to facilitate his escape. Again, Almásy is only pretends to be moved by the necessities, unless there are erotic necessities.

14. Elizabeth Kella understands the group at the monastery in Ondaatje's novel to be "a microcosm of the family of man" (*Beloved Communities: Solidarity and Difference in Fiction by Michael Ondaatje, Toni Morrison, and Joy Kogawa* [Upsala, Sweden: Akademitryck, Eds-bruk, 2000], 92). Kella argues that this "small community outside of pre-existing social net-works" and "stripped of the claptrap of national identities" resembles the community of "es-sential selves" Almásy envisions in the desert (Kella, *Beloved Communities*, 92 and 89). Although I believe that she is right about Almásy's vision, it is corrected by the film's atten-tion to adjectives.

15. Ondaatje, *The English Patient*, 240.

16. Kella argues that Madox's suicide in the novel, inasmuch as it occurs upon the news of England's declaration of war, "lends weight" to "the concept of a community of essential selves separate from and superior to the politics of nations" (Kella, *Beloved Communities*, 89).

17. Douglas Stenberg, "A Firmament in the Midst of the Waters; Dimensions of Love in The English Patient," *Literature/Film Quarterly* 26 (1998):256. See also George Hatza, "'The English Patient*: Extraordinary Romance," *Reading Eagle/Reading Times* 4 (December 1996): A9.

18. Mingella, *The English Patient*, 145-46.

19. Ondaatje, *The English Patient*, 284-86 and 291. A draft of the screenplay includes the episode, although it was excised from the film (revised draft, August 28, 1995. Jonathan Coe quotes the words of Saul Zaentz, the film's producer, about a conversation he had with Mi-chael Ondaatje: "I told Michael I didn't think the atom bomb thing was right. I was in the war, I was there, nobody knew what the atom bomb was all about" ("From Hull to Hollywood: Anthony Minghella Talks about His Film," *New Statesman* [March 7, 1997]: 39).

20. Kella, *Beloved Communities*, 84 and 81. See also Sadashige, "Sweeping the Sands," 245.

21. Sadashige claims to have been seduced by the novel, but betrayed by the film ("Sweeping the Sands," 242; see also 247).

22. Sadashige, "Sweeping the Sands," 250. See also Raymond Aaron Younis, "Nation-hood and Decolonization in *The English Patient*," *Canadian Journal of Film Studies* 26 (1998): 5.

23. Scobie argues that the characters in the novel, including the English patient himself, "project a fiction of identity onto the blank screen of his . . . burned body." For example, Caravaggio feeds him sufficient morphine so that he "becomes the central figure in one of Caravaggio's spy dramas. . . Whether Caravaggio's version of the English patient's identity is true or not scarcely matter," ("The Reading Lesson," 98). See also Sadashige, "Sweeping the Sands," 244.

24. Sadashige, "Sweeping the Sands," 249. See also Younis, "Nationhood and Decolonization," 5.

25. Sadashige quotes this characterization of Almásy's love from the film's home page as if this meant the film's valorization of such love ("Sweeping the Sands," 248).

26. Sadashige, "Sweeping the Sands," 248.

27. For a good account of the place of Sam in *Casablanca*, at the intersection between "old Negro manners" and "the racial liberalism" arising from American war aims, see Thomas Cripps, "Sam the Piano Player: The Man Between," *Journal of Popular Film and Television* (Winter 2000).

28. That neither the actors nor script writers knew how the film would end during its production is legend. One ending discussed was Laszlo's death, followed by the union of Rick and Ilsa. One of the script's writers, Howard Koch, recalls Bergman asking him how she would be able to play one of the film's love scenes without knowing which man she was going to end up with (Scott Eyman, "We're Still Looking at You, Kid," *Palm Beach Post* [August 2003]. For an excellent defense of the coherence that its director, Michael Curtiz, gave to the film—in spite of its somewhat chaotic making—see Gary Green, "The Happiest of Happy Accidents? A Re-evaluation of *Casablanca*," *Smithsonian Studies in American Art* I, 2 (Autumn 1987): 2-13.

29. Thus I do not entirely agree with Thomas Hurka that in *Casablanca* "Rick sacrifices his love for a larger political cause," ("The moral superiority of *Casablanca* over *The English Patient*," http://www.broadviewpress.com/writing/PdfFiles/HurkaArticle.pdf). For similar understandings of the film's message as "the necessity of self-sacrifice for the greater good," see Jack Nachbar, "Doing the Thinking for All of Us: *Casablanca* and the Home front," *Journal of Popular Film and Television* (Winter 2000).

30. Hurka, "The moral superiority of *Casablanca*." David Aaron Murray also criticizes *The English Patient* for its celebration of lovers whose "troubles don't just amount to less than a hill of beans," but whose "tawdry love affairs and betrayals acquire the drama of armies marching and empires collapsing." In contrasting the later movie with the earlier one, Murray finds that "the fundamental things definitely do not apply" (" *The English Patient* Plays *Casablanca*," *First Things* [May 1997]: 10-12). Others note this difference with approval: "*The English Patient* is revolutionary in a very important and often overlooked way. This is one of the few war movies in which, to paraphrase another great war romance, the troubles of two little people amount to more than a hill of beans" (http://www.soyouwanna.com/site/movies/romance/romance2.html).

31. Stanley Kauffmann finds John Seale, the Australian cinematographer, to be "the hero of *The English Patient*" ("Stanley Kauffmann on Films," *The New Republic* [December 9], 1996: 26).

32. Although *Casablanca* also won an academy award for best black-and-white cinematography, it lacked *The English Patient's* sweeping scenes of the desert. *Casablanca*, in fact, was filmed in Hollywood studios.

CHAPTER 5

AN AMERICAN FANTASY?
LOVE, NOBILITY, AND FRIENDSHIP IN *CASABLANCA*

PETER AUGUSTINE LAWLER

What moves us throughout *Casablanca* is Rick's rather consistent moral self-sufficiency, which is only compromised to some extent by love. We want to believe that Rick is the model American—both a rugged individualist and a loving man; and he may well be the most attractive American character in the history of film. We are characteristically anxious that our proud individualism is merely pretentious, but our individualism also leads us to think that love is for suckers. Our radical rebellion against what we've been given by nature and tradition—the habitual or dogmatic skepticism Tocqueville describes—ends up producing a disorienting inner emptiness that causes us to end up embracing a degrading social conformism—what Tocqueville describes as a thoughtless and desperate deference to public opinion. Our relentless pursuit of happiness is at the expense of love and nobility and never produces happiness itself.

But Rick reassures us that personal and emotional isolation need not culminate in hedonism or conformity. He never lives in the eyes of others; he never really denies that happiness is to be found in love or nobility; and he is never really dead to the truth that the secret to human happiness lies in responsible, unselfish devotion, in renouncing the right to the pursuit of happiness. The most moving moment of the film is when he renounces all that is selfish above love; nobility turns love into an idealized memory of a Parisian paradise that perhaps never existed. Rick does fall short—far short, in fact—of the stoic ideal of manly indifference to inevitable misfortune, but we want to believe that even a real man needs and finds love.

RICK'S

Rick never loses the point of view by which he judges and finds wanting his own actions and the actions of others. He is the living refutation of our nonjudgmentalism. Rick has character, not mere personality. Despite his most precarious situation in Casablanca—his nightclub is a sort of oasis of civilization in the midst of a state of nature dominated by vultures—he never uses flattery to gain favor with those on whom his success depends. In that respect, he really is, as he says, a "poor businessman." The method he uses with authorities—such as Renault—is bribery. And he makes clear that those who are compelled to bribe to survive are morally superior to those who accept bribes. Rick treats those with whom he must deal with ironic contempt.[1]

Early in the film, Rick's contempt for his customers is pretty open and more or less universal. He won't have a drink with any of them, and that's not because he's not given to drink. They are all ineffective or corrupt—refugees and the "scum of the earth" that prey on them. They are all morally weak in one way or another. They are all compromised by their slavish dependence on the opinion of others. So Rick repeatedly rebuffs the smart and affable Renault's offers of friendship. Rick will ally with the chief of police in the pursuit of mutual beneficial goals, but he refuses to respect or trust him. The Frenchman's shameless flattery of his superiors, his cynical use of his power to acquire sexual favors and line his pockets, and his empty boasts about his independence make him too unlike Rick for friendship to be possible. The one flash of insight Rick shares with Renault is that they are both to some extent better than they say; they both cannot help but sympathize secretly with the Free French. But Rick's actions are to the extent possible guided by his not completely secret sympathies. Renault's really are not, despite his occasional ironic remark. Rick had to change a little, and Renault much more, for their friendship to become possible. Renault's self-denial was so deep that it really almost completely turned his character into personality, but Rick never really lost sight of that distinction.

Rick, unlike Renault, seems at first to act consistently without illusions about the limits of his independence. That's one reason why he won't stick his neck out for anyone; in Casablanca, he couldn't save anyone anyway. He's against gratuitous acts of courage that would have no effect. His famous cynical remark about "German clerks" becoming "Honored Dead" is really about the fact that their deaths were utterly pointless. And when he wonders whether fighting for the cause is "worth all this" to Laszlo, his thought is really a reflection of the futility of his own earlier anti-Fascist efforts. Laszlo is perfectly and obviously right that when Rick says the world needs to be put out of its misery his words don't correspond to what he believes "in his heart," not to mention his actions in the world he can control—Rick's.

When the Germans question him, Rick shows no fear; his remarks are free of flattery and tinged with contempt. But he doesn't insult them openly, and he proclaims his neutrality in their political struggle. The deal he makes with the political authorities is "you run your business, and let me run mine," and he excuses himself from a political discussion with those authorities by saying, "Your business is politics; mine is running a saloon." Claiming to reduce politics to business is Rick's way of refusing to identify morally with evil without suicidally declaring war on it. Such comments are less cynical than strategic, and those who perceive Rick as a cynic are not particularly astute. (Renault does not make that mistake, which is why he reinforces Rick's rhetorical display with the Germans.) From the beginning, Rick opposes the Germans as much as he can and still keep his nightclub open. He understands it must be in the self-interest of the political authority for it to exist, and of course the nightclub doesn't exist primarily for Rick's self-interest. He's no ordinary businessman, and despite his crowded nightclub, rigged gambling, and excellent cash flow, he's clearly not getting rich. (He estimates he will be broke a couple of weeks after his nightclub is closed.)

The moral tightrope that Rick walks is for a man who thinks he is all alone in the world. He has been abandoned by his country and his love, and his cause—which he failed—seems doomed. His self-consciousness is not consciousness with someone else, and one of the film's most compelling themes is that such solitude is finally humanly unendurable. Radical moral autonomy — living without reference to anyone else at all—is inhuman and self-destructive. If love and honor are illusions for suckers or just for lucky other people, then life is pretty much unendurable. For many reasons, the Rick we see at the film's beginning seems not to have much of a future at all, which is why he refuses to live with the future in mind.

The film opens with Rick playing chess alone. He thinks he is compelled to manipulate all those around him just to survive. He can't even leave the outcome of games of chance to chance. He does have a minimal emotional connection with his employees—especially Sam. His life is not completely free from friendship and trust. But those connections are basically paternalistic. Rick has assumed complete responsibility for the well-being of those who work for him. Critics can't help but think that Rick's relationship with Sam is somehow racist; it is not, after all, a friendship between equals. On the one hand, Rick seems to be the only man in Casablanca above the buying and selling of human beings; only the American is morally opposed to slavery. On the other hand, Sam, although certainly not Rick's slave, does take his pay partly in money and partly in security. Sam is not Rick's equal—not because he's black, but because he freely gives himself over to Rick's protection.

Rick is Sam's prince, and he consents to be governed. The extent to which Sam trusts Rick is rather extraordinary. Otherwise, what would a black American be doing in a city on its way to becoming Nazi? Sam's trust seems fully justified; Rick secures his future as well as he can when he closes the nightclub and abandons Casablanca. And of course everyone gets paid when the nightclub is ordered closed by the authorities. Rick's paternalism of character provides more security than American capitalism, but the affection between Rick and Sam, although real, remains rather limited.

When Rick says he won't stick his neck out for anybody, we know early on he's not speaking the truth. He would risk everything for his friend Sam. And so we also know that his declaration of emotional independence is partly bragging and partly whining. It calls to mind the American's bragging about his moral freedom that Alexis de Tocqueville describes in his famous chapter on "self-interest rightly understood." The American brags that even when he works with or appears to help out others it is always with his self-interest in mind. He knows he can be more effective in pursuing his own interests if he secures the cooperation of others. The American doctrine is that all human sociality has the character of an alliance; the American brags that emotionally he always remains a free individual. The nastiest side of that doctrine, of course, is that such a free individual brags, in effect, that he would never stick his neck out for someone else, even to save someone from the Nazis.

Tocqueville observes that the American is better or less emotionally free than he says: He frequently gives way to love, showing that he is not only a free individual after all. Tocqueville himself affirms the American doctrine as a way of reducing the tension between the isolating demands of free individuality and the fulfillment of those social passions that really make life worth living. We see that Rick is never as free—as neutralist or isolationist or unsentimental—as he claims to be; he is less realistic about the emotional than the practical limits of his freedom. But his bragging is not the salutary self-deception of a free man of which Tocqueville approves. Those apparently cynical words are largely the whining of a wounded soul, and so they are the best evidence that an isolationist policy can't work for Rick over the long run.

Unlike the American Tocqueville describes, Rick does not seem to enjoy or take pride in his emotional independence. Playing chess alone in public is a form of whining. Nobody would do that, of course, if a decent opponent were available. His isolation is clearly a sign of his social failure, and it might even be understood as a rather pathetic overreaction to that failure, to his disappointments in love and politics. Rick, again, is no stoic. So in some ways Rick in Casablanca seems to fall prey to what Tocqueville calls the apathetic misguided judgment of individualism. In Rick's judgment, the heart-enlarging passions— the various forms of human love—are more trouble than they're worth. Rick feigns indifference to political life, to women, to both past and future. Time— somehow both the product and the cause of our self-conscious sociality—means nothing to him. The reason he can't have a real connection with a woman is he refuses to think far enough ahead to imagine their next encounter. He claims to be regressing, in effect, toward the subhuman, utterly self-sufficient contentment of the Rousseauean state of nature.

But of course Rick's life is really far from apathetic. His emotional withdrawal is, in fact, the cause of his obsessive calculation. Unable to love or trust or engage in political deliberation, he's stuck with taking solitary responsibility for his nightclub's always-precarious future. He attempts to limit his world to what he can control. Within that world, his emotional independence really does allow him to think very clearly and effectively. Rick's Café Américain really is a fabulous nightclub located in the middle of nowhere. It is an accomplishment of which he can quite legitimately take pride and would immediately disappear without his constant guidance. It is a triumph of American frontier ingenuity, but without a hint of American vulgarity or provincialism.

We see plenty of evidence that Rick's life is not as worthless or as ineffective as he whines; the very existence of the nightclub does lots of desperate people lots of good. There they can with some safety make the deals that will gain them freedom. There they can lose themselves in the sophisticated pleasures, forgetting momentarily the danger and rather dire necessity that characterizes human life in Casablanca. There people seem to transcend the ordinary limits of human embodiment. Everybody drinks, but nobody (except the Nazi Strasser) ever eats, and everyone, despite their real circumstances, looks their best. The truth is, the most impressive accomplishment of Rick's life is the café, and that accomplishment is a necessary prelude to his recovery of his self-conscious nobility, his greatness of soul.

Through the café, Rick is sticking his neck out for all the good people in Casablanca all along. He won't drink with them; they're not his equals. But he will do what he can to protect them. His seemingly sentimental decision to rig the gambling result to aid a loving couple in big trouble is far from surprising and actually prudent enough. He knows Renault will have to let him get away with it in the interest of his own fraudulent winnings. There are plenty of reasons why everyone has heard of Rick's, and everyone—those in trouble and those just looking for civilized and sophisticated human enjoyment—goes to Rick's. Even the austere and noble Laszlo is moved to congratulate Rick for his café.

NOBILITY

The action of the film is Rick's rediscovery of his consciousness of his own nobility, which anyone at Rick's can see he never really lost. When he tells Ilsa that "I'm no good at being noble" at the moment of their separation, nobody believes that he really thinks that anymore. Laszlo and Ilsa, in effect, appear to redeem him, although he, in fact, saves them. By saving them—being effective in the cause's service—he redeems himself. By, in effect, providing the miracle that gets Laszlo out of Casablanca, Rick almost miraculously secures a noble future for himself.

Laszlo, the film's most perfectly admirable character, tells Rick that "each of us has a destiny, for good and evil," and a man who denies that is "trying to convince himself of something he doesn't believe in his heart." Rick, of course, thought that he had no choice but to engage in such self-denial, which was always, in his case, ineffective. His cynical words never really transformed his sentimental and noble heart, and so Rick could never really forget what good and evil are. Part of the power of the film is that it doesn't leave us in doubt about what good and evil are, and it allows us to judge love, death, nobility, and friendship according to what is good. All the characters that end up being good—Laszlo, Ilsa, Rick, and Renault—know exactly what doing good is. And so the good and the noble are identical.

NOBILITY AND LOVE

In the film's clear scheme of judgment, love is basically ambiguous and ranks lower than nobility. The appearance of Ilsa pulls Rick out of his self-deceptive isolation and leads him to become "quite human" again. But being merely human is to fall short of nobility. Insofar as Laszlo loves Ilsa he is merely a man; otherwise, he is willing to accept the view held by others that he is a sort of superhuman leader of "a great movement." Love causes him to prefer Ilsa's safety to his own, although the cause—the very future of human freedom—depends on his remaining alive. It also caused him to have put her life in constant danger as she followed him from place to place in endless flight. Laszlo never thinks sensibly when she is concerned. And love, of course, causes Rick briefly to want to act selfishly against the very embodiment of human courage and effectiveness in the service of freedom's future. Love keeps both Rick and Laszlo from acting consistently on what they really know.

From the perspective of the cause, Ilsa's life is of no consequence. It is only because of his perception of Laszlo's merely human weakness that Rick believes that Ilsa must remain with that noble hero. It would be easy to accuse the film of sexism: even the best women lack nobility, and men would be better if they could do without them. Ilsa imagines that Rick is vengefully sulking in Casablanca out of scorned love, and Laszlo imagines his problem must be ineffective self-denial concerning his nobility. They are, of course, both partly right. But Ilsa can still love Rick while thinking less of him, and we can still love Ilsa while thinking less of her.

But we can also see that Rick means to help Ilsa rediscover her attraction to nobility that brought her to Laszlo, that attraction she once mistook for love. Her nobility consists in sacrificing all the satisfactions that come with erotic love for the sake of the Cause; she surely believes it when Rick tells her that its future depends on her. Rick tells her that her destiny is not to live for love or even for herself; her future is merely as "part of his [Laszlo's] work." She is convinced by Rick that love without virtue is empty, and so it is finally impossible to choose love over nobility. Such choices always produce regret, "for the rest of your life."

We can even see Rick's ordinary respect for marriage. In Paris, he pushed Ilsa to see that their love points to marriage, and in Casablanca he refuses to steal another man's wife, even when she is perfectly willing to be stolen. Both Rick and Laszlo actually are more concerned with the institution of marriage than Ilsa, because they more readily connect love with human responsibility. Women are ordinarily more marriage oriented than men, but that's because they think of themselves as both wives and mothers. Ilsa shows us what female love is like when detached by extraordinary circumstances from maternal concerns. One reason the film is so romantic, of course, is that no one need be brought down to earth by thinking about the children. In the absence of children at least, the most solid foundation for marriage is nobility, not love. And it seems that women teach men about love, and men have to teach women about nobility.

The film leaves us with the noble thought that love is unsatisfying if detached from other human responsibilities. Rick says they will always have Paris, where in his mind their love had a future. There he thought of marriage; they almost lost Paris when he vengefully plotted to wreck a marriage. The true love of Rick and Ilsa can persist only in their memories, in their imaginations, and so we reach the conclusion that true love can be detached from sexual satisfaction. And we have to reach that conclusion for justice to prevail. But Rick's surrendering his future with Ilsa to preserve the memory of their past is less of a sacrifice than it seems. The plane to Lisbon is only liberation if it is one step on the way to America, but America is not an option for Rick. There is no way he could have gotten on that plane, and so there is no way he could have had a future with Ilsa.

The film is actually a bit more nuanced about love. We can't forget that Laszlo is less of a man than Rick. Nobody in the film, and surely hardly any viewers, find Laszlo lovable. His love for Ilsa is not reciprocated; she will not even say that she loves him. She looks up and learns from him, and she thinks of him unerotically—as a teacher and father—and not as a man. Rick taught her the difference between admiration for moral and intellectual greatness and love. Any real woman cannot help choosing the love of a real man over devotion to almost disembodied idealism. So we don't blame Ilsa for so quickly dumping her devoted husband for Rick, although her choice surely is against nobility.

LASZLO AND RICK

Critics have found Laszlo's idealistic devotion rather repulsive, because it is too pure to ring true. His intensity, the thought is, could serve tyranny just as well as freedom. The tyranny Laszlo seems to impose on his own nature is more attuned to Fascism than to the diverse flourishing of human nature found in a free country. And for the most part he is presented more as what we call a superhero than a real man. Every Nazi effort to contain or kill or break him—even in a concentration camp—fails.

This sort of criticism is contrary to the intention of the film, which is to present him as a great man. Laszlo admits that he is afraid, although he is never actually moved by fear. And he, of course, loves. He's no fanatic; he is a man of learning as well as action. He opened Ilsa to "a new world of knowledge and thought and ideals," and he has chosen rather than thoughtlessly embraced his cause. And that cause of freedom is exactly the opposite of any kind of Fascism or even nationalism. Laszlo is certainly not primarily a Czech patriot. His cause is universal; he has followers everywhere, and the cause is so rooted in human nature itself that it cannot be finally defeated. Laszlo, in fact, is amazingly undistorted by anger. Despite his love for Ilsa, he says he does not blame Rick and Ilsa for their love for each other. Where's the blame in something that can't be helped? How many lovers can think that dispassionately and still be in love?

We return to the thought that because we can't understand Laszlo's own passion that we can't find him lovable. But he is presented both as having the human passions and as having brought them under conscious control. Laszlo is, in truth, the most stoic of the characters. He has the virtue required to bear reasonably well the inevitable fluctuations of fate, and it may well be characteristically American—at least since the defeat of the Southern aristocracy—to mistake stoicism for inhuman moral fanaticism.

Laszlo, in fact, reminds us in many ways of Socrates. He does not have Socrates' ambivalence about action, which makes him in that respect the better man. Also missing in Laszlo is Socrates' (or even Rick's) irony, which arguably is also to Laszlo's credit. Socrates never nobly took responsibility for the freedom of everyone. But most of all, Laszlo lacks Socrates' famous eros. His love for Ilsa seems rather disembodied or unerotic, which is why it's relatively unselfish. And she's attracted to him in every way but erotically; clearly, they don't have much of a sexual relationship at all. Laszlo's idealistic devotion makes his love, we might say, rather "platonic"—the desexualized love Socrates inspired in the idealistic Glaucon in the pursuit of justice. His love of justice is so extreme that it even sublimates his love of a particular woman. We are tempted to say that Laszlo's shortcomings—which are evident, by contrast, in Rick's irony and magnetic erotic attractiveness (which affects even the womanizer Renault)—are the film's Socratic reservations about all modern idealism, maybe about communism in particular.

We have to add that Rick himself does not have such reservations about Laszlo and his cause. In general the fight for freedom in 1941 was not understood as a fight against communism. Even the film's affirmation of the superiority of Rick's American way of life is not quite that of an American citizen, and Rick ends the film not only by imitating Laszlo with his nobility but also by sublimating his love for Ilsa. But if for some reason Laszlo loses Ilsa, he will continue to be unlovable. Rick, having cured himself of his bitter mooning over Ilsa by containing their love to the past, is now free to very successfully play the field—and meet another woman he loves—again.

Rick says the womanizer Renault is like other men, but only more so. On that basis, we can say that Laszlo is like other men, only less so. That fact seems to deprive him not only of love of women, but friendship with other men. The two "real men"—Rick and Renault—become noble friends at the film's end, but more than nobility links them together. Laszlo says Rick is the kind of man to whom he would be attracted if he were a woman. That doesn't mean he's a closeted homosexual, just that male friendship—the attraction of like to like—has many dimensions and depends on all sorts of shared experiences.

The three human goods—love, friendship, and nobility—come together for Rick, and Rick only. Friendship and nobility come together in Renault. He also gets lots of sex, and his new nobility holds open the promise of love. Laszlo's nobility is pretty lonely, and it's only an exaggeration to say that nobody cares about what happens to him in particular. With Rick and Renault ready for action, few watching the film's end really believe that the future of the cause any longer depends on Laszlo alone. It turns out that courageous and clever Laszlo was not a superhero after all. He had no way out of Casablanca without Rick's help. Rick ends the film as noble as ever but more clever and effective than Laszlo, and Laszlo tells Rick that with him back in action their side will now win. At one level, the ending means that America's entry into the war ensures the victory of the cause, and the film celebrates the natural superiority of American ingenuity. But it's also the case that the American is more of a man; only he at his best combines all the best human qualities into an admirable and attractive whole. The only whole character—the only character who is not clearly a caricature—in the film is Rick, and so the film might be criticized as rather chauvinistic.

RICK'S AMBIGUOUS PATRIOTISM AND HIS FRENCH FRIEND

Still, Laszlo is not a disembodied idealist in the sense of caring only about intentions and being indifferent to results. Like Rick, he knows there's little point in being courageous if you can't be clever too. To Rick, he's admirable primarily because he's been effective, whereas Rick sulks in Casablanca, in part, because of his own past ineffectiveness. Rick will drink with Laszlo because he's both noble and effective. The film's clearest standard is finally noble and effective anti-Fascist action; all other human goods depend on that effectiveness. It means to awaken America to the truth Rick and Laszlo share. The comparison between Rick and America is obvious, even overbearing. America followed an isolationist foreign policy in the 1930s, one that was not completely abandoned in 1941. The official reason was self-interest; it was what's best for business. But to some extent America was sulking because of its ineffectiveness in reconstructing Europe in its own image after World War I. The combination of selfishness and vengefulness produced a failed policy, one the Americans abandoned for reasons of both self-interest and nobility.

When it comes to the universal principles of liberty and democracy, Americans are never at heart neutrals, and any indifference they show to the fate of others is partly feigned and partly self-deceptive. By the film's end, we imagine that the Americans, following Rick's example, will not remain oblivious to their political destiny. It is their destiny to fight for good and against evil everywhere, and we can't forget that Laszlo had to redeem Rick by reminding him of that fact. From that view, we connect Rick with Franklin Roosevelt and Laszlo with Winston Churchill, and we see why America will replace Britain as the noble and effective guardian of freedom everywhere.

The obvious irony of the comparison of Rick's neutralist and isolationist moral and political policy as a nightclub owner with the American foreign policy of the 1930s is that Rick himself was a critic of that policy. Violating laws based on America's neutrality principles, he worked for the Ethiopians against Mussolini's Italy and for the republicans in Spain against Franco's Fascists. By siding with the anti-Fascist underdogs, he alienated himself from his own country. Presumably he can't return to America because he would be a criminal there. His standard was higher than his own country's laws—his own country's universal principles. The result is that his country is no longer really his own. He calls his café Américain because it reflects his style and his convictions. But he only admits to being born in Brooklyn; he doesn't regard himself as an American citizen. So the film's land of hope—his homeland—is closed to him. Rick, in fact, is from nowhere in particular; it's neither his Brooklyn nor his Paris. And so he's stuck in nowhere in particular, a place that seems to be the homeland to nobody, somewhere where people are compelled to come and hope soon to leave—Casablanca. America's amoral neutralism is what led Rick to cynically but understandably adopt the same policy; Rick had better reasons to believe that he had no choice but to withdraw into himself. But even his choice was self-indulgent and needlessly shortsighted. The choice of effective nobility is always what secures best one's own self-interest.

When Renault says that Rick has become a patriot, he must mean that he has returned to his country in principle, which means that that particular word is given a universal connotation. There's nothing in his cause that reflects America in particular. The song of freedom—played at the initiative of Laszlo and Rick—is the "Marseillaise." And Rick goes off to fight with Free French at a time when America still recognized the legitimacy of the Vichy government, again replacing his country's policy with his own. Renault's patriotism is more nationalistic than Rick's; he's for France as much as he's for freedom. And in some measure the film is about Renault and Rick choosing nobly to serve the true cause of France—liberty, equality, and fraternity. A very small multinational band of brothers goes off to join those who would return France to her revolutionary, republican liberty.

We are shown how liberty and equality generates fraternity, and so perhaps a criticism of the incompleteness of the individualistic American Declaration of Independence. The superiority of Rick to Renault is evidence of why de Gaulle's France will end up deferring to American leadership, but with the selfish or Lockean side of American principle ennobled somewhat by the more fraternal or Rousseauean French. The film is French enough to applaud American business ingenuity while criticizing, perhaps excessively, American business ethics. The film surely agrees with the Frenchman Tocqueville with its portrayal of the cynical doctrine of self-interest rightly understood as really the cry of a wounded soul.

CASABLANCA FOR US

Despite such criticism, we can hardly say that the film challenges the American viewer much. All in all it is a pretty self-indulgent fantasy. No character we care about dies, and the one embodiment of evil—Major Strasser—is shot by Rick— by then the very embodiment of good. And Rick gets away clean with what remains legally murder, and we are led to assume that he and Renault have no problem getting to the Free French garrison at Brazzeville. Our optimism for their future is enhanced by our knowledge—that original viewers, of course, did not have—that the Free French end up on the winning side. After the war, we cannot help but think that an ennobled America will repudiate its selfish foreign policy errors of the 1930s and welcome Rick back as a hero. Renault's Vichy service will also be forgotten, and he'll fare well under de Gaulle. Even Laszlo is off to America, where apparently he'll be stuck with serving the cause in relative safety.

Casablanca is a desperate, dangerous, vulture-ridden place; we are told and see some evidence of that. For a while, all our favorite characters, even Renault, seem doomed. Laszlo's life has been one long brush with death, and the suffering he experienced in the concentration camp must have been horrible. But none of those characters suffer any physical suffering or even deprivation in the film, and none shows courage in the immediate face of death. There is none of the suffering and death experienced by so many Americans on the battlefield. This film is about Casablanca as limbo or purgatory, and it is some distance from the real hell of war. As a tale of courage, it is a stylized, romanticized fantasy.

What this film does is awaken our longing for nobility. Its message is that the real American is a real man, a man in full, and we don't even notice that Rick is never quite that. We long for the circumstances for which we could be like Rick, to be put into a dangerous situation in which we could display our capabilities and virtues while not actually suffering very much. We long to be men of character, and not stuck with merely being pleasing to others. We long for good and evil to be clear and compelling; we wish we didn't live in a world that rewards nonjudgmental wimps and therapeutic experts. We long to be free from our pedestrian jobs and our ordinary families; we really long to be freed from the boring responsibilities and compromising positions that characterize our lives under the good government that secures peace and makes prosperity fairly easy for us. We wish we could spend most of our time in Rick's, a fabulous place. We wish we didn't have to eat, but could spend our time lost in conversation enlivened by music and drink.

We also know that Rick and Laszlo—like de Gaulle and Churchill—would be miserable living in our world. What would Laszlo, in particular, be like without a cause worthy of consuming his whole being? Fighting for the cause for him is like breathing; without it, he says, he would die. *The Last Days of Disco*, another fine nightclub movie, shows better the rather daunting difficulty of living nobly in our yuppie or bourgeois bohemian world, where nothing like Rick's and Laszlo's opportunities to display their virtue seem available, and nobody seems to have Rick's magnetic erotic attraction. But that's not to say that *Casablanca* is not good for us. The character played by Woody Allen in *Play It Again, Sam* imagines that he is Bogart when he does the decent thing by not stealing his best friend's wife—the only woman he loves and who loves and understands him. Love is real, but love is empty without virtue, and love might be a source of virtue that transcends or sublimates merely erotic satisfaction—these truths are surely neglected in our time. *Casablanca*, in its way, takes a strong stand against home wrecking and against the idea that our right to personal happiness trumps our responsibilities.

Anything that can steel us against nonjudgmentalism and easy cynicism is worthwhile, as is anything that counters our misguided individualistic judgments—those that conclude that love and the other heart-enlarging passions are more trouble than they're worth. The view of America as soaring higher than isolationist self-interest in the direction of principled universalism also has to do us good. But even there, isolationism doesn't get a fair shake; at its height, it is not only about American business but about American virtue too. We can certainly argue about how the certainly well-intentioned and somewhat universalistic American empire created by the outcome of World War II has been for the nobility of American citizens. Its positive effect seems to depend on good and evil being relatively unambiguous and ordinary Americans actually being ennobled by direct involvement in the struggle. Today especially, our fascination with *Casablanca* must be criticized in part as a diversion from the real problems of living virtuously in a free and prosperous country defended so effectively by a tiny professional armed forces.

NOTES

1. All quotes from *Casablanca* can found at:
http://www.geocities.com/classicmoviescripts/script/casablanca.pdf.

CHAPTER 6

CASABLANCA AND THE PARADOXICAL TRUTH OF STEREOTYPING: RICK AND THE AMERICAN CHARACTER

JAMES F. PONTUSO

CATEGORIZATION AND STEREOTYPES

As far back as I can remember, *Casablanca* has been my favorite movie. Whenever I discover it showing on television I either watch it again for the hundred-somethingth time or channel surf back to catch some of my favorite bits. Despite the many times that I have watched it, I am still thrilled when Victor Laszlo sings the "Marseillaise" or when Rick lets Jan Brandel win at roulette so that Annina can remain virtuous. I have had a crush on Ingrid Bergman's Ilsa for at least fifty years. While I am pleased that many fans clearly share my fondness for the film, I am amazed that so few people seem to notice its most striking feature: *Casablanca* is replete with racial, ethnic, and gender stereotypes. Indeed, Umberto Eco maintains that the stereotypes and clichés provide the film's only strength. He explains that

> aesthetically speaking (or by any strict critical standards) *Casablanca* is a very mediocre film. It is a comic strip, a hotch-potch, low on psychological credibility, and with little continuity in its dramatic effects. . . . When all the archetypes burst in shamelessly, we reach Homeric depths. Two clichés make us laugh. A hundred clichés move us. For we sense dimly that the clichés are talking *among themselves* and celebrating a reunion. Just as the height of pain may encounter sensual pleasure, and the height of perversion border on mystical energy, so too the height of banality allows us to catch a glimpse of the sublime.[1]

We live in an age when a remark even hinting at a stereotype can have disastrous repercussions. Sports figures such as Al Campanis, Howard Cosell, and Jimmy "the Greek" Snyder lost their jobs for making insensitive comments about ethnic minorities—the latter because of a statement intended to praise African-Americans for their superior athletic prowess. Rush Limbaugh lasted one week as a commentator on Monday Night Football after he criticized the media for their positive coverage of an African-American quarterback.

Political figures are just as vulnerable. Trent Lott (R-Mississippi) was pressured to resign as senate majority leader when he made complimentary remarks at the one hundredth birthday party for Strom Thurmond (R-South Carolina), the once segregationist leader who later in life received an award from the NAACP. Senator Hillary Clinton (D-New York) barely escaped a scandal when she light-heartedly joked about Mahatma Gandhi running a gas station in St. Louis. During the 2004 presidential campaign, Democratic candidate Howard Dean had to apologize both to Southerners and African-Americans for mentioning the Confederate flag.

In academics, the ban on ethnic slurs has become almost religious dogma. At a major Southern university, an employee objected to a sports team named after American Indians, comparing the nickname to the "n-word" used to insult African-Americans. Despite the employee's clear intention to indicate her aversion to racial or ethnic epithets, the president of the university issued a public apology and the employee narrowly escaped dismissal. Most institutions of higher learning have restrictions against harassment, which often include bans on name calling and verbal abuse.

Why are stereotypes so taboo? James M. Jones defines the concept as follows:

> Literally, a stereotype is a metal plate that is used to make duplicate pages of the same type. Social commentator Walter Lippman borrowed this term back in 1922 to describe what he considered to be a biased perception. The bias was evidenced by comparing those "pictures" we had in our heads of someone and the reality the person presented to us. The bias resulted from preconceptions that were the result of the stereotyping process, whereby we "stamped" every member of the group as a duplicate of every other member—in other words, we created a stereotype. When we encountered a member of the group, we did not see him or her realistically. Instead, we saw the image of him or her filtered through this mental picture of the group we had stereotyped.[2]

Jones concludes that ethnic stereotypes are "the engine that drives prejudice. . . . Stereotypes are prejudicial because they involve generalization."[3]

Milton Kleg explains that "when tied to prejudiced attitudes, stereotypes help create a number of behaviors ranging from avoidance to violence. Our review of stereotypes indicates that one's perceived reality is not reality itself, but is a mixture of fact and fiction."[4]

In our age of political correctness, Jones and Kleg's views are the norm. Yet, for all the efforts to weed out generalizations about ethnicity, religion, and gender, stereotyping is alive and well. What accounts for the staying power of stereotypes? Is their survival in the face of the academy's relentless assault evidence of the maliciousness of the human psyche and of the human need to ridicule or disparage "the other," those who are different? Or could our tendency to stereotype simply reflect the fact that culturally determined and identifiable behavior and personality traits exist? Perhaps groups, including national cultures, have the power to shape individual character and behavior, and stereotypes are nothing more than acknowledgment of that fact.

In his classic study of prejudice, Gordon Allport explains that natural divisions occur between groups based on self-identification. He writes:

> Everywhere on earth we find a condition of separateness among groups. People mate with their own kind. They eat, play, reside in homogeneous clusters. They visit with their own kind, and prefer to worship together. Much of this automatic cohesion is due to nothing more than convenience. There is no need to turn to out-groups for companionship. With plenty of people at hand to choose from, why create for ourselves the trouble of adjusting to new languages, new foods, new cultures, or to people of a different educational level?
>
> Thus most of the business of life can go on with less effort if we stick together with our own kind. Foreigners are a strain. So too are people of a higher or lower social and economic class than our own. We don't play bridge with the janitor. Why? Perhaps he prefers poker; almost certainly he would not grasp the type of jests and chatter that we and our friends enjoy; there would be a certain awkwardness in blending our differing manners. It is not that we have class prejudice, but only that we find comfort and ease in our own class. And normally there are plenty of people of our own class, or race, or religion to play, live, and eat with, and to marry.
>
> It is not always the dominant majority that forces minority groups to remain separate. They often prefer to keep their identity, so that they need not strain to speak a foreign language or to watch their manners. Like the old grads at a college reunion, they can "let down" with those who share their traditions and presuppositions. . . .
>
> The initial fact, therefore, is that human groups tend to stay apart. We need not ascribe this tendency to a gregarious instinct, to a "consciousness of kind," or to prejudice. The fact is adequately explained by the principles of ease, least effort, congeniality, and pride in one's own culture.
>
> Once this separatism exists, however, tire ground is laid for all sorts of psychological elaboration. People who stay separate have few channels of communication. They easily exaggerate the degree of difference between groups, and readily misunderstand the grounds for it. And, perhaps most important of all, the separateness may lead to genuine conflicts of interests, as well as to many imaginary conflicts.[5]

Allport describes what is often taken to be prejudice as simply an effort to categorize and understand a complex world.

> The human mind must think with the aid of categories (the term is equivalent here to generalizations). Once formed, categories are the basis for normal prejudgment. We cannot possibly avoid this process. Orderly living depends upon it. . . . [T]he process of categorization . . . forms large classes and clusters for guiding our daily adjustments. We spend most of our waking life calling upon preformed categories for this purpose. When the sky darkens and the barometer falls we prejudge that rain will fall. We adjust to this cluster of happenings by taking along an umbrella. When an angry looking dog charges down the street, we categorize him as a "mad dog" and avoid him. When we go to a physician

with an ailment we expect him to behave in a certain way toward us. On these, and countless other occasions, we "type" a single event, place it within a familiar rubric, and act accordingly. Sometimes we are mistaken: the event does not fit the category. It does not rain; the dog is not mad; the physician behaves unprofessionally. Yet our behavior was rational. It was based on high probability. Though we used the wrong category, we did the best we could.

What all this means is that our experience in life tends to form itself into clusters (concepts, categories), and while we may call on the right cluster at the wrong time, or the wrong cluster at the right time, still the process in question dominates our entire mental life. A million events befall us every day. We cannot handle so many events. If we think of them at all, we type them.

Open-mindedness is considered to be a virtue. But, strictly speaking, it cannot occur. A new experience must be redacted into old categories. We cannot handle each event freshly in its own right. If we did so, of what use would past experience be? Bertrand Russell, the philosopher, has summed up the matter in a phrase, "a mind perpetually open will be a mind perpetually vacant."[6]

If group qualities exit, then we must ask whether pointing out the distinctive characteristics exhibited by individuals in those groups is really prejudice. The oddest thing about academia's current insistence on politically correct speech and attitudes is its equally intense obsession with multiculturalism. Multiculturalism posits that there are distinct cultures or ways of life that must be recognized and even embraced. Gregory Jay states that multiculturalism

needs to be understood from both an historical and a conceptual perspective. Historically, "multiculturalism" came into wide public use during the early 1980s in the context of public school curriculum reform. Specifically, the argument was made that the content of classes in history, literature, social studies, and other areas reflected what came to be called a "Eurocentric" bias. Few if any women or people of color, or people from outside the Western European tradition, appeared prominently in the curriculums of schools in the United States. This material absence was also interpreted as a value judgment that reinforced unhealthy ethnocentric and even racist attitudes.

Observers noted that teaching and administrative staffs in schools were also overwhelmingly white and/or male (whiteness being pervasive at the teaching level, maleness at the administrative level, reflecting the politics of gender and class as well as race in the educational system). Eventually parallel questions were raised (once more) about the ethnoracial or cultural biases of other institutions, such as legislatures, government agencies, corporations, religious groups, private clubs, etc. Each of these has in turn developed its own response and policies regarding multiculturalism.

Finally, "multiculturalism" may also have become a popular term as "race" lost much of its former credibility as a concept. Scientists agree that, in terms of DNA genetics, "race" has no significant meaning as a way of categorizing human differences. Intermarried families offer the puzzle of a parent and child considered as belonging to two different races—clearly an absurd idea given that race was thought of as biologically passed from parent to offspring. Thus "culture" began to replace "race" as a term for distinguishing among distinct human groups.[7]

Although Jay's view implies that multiculturalism and politically correct speech derive from the same concern, in reality the two are at odds. If both principles were true, there would be no denying that distinct human characteristics exist, but we would be barred from talking about them.

It is the thesis of this essay that multiculturalism ought to be taken seriously and that we should not fail to recognize characteristics common to particular cultural, ethnic, and gender groups, even if those traits are occasionally less than flattering.

CASABLANCA'S MANY STEREOTYPES: THE NEGATIVES

Given America's sensitivity toward stereotypes it is a bit of a mystery why *Casablanca* has not been attacked for its use of typecast characters, and, in fact, remains popular with critics and the public alike. Of course, there is no public disapproval of the evil Nazi Major Strasser: portrayals of maniacal characters with German accents are so common that no one objects and Germans seem too embarrassed by their part in Adolph Hitler's regime to protest.

Other not-so-enlightened stereotypes in *Casablanca* include the Italian Officer Tonelli and the Frenchman Lieutenant Casselle, both displaying the Latin mannerism of over-exuberance, talking too much and too quickly. Even more disquieting is one of the first characters the audience meets in the film: a pickpocket. Latter-day screenplays identify him as a European, but earlier versions of *Casablanca* describe him as a "dark European." Most likely the character was supposed to be a Gypsy or Roma, according to the current usage. Surely it is unfair to stereotype all Gypsies as pickpockets and thieves. Yet, for anyone who has lived in Central Europe and experienced the astonishing dexterity of Roma pickpockets at work, it must be acknowledged that the art is part of the Roma national culture.

An English couple, who seem to be on tour despite the war, are the perfect targets of the deft fingers of the dark European. They are civil, polite, and unsuspecting. Perhaps the British are so gullible and vulnerable to criminals because the rule of law has been the norm in their country for centuries. The police, courts, and community pressure all have had the effect of reducing petty crime in Britain, especially in upper-middle-class areas where Casablanca's vacationing couple no doubt resides.

Another negative stereotype is Yvonne, the young attractive French woman who has fallen for Rick and makes a scene when he responds nonchalantly to her advances. The evening after Rick spurns her affections, Yvonne shows up at Rick's Café Américain with a German officer, much to the consternation of a French soldier drinking at the bar. Obviously she hopes to flaunt her independence from Rick by attaching herself to a man whose political leanings he likely detests. Yvonne's relationships define her personality; she is dependent on men. She is a caricature of the kind of needy woman that women's liberation advocates criticize.

It is not exactly clear what nationality either Ugarte or Ferrari are, although the latter is described as Italian in some latter-day notes on the cast. But Ferrari, who may have Arab ancestry, thrives within Arab culture, and he certainly represents stereotypical Arab mores. When he first appears on screen entering Rick's Café Américain, he sits at a table with customers dressed in the Hollywood version of traditional Moroccan garb and salutes them by touching his chest, lips and forehead in what seems to be 1942 Hollywood's version of a Muslim greeting. Ferrari admits to being the "leader of all illegal activity in Casablanca."[8] He shorts Rick's Café with every shipment. Yet for all his purported illegality, Ferrari is not very sinister. He does not take advantage of the young Jan and Annina Brandel even though he knows they are desperate to leave Casablanca. He even helps Ilsa and Victor Laszlo by sending them to Rick to obtain their exit visas.

Ferrari's disposition can best be understood through the behavior of another character: the Arab street vendor attempting to sell Ilsa some tablecloths. The vendor claims that she could "not find a treasure like this in all of Morocco," while boasting that he is charging "only seven hundred francs." When Rick walks up and tells Ilsa that she is being cheated, the vendor drops the price to two hundred francs because the lady is a friend of Rick's. When Ilsa walks off, the vendor produces a sign which reads "100 francs."

In Arab cultures, as in many places throughout the world (and in almost all times past), goods are exchanged by barter. There is no fixed price for merchandise. The price is, as Adam Smith would say, whatever the buyer is willing to pay. There is nothing dishonest in this practice, but it is perhaps not the best policy from a business point of view. Consumers feel cheated if they purchase goods and then discover that their neighbor or friend bought the same goods at a substantially lower price. They may seek other suppliers that they deem more trustworthy. Perhaps this consumer aversion to being cheated is why all advanced industrial economies have adopted standard or fixed prices on most retail products and services. The glaring exceptions to the fixed-price regime in the United States are car dealerships, where prices are set partially by barter and partially fixed. It is for this reason that consumers have a low estimation for the honesty of automobile dealers.

Why have advanced industrial economies adopted a standard or fixed price system? Probably because it is more efficient, less time consuming, and more profitable. In other words, the fixed price system is based on the mode of exchange that consumers most often prefer and that retailers therefore adopt, called consumer sovereignty by economists and "self-interest rightly understood" by Alexis de Tocqueville. We can now surmise the origin of Ferrari's business dealings. He adopts the more traditional, culture-bound practice that takes it's bearing from the short-term gain of the individual over the long-term advantage of the business. As shrewd as he is, Ferrari fails to understand the demands of consumer sovereignty. He does not realize why the Blue Parrot is not as popular as Rick's Café Américain. He thinks that the competition is beating him only because Sam's musical talents give Rick's a comparative advantage. He fails to comprehend that Rick's Café Américain is more honest and gives customers more for their money. Ferrari is not so much dishonest as he is short-sighted.

THE POSITIVES

The negative stereotypes in *Casablanca* are balanced by characters with positive traits. The malevolent Major Strasser must be compared to the kindly Carl, described as a "fat, jovial German refugee." Rick's doorman, Abdul, respectfully calls Carl "Herr Professor," reminding us that for much of the twentieth century Germany was the intellectual, cultural, and artistic center of Europe and the world.

There is also the sweet and gentle portrayal of a German Jewish couple who are emigrating to the United States. Evidently they have obtained exit visas and are enjoying an evening out before they embark. Carl is conscious of their good fortune as he waits on their table and serves them a drink:

MR. LEUCHTAG: Carl, sit down. Have a brandy with us.
MRS. LEUCHTAG: (beaming with happiness) To celebrate our leaving for America tomorrow.
    Carl sits down.
CARL: Thank you very much. I thought you would ask me, so I brought the good brandy and a third glass.
    He produces a glass from a back pocket.
MRS. LEUCHTAG: At last the day has came.
MR. LEUCHTAG: Frau Leuchtag and I are speaking nothing but English now.
MRS. LEUCHTAG: So we should feel at home ven ve get to America.
CARL: A very nice idea.
MR. LEUCHTAG: (raising his glass) To America.
    Mrs. Leuchtag and Carl repeat "To America." They clink glasses and drink.
MR. LEUCHTAG: Liebchen, uh, sweetness heart, what watch?
    She glances at her wristwatch.
MRS. LEUCHTAG: Ten watch.
MR. LEUCHTAG: (surprised) Such much?
CARL: Er, you will get along beautifully in America, huh.

The scene stresses the importance of family in Jewish culture. Since the time of Abraham, the Jewish people have placed dedication to family over almost every other motivation, with the obvious exception of obedience to God. After all, God made Abraham the instrument through which He created the chosen people. Therefore, the procreation and rearing of children is the fundamental link between God and the Jews. If Abraham is compared to other cultures' ideal men—for instance, the *Iliad*'s Achilles—one cannot help but be struck by the intense, almost single-minded attachment to private and family concerns as compared to the Greeks' love of honor and distinction. Carl is correct that no matter the inadequacies of their English, the Leuchtags will get along beautifully in America. They will be left alone to pursue their private goals, which for them will likely entail being law-abiding citizens, for in that role they can best provide for their family.

PATRIARCHY

Casablanca gives us another stereotypical family, Bulgarians Annina and Jan Brandel. In 1941 Bulgaria was a traditionally patriarchal society, where men were the head of household and woman did their bidding. On the surface, Annina is a compliant, vulnerable woman, willing to do anything for her husband. The newlyweds have no money to buy an exit visa and fear going home to what was in the 1940s a brutal Fascist regime. Like many others, they are trapped in Casablanca. When Captain Renault learns of their plight, he offers to help, but the price is that the beautiful young Annina must submit to the Frenchman's appetites. Annina seeks Rick's advice on whether she should accept Renault's offer.

> ANNINA: He tells me he can give us an exit visa, but we have no money.
> RICK: Does he know that?
> ANNINA: Oh, yes.
> RICK: And he is still willing to give you a visa?
> ANNINA: Yes, Monsieur.
> RICK: And you want to know.
> ANNINA: Will he keep his word?
> RICK: He always has.
>> There is a silence. Annina is very disturbed.
> ANNINA: Oh, Monsieur, you are a man. If someone loved you very much, so that your happiness was the only thing that she wanted in the whole world, but she did a bad thing to make certain of it, could you forgive her?
>> Rick stares off into space.
> RICK: Nobody ever loved me that much.
> ANNINA: And he never knew, and the girl kept this bad thing locked in her heart? That would be all right, wouldn't it?
> RICK: (harshly) You want my advice?
> ANNINA: Oh, yes, please.
> RICK: Go back to Bulgaria.
> ANNINA: Oh, but if you knew what it means to us to leave Europe, to get to America! Oh, but if Jan should find out! He is such a boy. In many ways I am so much older than he is.
> RICK: Yes, well, everybody in Casablanca has problems. Yours may work out. You'll excuse me.

Despite her roots in a traditional male-dominated society, Annina is well aware of the sacrifices that sometimes need to be made in order to protect oneself and one's dear ones. She has a more realistic understanding of the world than her husband. Annina exhibits one of the keys to understanding patriarchal societies: In spite of their unequal status, women in those societies are sometimes wiser than men. Women must submit to male judgments even when those judgments are parochial, uninformed, and stupid. The men often live in artificial family situations where their decisions are accepted even when they are wrong. Men in patriarchal societies may come to believe in their own infallibility because they are always obeyed. Because social mores in such cultures generally do not allow women to challenge men, the men become blind to their inadequacies, and their egos may give them a false sense of their capabilities. Women, on the other hand, usually understand that they must pretend that males are superior. By submitting to the rule of males, tending their puffed-up egos, and experiencing the sometimes harmful consequences of men's decisions, women tend to gain a clearer understanding of how the world really works. Georg Hegel explains how people of inferior status become more knowledgeable about the world in a passage from *The Phenomenology of Mind* that became the basis for all of Karl Marx's work.

> In the master, the bondsman feels self-existence to be something external, an objective fact; in fear self-existence is present within himself; in fashioning the thing, self-existence comes to be felt explicitly as his own proper being, and he attains the consciousness that he himself exists in its own right and on its own account (*an und für sich*). By the fact that the form is objectified, it does not become something other than the consciousness moulding the thing through work; for just that form is his pure self existence, which therein becomes truly realized. Thus precisely in labour where there seemed to be merely some outsider's mind and ideas involved, the bondsman becomes aware, through this rediscovery of himself by himself, of having and being a "mind of his own."[9]

Annina summarizes the concept much more succinctly when she affirms that her husband "is such a boy," adding, "In many ways I am so much older than he is."

ILSA'S STRENGTH AND VULNERABILITY

If Carl and the Leuchtags are the opposite of Strasser and represent positive German stereotypes, Ilsa is the opposite of the stereotypical dependent woman, Yvonne. At first glance Ilsa seems to be quite like Yvonne. She gives up her own life to follow her husband. She is incapable of controlling her attachment to Rick even when she wants to.

> ILSA: Richard, I tried to stay away. I thought that I would never see you again, that you were out of my life. . . . The day I left, if you know what I went through! If you knew how much I loved you, how much I still love you. . . . I'll never have the strength to leave you again. . . . I can't fight it anymore. I ran away from you once. I can't do it again. Oh, I don't know what's right any longer. You'll have to think for both of us, for all of us.
> RICK: All right, I will. Here's looking at you kid.
> ILSA: I wish I didn't love you so much.

Although it might be argued that Ilsa plays an inferior role to the men in her life, we should not forget that she is clearly capable of taking care of both herself and her men if need be. She abandons Rick, the man she really loves, to aid her heroic husband. She helps Victor escape capture everywhere in Nazi-occupied Europe. She stands her ground in a spirited exchange with Major Strasser. She comes very close to shooting Rick to obtain the letters of transit that will allow her and Victor to escape sure arrest and possibly death in Casablanca.

How can we account for Ilsa's combination of neediness and autonomy? Perhaps because we are accustomed to think in terms of opposites when the true nature of women is more complicated than a simple polarity suggests. Simone de Beauvoir captures this polarity in her classic analysis of women:

> The "feminine" woman in making herself prey tries to reduce man, also, to her carnal Passivity; she occupies herself in catching him in her trap, in enchaining him by means of the desire she arouses in him in submissively making herself a thing. The emancipated woman, on the contrary, wants to be active, a taker, and refuses the passivity man means to impose on her. [Feminine women] deny the values of the activities of virile type; they put the flesh above the spirit, contingence above liberty, their routine wisdom above creative audacity. But the "modern" woman accepts masculine values: she prides herself on thinking, taking action, working, creating, on the same terms as men; instead of seeking to disparage them, she declares herself their equal.[10]

Ilsa may be a stereotype, but she is neither the feminine nor the feminist dichotomy elucidated by de Beauvoir. Rather she represents the image that American men have of sophisticated, independent, yet feminine European women. The contours of Ilsa's character were shaped by Casey Robinson, whom Hal Wallis assigned to work on the screenplay for three weeks just as the movie began production in May 1942. Robinson knew something about strong yet vulnerable women; he was probably having an affair at the time with the Russian actress Tamara Toumanova, whom he later married.[11] Robinson provided balance to the film, making it less cynical than the versions written by Julius and Philip Epstein, and less idealistic and moralistic than the outlines written by Howard Koch. It was Robinson who illuminated the depth of the love triangle between Ilsa, Rick, and Laszlo. Robinson did so by establishing a tension in Ilsa's persona. She could be quite strong when she needed to be, but her strength did not cause her to lose her femininity. If she was subordinate in her relationship with Rick, it was not because she depended on men to give her life meaning, but rather because she—like Rick—was in love.

THE PARADOXICAL CZECH COURAGE

It is eerily prescient that *Casablanca*'s leading moral spokesman should be a well-spoken, light-haired, freedom-fighting Czech writer. His tyrannical adversary, Major Strasser, claims that "Victor Laszlo published the foulest lies in the Prague newspapers until the very day we marched in, and even after that he continued to print scandal sheets in a cellar." Laszlo escaped the Nazis three times while continuing his underground resistance against them. Even the cynical

Captain Renault "must admit he has great courage." Laszlo is connected with the underground movement throughout Europe and taunts Strasser that he knows the anti-Nazi leaders in Berlin. Even after enduring the Nazi's "persuasive methods" of interrogation for a year in a concentration camp, he has not given up their identities. Laszlo is the only person in the movie who impresses Rick. The similarities between Laszlo and the remarkable writer, dissident, and for-mer-Czech president Václav Havel are striking. Both are singularly brave, elo-quent, and the focal point of opposition to a totalitarian regime.[12]

Laszlo's courage is all the more remarkable when put in the context of the situation in Czechoslovakia in 1941. Hitler had incorporated the Sudaten Ge r-man-speaking areas of the Czech lands into the German Reich and had placed the Czech areas under a Reich protectorate. Slovakia had become an independ-ent country, but its leader was virtually a Nazi puppet. Despite having a comp e-tent army and perhaps the most technologically advanced military equipment in Europe—so advanced that Hitler believed that the Czechs would have put up a stiff resistance to invasion—the Czechs did not oppose Nazi aggression. Hitler triumphantly entered Prague without firing a shot.

How then can we account for Laszlo's individual courage and the timid response of the Czech nation to conquest and defeat? To understand the stereo-type of the Czech character, we need to delve a bit into its history. The Czechs seem to combine extraordinary examples of personal courage with a tendency toward more general national trepidation and even appeasement. A clue to the Czech character is found in Jaroslav Hašek's *The Good Soldier Švejk*, the sym-bol of Czech resistance to domination and oppression to Austro-Hungarian rule. Švejk hates war, but he also hates confrontation with those who order him to war. He readily and overenthusiastically complies with the letter of the com-mands given by his Austro-Hungarian leaders, but always in a way that under-cuts the spirit of those orders.[13]

Perhaps because the Czechs inhabit such a small country, numbering even today only about ten million, they are not a martial people. Prague is one of the few major European cities not seriously damaged in the two world wars. The Czechs were reluctant combatants in World War I, perhaps because their loyal-ties were with their fellow-Slav Russians—their opponents in the war—not their German-speaking overlords. In fact, a Czech brigade defected to the Russian czar's side, only to be caught behind enemy lines when the Bolshevik Revolu-tion broke out at the front. In one of the oddest incidents in military history, the Czech brigade retreated across the vast stretches of Siberia until reaching Vladi-vostok. The survivors were evacuated by American transport ships sent by Woodrow Wilson and eventually sailed back to the newly created Czechoslova-kia, ma king them the only military unit to retreat all the way around the world.

The Czechs initially resisted the Soviet invasion in 1968, but soon com-plied. They adapted, if reluctantly, to the "era of normalization," a dull, depress-ing period in which the Communist government sought to maintain order by squelching spontaneity, personal initiative, and anything that deviated from the Soviet model. Most Czechs retreated into their private lives, concentrating on careers, vacations, or, often the most important priority, their weekend get-away houses in the country.

On the other hand, in all the instances cited above, there were astonishing acts of individual bravery. Although the Czech brigade retreated from the vastly numerically superior Red Army, it did so with discipline, skill, and valor. It captured much of the trans-Siberian railroad and, at times controlled more territory in Russia than either the Red or White forces.

While the Czechs capitulated to the Nazi occupation of their country, members of the Czech underground killed Reinhard Heydrich, the Reich Protector of Bohemia and Moravia and the highest ranking Nazi to be assassinated during the war. At about the same time Czech fliers were exhibiting skill and audacity during the Battle of Britain; one Czech airman was the most decorated soldier of that conflict.

After the Soviet invasion and suppression of the Prague Spring—a short-lived period of freedom during the Communist era in central Europe—Czechs developed one of the most successful dissident movements in the Soviet bloc. Professor Alená Hromádková, now of Charles University in Prague, was a central figure in the creation of an underground, or "black" university. She helped sponsor seminars on history, philosophy, ethics, and religion—topics barred by Communist bureaucrats.[14] She and those in her seminars were hounded by the state security police. More well-known is Charter 77, the human-rights watch group established by Václav Havel, who, like Victor Laszlo, spent years in jail for refusing to renounce the group's activities. Laszlo is an exemplar of extraordinary individual courage that occasionally rises up in an otherwise compliant Czech society.

THE FRENCH AND WORLDLY CYNICISM

Captain Louis Renault is the most cynical character in *Casablanca*. He seems to care nothing for moral, ethical, or political principles and is quite willing to subordinate himself to the Free French, the Vichy government, or even the Nazis if his personal security is at risk. When asked by Major Strasser whether he expects the Third Reich to be succeeded by others, Renault answers, "Well, personally, Major, I will take what comes." He claims to "have no conviction." He says, "I blow with the wind, and the prevailing wind happens to be Vichy." He praises Rick, who he believes at the time is selling out Laszlo, as "the only one in Casablanca who has even less scruples than I."

Renault is an inveterate and even predatory womanizer. When, after rejecting her, Rick sends Yvonne home because of the drunken scene she has caused, Renault comments snidely, "How extraordinary you are, throwing away women like that. Someday they may be scarce." Renault then considers calling on Yvonne to "get her on the rebound." When Renault meets Ilsa, he turns on the charm: "I was informed that you were the most beautiful woman to visit Casablanca. That was a gross understatement." Renault arranges what he refers to as "a little romance" with the young, innocent, and newly married Annina Brandel in exchange for her and Jan's exit visas. When Rick spoils the scheme by allowing Jan to win at roulette, making it possible for the Brandels to buy exit visas, Renault is not particularly angry, but he encourages Rick, a casino owner, to help him out: "I forgive you this time. But I'll be in tomorrow night with a breathtaking blonde. And it will make me very happy if she loses."

Renault is equally sarcastic about his work. When Major Strasser arrives in Casablanca not long after the murder of two German couriers, Renault quips, "Realizing the importance of the case, my men are rounding up twice the usual number of suspects." But, the mass arrests are made only to curry favor with the Germans, since Renault knows that Ugarte has committed the crime. Renault hopes to impress Strasser with a "demonstration of the efficiency" of his "administration" by making Ugarte's arrest while the Major is socializing at Rick's. After Ugarte is arrested without the letters of transit, Renault has Rick's Café searched, telling his "men to be especially destructive. You know how that impresses Germans." Renault is complicit in Ugarte's murder. He remarks, "I am making out the report now. We haven't quite decided whether he committed suicide or died trying to escape."

Renault is also dishonest. He offers to buy Victor Laszlo a drink with the admission: "No. Please, Monsieur, it is a little game we play. They put it on my bill. I tear up the bill. It is very convenient." He even admits to being "only a poor corrupt official." Renault's unscrupulous disposition leads to perhaps the funniest line in the movie when Strasser insists that Rick's be closed:

> RENAULT (loudly): Everybody is to leave here immediately! This café is closed until further notice!
> RICK: How can you close me up? On what grounds?
> RENAULT: I am shocked, shocked to find that there is gambling going on in here!
> CROUPIER (handing Renault a roll of bills): Your winnings, sir.
> RENAULT: Oh. Thank you very much. . . . Everybody out at once!

Renault embodies every stereotypical, nasty quality that Americans think about the French. He is selfish, obsequious, proud, underhanded, and amoral. And yet, the screenplay described him as "debonair and gay, but withal a shrewd and alert official." Renault is also astute multiculturalist, aware of the traits of his own and other nations. He ironically introduces Rick to the malevolent Strasser with the comment, "We are very honored tonight, Rick. Major Stasser is one of the reasons the Third Reich enjoys the reputation it has today." When Rick begins to drink (alcohol) midday and lights up a cigarette, Renault's portrait as a stereotypically debauched Frenchman is cemented with his comment: "Well, Ricky, I'm pleased with you. Now you're beginning to live like a Frenchman." Renault recognizes Laszlo's courage, understands and perhaps approves of Rick's idealism, and, of course, decides to fight against Nazism and protect his friend Rick at the conclusion of the movie.

What then can explain the paradox in Renault's character? Perhaps it is rooted in his nation's history. For hundreds of years the French were a vigorous, warlike people. Frankish knights on the Fourth Crusade conquered Constantinople when the city was thought to be impregnable. The French can look back to centuries of war with the British. France was the fulcrum on which the balance of power revolved in Europe. The French experienced bloody religious war and the even bloodier horrors of the French Revolution. They were governed by Charlemagne, the Sun King, Robespierre, and Napoleon, just to name the highlights. France was for centuries the cultural center of the world; French was the language of diplomacy. But the French lost their empire and their greatness. They fought in costly and often fruitless wars. World War I, in which millions of Frenchmen died in trench warfare and 11 percent of the entire population suffered casualties, was the final blow to French pride and martial verve. Little wonder that the French are so reluctant to go to war or, like Renault, are more interested in private rather than political concerns. With such a national history, who can blame the French for their reluctance to enter combat? Who can fault Renault, as a stereotypical representative of his nation, for viewing rising powers, be they German or American, with a skeptical eye?

THE AMERICANS: SAM

Sam, as played by Dooley Wilson, is surely the least politically correct character in *Casablanca*. He is gracious, considerate, mildmannered, and deferential; in short, he is a portrait of the perfect sidekick or helper whose actions critics claim demean African-Americans. Sidekick roles degrade blacks, it is argued, because they convey the idea that blacks are subordinate, unable to guide, direct, or give meaning to their own lives without the leadership of whites. Although helpers are quite often sympathetic characters, as was Hattie McDaniel, who won the 1940 Best Supporting Actress Oscar for her portrayal of Mammy in *Gone with the Wind*, such characterizations usually sustain the stereotype of white superiority. Philippa Gates argues that such roles "tend to conform to white mainstream attitudes by placing the African-American buddy in a subordinate position as trusty sidekick to the white hero."[15] BET (Black Entertainment Television) vented its frustration at the black actor Morgan Freeman who, it said, raised "our collective ire by playing a servant in *Driving Miss Daisy*."[16] Freeman played Hoke Colburn, the patient, understanding, and wise chauffeur of the aging (white and Jewish) Miss Daisy and in the process reinforced the stereotype of the capable black helper nevertheless relegated to servant or "Uncle Tom" status by the white people he supports.

Critics may be correct that sidekick roles re-enforce long-standing preconceptions, but is there anything true about the stereotype of blacks as loyal, decent (even while subordinate) partners of whites? The most influential African-American leader in American history certainly did not think so. In his Atlanta Exposition Address, Booker T. Washington actually extolled the loyalty of American blacks in order to make them more attractive than immigrant labor to white employers. Aiming his comments directly at white business leaders, Washington declared:

Cast it down among the eight millions of Negroes whose habits you know, whose fidelity and love you have tested in days when to have proved treacherous meant the ruin of your firesides. Cast down your bucket among these people who have, without strikes and labor wars, tilled your fields, cleared your forests, builded your railroads and cities, and brought forth treasures from the bowels of the earth and helped make possible this magnificent representation of the progress of the South. Casting down your bucket among my people, helping and encouraging them as you are doing on these grounds, and to education of head, hand, and heart, you will find that they will buy your surplus land, make blossom the waste places in your fields, and run your factories. While doing this, you can be sure in the future, as in the past, that you and your families will be surrounded by the most patient, faithful, law-abiding, and unresentful people that the world has seen. As we have proved our loyalty to you in the past, in nursing your children, watching by the sickbed of your mothers and fathers, and often following them with tear-dimmed eyes to their graves, so in the future, in our humble way, we shall stand by you with a devotion that no foreigner can approach, ready to lay down our lives, if need be, in defense of yours, interlacing our industrial, commercial, civil, and religious life with yours in a way that shall make the interests of both races one.[17]

There is truth to the view that African-Americans patiently accepted their place in American society. Thomas Jefferson's fears that freed slaves would rise up in righteous indignation against their former masters never materialized. Despite the justification that the horrors of slavery provided, there were very few instances of revenge taken by former slaves against their masters. Most blacks were willing to disregard the cruelties they suffered if they could be left alone to get on with their lives. Moreover, few vestiges of African culture remained when blacks were freed. American ideals, hopes, and traditions were the only real choice for African-Americans, and those principles were embodied in the dominant white culture. To live in America, blacks had to work with and for whites, but, until recent history, almost never as their equals.

Sam represents a dignified acceptance of the unequal status that was common among African-Americans for a century after the end of slavery. If he were asked, no doubt Sam would object to the inequities that he suffered in his homeland—he is, after all, an émigré. It is just as well that Sam is out of earshot when Ilsa calls him a boy for he might have been more than a little offended. But Sam understands the world in which he lives and does what is necessary to get by and even flourish. (By way of comparison, how many assistant professors really want to publish multiple books and articles in order to get tenure?)

As with all the other employees of Rick's Café, Sam accepts Rick's leadership. When given the chance to work at the Blue Parrot for twice the salary, he refuses, claiming that he cannot spend all the money he currently makes. Sam is not debased by Rick's leadership, because his employment is based on consent; he left Paris with Rick as the Germans occupied the city and moved with him to Casablanca. Nor is Sam degraded by his inferior status. Quite the contrary— Sam is the true backbone of Rick's Café. It is his musical talent that draws the crowds and creates the congenial atmosphere, even in a war-torn city full of exiles seeking a safe haven. Sam's artistic abilities give him a kind of independence from and superiority over his social condition. It is perhaps true that to succeed African-Americans had to have twice the talent and work twice as hard as their white counterparts. But for those like Sam who did thrive in a world dominated by whites, there must have been a strong sense of inner achievement. Sam is a symbol of a black meritocracy, people who made a mark through hard work and ability despite the social roadblocks put before them. Sam is not just a sidekick, he is an American success story.

RICK AND THE AMERICAN CHARACTER

Rick Blaine, age thirty-seven, is an American, who cannot return to his country. We are not sure why his return to the United States is impossible, but we should be sure that Rick epitomizes the American character. There are actually two Ricks: the early, self-centered Rick who seems to care only for himself, and the later idealistic Rick who sacrifices personal happiness for the sake of his principles. Each Rick is a symbol of one aspect of the American character, because each follows the principles set forth in the Declaration of Independence, the origin of American ideals and most American practices. Americans hold as self-evident truths that "all men are created equal" and that all people "are endowed by their Creator with certain unalienable rights; that among these are life, liberty, and the pursuit of happiness." The founders believed our unalienable rights existed prior to the establishment of government, that they are part of our nature as human beings. Protection of rights is the primary reason for the creation of government. Rights are claims against the government, acting as standards by which to judge what the government can and cannot do.

Belief in the principles of natural rights tends to make Americans interested in their private concerns. After all, government exists to protect rights, and rights permit people to choose what they will do with their lives. Since most people's primary concerns are for their survival, security, comfort, and success, dedication to natural rights liberates the inclination of people to look out for themselves. They especially pursue wealth, which some people consider to be a primary precondition for comfortable self-preservation.

Rick typifies the American attachment to self-interest. He is engrossed in business, pleasure, love, and, of course, moneymaking. Rick's personal well-being overshadows dedication to country, community, or abstract principles. Rick succinctly asserts his preference for his own concerns by stating: "I stick my neck out for nobody." He professes that he is "not fighting for anything anymore, except myself. I'm the only cause I'm interested in." He claims that he will leave politics to the German Strasser and the Frenchman Renault, since, as embodiments of their respective cultures, their "business is politics," while his "is running a saloon." He contends that he is "not interested in politics. The problems of the world are not my department. I'm a saloon keeper." Renault praises Rick for his detachment from the world's problems, claiming that Rick's doctrine of "sticking his neck out for nobody" is "a wise foreign policy." Although they have quite different reasons for saying so, both the self-interested Ferrari and the selfless Laszlo warn Rick that "in this world today isolationism is no longer a practical foreign policy."

As do many Americans, Rick believes that his rights exist for self-protection. Despite his aversion to politics, Rick can even be assertive in protecting his privacy. He boldly takes his dossier out of Strasser's hands when the German reveals information the Nazis have collected on him: "Richard Blaine, American. Age, thirty-seven. Cannot return to his country." To which Rick sarcastically remarks: "Are my eyes really brown?"

Rick's self-interest does not lead him down the same road as Ferrari, however. He runs the most successful saloon in Casablanca, a place where everybody goes. He does not use his nightclub merely to satisfy his immediate personal gratification. He knows enough not to mix business with pleasure, follows sound business practices, and refuses to drink with his customers. He also treats his employees well, recognizes their talents, and rewards them accordingly. He gives the most important member of his staff, Sam, a 10 percent stake in the café. Rick treats his help with respect, acknowledges their natural rights, and refuses to "buy or sell human beings." It is not surprising that everyone at Rick's seems devoted to him.

The most important reason for Café Américain's success is that Rick takes care of his customers, clearly behaving better toward them than does his competitor at the Blue Parrot. Rick believes in fair business exchanges. He denies entrance to a customer who probably is in the habit of not paying his debts, despite the man's importance in the Nazi hierarchy. Rick does not discriminate; he serves anyone who is willing to pay, even Nazis, so long as they do not make a disturbance in his establishment. He complains because Ferrari shorts him on every delivery of goods, especially cigarettes. He tells Ugarte that he does not "mind a parasite. I object to a cut-rate one," implying that Ugarte gives shoddy goods or services to his clients. Rick attempts to negotiate a better salary for Sam rather than simply selling his entertainer's services to Ferrari. Although Rick could rig the roulette table so that the house gained an unfair advantage (he fixes the game so that Jan Brandel can win enough to purchase exit visas), he usually does not. For example, he loses twenty thousand francs for which he must make a special trip to his cash reserves. Rick realizes that if he were unfair, customers would eventually catch on, and he would lose their business. Rick may not *really* care about his customers, since he sticks his neck out for nobody, but he understands consumer sovereignty. Customers who feel cheated will not return to play again. Rick's trustworthiness is not so much an ethical principle as it is what Tocqueville singles out as the most prominent American virtue, self-interest rightly understood. However much Rick may desire to get ahead, he knows that he can out-compete Ferrari simply by being honest. Or as Carl puts it, Rick's Café Américain is "as honest as the day is long." Although, because of its proximity to the equator, Casablanca is not known for its particularly long days.

Although Rick's primary focus is on his own affairs, his dedication to individual rights does not make him parochial. Quite the contrary, like most Americans, Rick applies natural rights to everyone, accepting that people everywhere share common aspirations and desires. He has, therefore, a kind of universal perspective; his identity is not constructed by attachment to a particular place so much as by a dedication to a set of ideals that he believes are common to all humanity. When asked by Strasser, "What is your nationality?" Rick responds ironically, "I'm a drunkard." Exhibiting the typically French ability to make one example into a general theory, Renault adds, "That makes Rick a citizen of the world."

There is, of course, a downside to Rick's commitment to his own narrow concerns. As Ugarte says, Rick has become "a very cynical person." Ilsa's rejection has made Rick self-absorbed and almost narcissistic. Ilsa complains, "You want to feel sorry for yourself, don't you? With so much at stake, all you can think of is your own feelings. One woman has hurt you, and you take revenge on the rest of the world. You're a, you're a coward, and a weakling." Rick is not unlike those Americans who, as Peter Augustine Lawler points out, are so intent on finding happiness that they make themselves miserable when faced with even the slightest stress and misfortune in everyday life. They, and their doctors, identify the absence of happiness as an illness to be treated therapeutically with antidepressant drugs.[18] For Rick not to degenerate into self-indulgent therapeutic alcoholism, the drug of choice in 1941, he must have something higher to believe in, something that gives his life purpose. As Laszlo tells Rick, "I wonder if you know that you're trying to escape from yourself and that you will never succeed."

Casablanca would not have been much of a movie if, as in the original play, Rick surrendered to his passions and ran off with Ilsa, leaving Victor to his fate. For most of the film Rick seems not to appreciate the global crisis threatening the rights he acknowledges as natural, and therefore unalienable, and also his personal happiness and security. The cynical Rick takes some weak and ineffective steps to stymie agents of the malignant political system that he sees growing around him. He runs guns to anti-Fascists in Ethiopia and loyalists in Spain. He sides with the French officer against the Nazi when a scuffle breaks out in Café Américain after the singing of the "Marseillaise." He cautions Strasser that "there are certain sections of New York . . . that I wouldn't advise you to try to invade," warning the Nazi that Americans would defend their homeland more tenaciously than their outward devotion to commercial pursuits might suggest. But in typical American fashion it is only after suffering—to paraphrase the Declaration of Independence—a long train of indignities and injustices committed by Nazis, that Rick reaches a tipping point. He then understands the scope of the crisis, realizes that his personal difficulties "don't amount to a hill of beans in this crazy world," and determines to take a stand against an evil enemy.

What had made Rick so distrustful was the loss of Ilsa's love. Once she expresses her devotion, Rick's confidence is restored. He appreciates that Ilsa left him because of the duty she felt toward Laszlo, not because of a lack of affection for Rick. But, paradoxically, Rick's reunion with Ilsa also makes him fection for Rick. But, paradoxically, Rick's reunion with Ilsa also makes him aware that his commitment to self-interest has been shortsighted. In a world ruled by Nazis, Rick and Ilsa would not be free to pursue their happiness; the odds, as Rick says, are "nine chances out of ten" that they would "both wind up in a concentration camp." Even if they could find some corner of the world in which to hide from Fascist domination, the psychological effect of abandoning Laszlo, one of the bravest men in the world, would ruin their relationship.

> RICK: Inside we both know you belong with Victor. You're part of his work, the thing that keeps him going. If that plane leaves the ground and you're not with him, you'll regret it.
> ILSA: No.
> RICK: Maybe not today, maybe not tomorrow, but soon, and for the rest of your life.

Although the skeptical Renault believes that Rick is a sentimentalist who has invented a fairy tale merely to help Laszlo, Rick states that the distasteful consequences of forsaking Laszlo are true. Richard Corliss argues that "Rick can give Renault a sense of values, and Renault can give Rick a sense of proportion."[19] However, it is not Renault but Ferrari and Laszlo, who are correct. Both Rick's safety and beliefs are threatened by totalitarianism.

Rick's dilemma at the Casablanca airport raises one of the central questions of human existence: how much should we devote ourselves to what we love, what gives us pleasure, and makes us comfortable, and how much should we dedicate ourselves to ethical and moral principles that, as Laszlo says, help decide our "destiny, for good and for evil"? If we tilt the scale too much in one direction, we become like Ferrari or Ugarte, egocentric schemers whose desires dominate their lives. If, on the other hand, we become too self-sacrificing and willing to commit ourselves to a cause, we can become as fanatical as Strasser, or as passionless as Laszlo. In a sense, Laszlo is Strasser's doppelganger. His decent sacrifices would be unnecessary if it were not for Strasser's evil depravity. Laszlo defines his identity and the meaning of life generally by opposition to evil. He declares that "We might as well question why we breathe. If we stop breathing, we'll die. If we stop fighting our enemies, the world will die."

Laszlo's passionless idealism reminds us of Aristotle's criticism of the Spartan regime in the *Politics*. The Spartans were so public spirited that they neglected their wives, sometimes even sharing them with their comrades. The result of Spartan civic-mindedness was that the women were left alone too much and became dissolute. The Spartan men had to make such enormous sacrifices for the community that they resembled bees, who merely do what is best for the colony, more than humans, who need personal fulfillment in order to make their lives worthwhile. Rick has to remind Laszlo that fidelity to abstract principles, no matter how noble, cannot take the place of the relationship between lovers. In the heat of the struggle against mankind's enemies, Laszlo may believe that he is not jealous because Rick and he are "in love with the same woman," but "it may make a difference" to Laszlo "later on" if Ilsa has been unfaithful. Rick attempts to make Laszlo believe that if Ilsa has been unfaithful it was because she sacrificed herself for Laszlo's safety and for the good of the cause. "She tried everything to get" the letters of transit, Rick reveals to Laszlo, "and nothing worked. She did her best to convince me that she was still in love with me, but that was all over long ago. For your sake, she pretended it wasn't, and I let her pretend."

For Rick, the chances for true love are not so promising. As the Bureau of Motion Pictures stated during World War II, *Casablanca* shows "that personal desires must be subordinated to the task of defeating fascism."[20] Roger Ebert points out that "The great break between *Casablanca* and almost all Hollywood love stories—even wartime romances—is that it does not believe that love can, or should, conquer all."[21] Unlike Laszlo, Rick never underestimates the power of love; he sacrifices Ilsa's presence in his life only out of necessity. But Rick finally sees that fascism is a threat to the very rights that allow him to pursue private happiness. Rights are in need of a defense that cannot be based on rights. Rights can only be preserved, as the Declaration of Independence makes clear, if their supporters pledge their lives, fortunes, and sacred honor.

The key to understanding Rick, and along with him the American character, is that lurking behind the omnipresent acquisitive efforts and self-promoting activities is an intense idealism. In peaceful and ordinary times Americans exercise their rights by pursuing their interests, but when the rights that protect their interests are jeopardized, Americans act decisively to protect their ideals. Because of the dichotomy between how Americans usually behave and how they react to a crisis, their intentions are often misunderstood. For example, the sophisticated Renault mistakes Rick's commitment to a cause as sentimentalism, echoing the mistaken criticism the worldly French often make of American amateurism and naïveté in international diplomacy.

Others ascribe sinister materialistic motives to American policy, insisting that Americans never waver from self-interested pursuits and that every decision taken by the government must have a monetary objective as its end. For instance, critics charged that America went to war in Vietnam to assist Dow Chemical, the manufacturer of napalm, or to exploit Vietnam's natural resources. President Ronald Reagan was charged with conspiring to enlarge the military-industrial complex when he claimed that a strong military was necessary to resist Communist totalitarianism. Critics charged that President Bill Clinton bombed Al Qaeda training camps in order to divert attention from the Monica Lewinsky affair, rather than for the stated reason of protecting American national security. The United States was accused of going to war in Kuwait and Iraq to secure their oil or to help the Halliburton company turn a profit. But if American policy were crafted merely to improve the bottom line or enhance the careers of politicians, it would have been much easier and more profitable to pay companies direct subsidies rather than enlist them in the war efforts, trade with Communist governments rather than oppose them, act cautiously toward Al Qaeda (Clinton was President before the terrorist attacks of September 11,

2001) rather than attempt to destroy it, and buy oil from Saddam Hussein rather than topple him.

What sophisticated critics find unbelievable (and those who maintain that America's leaders act only on the basis of self-interest always think of themselves as more sophisticated than those who support the leadership) is that Presidents Lyndon Johnson, Ronald Reagan, George H. W. Bush, Bill Clinton, and George W. Bush actually believed what they were saying. As simple and naïve as it sounds, they maintained that they were going to war to protect and defend freedom. Like Rick, most Americans think that rights are not only natural, but also universally applicable. When a serious threat to those rights exists, many Americans feel justified in taking—and perhaps, again like Rick, compelled to take—action. An argument might be made that American idealism, not American cupidity, has been the cause of most American military intervention.

The most grievous misjudgment made about America is to underestimate the nation's resolve, seeing only that side of the national character that seeks comfortable self-preservation, viewing all Americans as self-interested Rick Blaines. Strasser makes this error when he pronounces Rick to be "just another blundering American," to which Renault responds, "But we mustn't underestimate American blundering. I was with them when they 'blundered' into Berlin in 1918." In its two-hundred-plus years of existence, America has consistently opposed forms of government that reject the principles of natural rights. It has helped destroy monarchy, aristocracy, fascism, and communism. It has shaped a world in which the only principled alternatives to liberal democracy—the regime that most fully protects natural rights—are fanatical theocracies that hope to turn back the tide of history by thwarting the human longing for material advancement, scientific inquiry, physical pleasure, and individual freedom. It is doubtful that the mass of humanity will adopt such narrow views.

Movie critics have long debated which is the greatest American film. *Citizen Kane* usually wins. But the critics are wrong. *Citizen Kane* shows only half the American personality. Kane becomes more and more cynical, selfish, and self-indulgent as he gets older.[22] But, as accurate as this portrait might be of William Randolph Hearst, it is not a genuine interpretation of the American soul. Americans are like Rick Blaine. They stick their necks out for nobody, until some dire threat stirs in them the noble impulse to guard their sacred honor.

CONCLUSION

Casablanca is full of stereotypes, but that is what makes it such a great motion picture. *Casablanca* was multicultural before its time. It recognized that nations and cultures produce distinctive ways of life. As the real-life Czech champion of human dignity, Václav Havel, argues, human beings establish their identities by what they define as their home. He explains that human beings want to be

anchored in one way or another to the world that surrounds us. Our family, our friends, the spiritual and social environment we are associated with, the community, town, or region where we grew up and lived, and to which we accustomed ourselves, our country, our nation, our home in the broadest sense of the word—all these are our anchors in this world, and more: they are integral components of our identity; indeed, they are part of ourselves. We have taken roots in our home, and our home has taken roots in us.[23]

Of course, within every national, cultural, or gender group, there are vast individual differences. These distinctly individual qualities cause thoughtful people to be hesitant about making generalities. Yet even in the era of globalization, we cannot dismiss the effect of culture, nationality, or sex on individual personality.[24] Multiculturalism is the proper way to understand the complexity and diversity of the human race. But if we accept accuracy of multiculturalism, we cannot forego discussing the traits that make us different. Like *Casablanca*, we must accept that there may be much more than a grain of truth in our stereotypes.

NOTES

1. Umberto Eco "*Casablanca*: The Clichés Are Having a Ball," in *Signs of Life in the U.S.A.: Readings on Popular Culture for Writers*, Sonia Maasik and Jack Solomon, eds. (Boston: Bedford Books, 1994), 260, 264.

2. James M. Jones, *Prejudice and Racism* (New York: McGraw-Hill, 1997), 167.

3. Jones, *Prejudice and Racism*, 201.

4. Milton Kleg, *Hate, Prejudice, and Racism* (Albany: State University of New York, 1993), 155.

5. Gordon W. Allport, *The Nature of Prejudice* (Garden City, New York: Doubleday Anchor Books, 1958), 17-19.

6. Allport, *The Nature of Prejudice*, 19-20.

7. Gregory Jay, "What Is Multiculturalism?" online at http://www.uwm.edu/~gjay/Multicult/Multiculturalism.html.

8. All quotes from *Casablanca* can found at: http://www.geocities.com/classicmoviescripts/script/casablanca.pdf.

9. G.W.F. Hegel, *The Phenomenology of Mind*, trans. J. B. Baillie (New York: Harper & Row, 1967), http://www.marxists.org/reference/archive/hegel/works/ph/phba.htm.

10. Simone de Beauvoir, *The Second Sex*, trans. and ed. H. M. Parshley, (New York: Alfred A. Knopf, 1952), 676. For a exhaustive treatment of gender differences see Steven E. Rhoads, *Taking Sex Differences Seriously* (San Francisco: Encounter Books, 2004).

11. Aljean Harmetz, *Round Up the Usual Suspects: The Making of Casablanca—Bogart, Bergman, and World War II* (New York: Hyperion, 1992), 174-79.

12. For an account of Havel's valor see James F. Pontuso, *Václav Havel: Civic Responsibility in the Postmodern Age* (Rowman & Littlefield, 2004).

13. Jaroslav Hašek, *The Good Soldier Švejk and His Fortunes in the World War*, trans. Cecil Parrott, with the original illustrations by Josef Lada (New York: Crowell, 1974).

14. Barbara Day, *The Velvet Philosophers* (London: Claridge Press, 1999).

15. Philippa Gates, "Being a Buddy: The Black Detective on the Big Screen," online at www.crimeculture.com/Contents/Articles-Summer03/Gates-BlackDet.html.

16. BET, http://www.bet.com/articles/0%2C%2Cc31gb2729-3391%2C00.html.

17. Booker T. Washington, Atlanta Exposition Address, http://www.bartleby.com/1004/14.html.

18. Peter Augustine Lawler, *Aliens in America: The Strange Truth about Our Souls* (Wilmington, Del.: ISI Books, 2002).

19. Richard Corliss, "*Casablanca*: An Analysis of the Film," in Howard Koch, *Casablanca: Script and Legend* (London: Arum Press, 1992), 233.

20. Harmetz, *Round Up the Usual Suspects*, 289.

21. Roger Ebert, *Casablanca* at Fifty," in Howard Koch, *Casablanca: Script and Legend* (London: Arum Press, 1992), 250.

22. For an analysis of *Citizen Kane*, see Pauline Kael, "Raising Kane," *The Citizen Kane Book* (New York: Limelight Editions, 1984), 3-84.

23. Václav Havel, "Speech on National Day of the Czech Republic," Prague, October 28, 1995. Downloaded from the Czech President's website, http://www.hrad.cz/.

24. For a discussion of popular culture in that age of globalization see, Paul A. Cantor, *Gilligan Unbound: Pop Culture in the Age of Globalization* (Lanham, Md.: Rowman & Littlefield, 2001) and James F. Pontuso, "Trevanian's *Shibumi:* The Perfect Postmodern Tale," *Faith, Reason, and Political Life Today*, eds. Peter Augustine Lawler and Dale McConkey (Lanham, Md.: Lexington Books, 2001), 139-61

CHAPTER 7

ILSA'S CHOICE: LOVE AND TRAGEDY IN *CASABLANCA*

NIVEDITA N. BAGCHI

LOUIS: No matter how clever [Laszlo] is, he still needs an exit visa. Or I should say two.
RICK: Why two?
LOUIS: He is traveling with a lady.
RICK: He'll take one.
LOUIS: I think not. I've seen the lady.[1]

Casablanca is one of the classic love stories in American movie history. It is also more than a love story, for it is about something more important than the usually love story with a happy ending. *Casablanca* is a movie about redemption—redemption through love. Casablanca is a place where people exhibit their best and worst traits, where policemen are corrupt, casinos fix roulette wheels, and most everyone will do most anything to escape. Greed, selfishness, and domination are ever present. In *Casablanca* we see that the worst human proclivities can be redeemed through the purest human emotion—love. But nothing comes easy in Casablanca. Even though love proves redemptive, it does not win out—in Casablanca the allure of love must compete against life's duties and responsibilities. No better character epitomizes the competition between love and other obligations than the mysterious Ilsa Lund. By comparing Ilsa to the other characters in the film we can best appreciate the redemptive power of love and the conflicting pull of love and duty.

Distant yet alluring, enigmatic yet endearing, Ilsa Lund portrayed by Ingrid Bergman is one of the unforgettable performances in film history. Ilsa's character demonstrates the complicated nature of love and its affects on the human soul. What is to be learned from Ilsa's choices? Through her we see that love strengthens when we love a virtuous person—at least, it is easier to love virtue than vice. In the dialogue *Symposium* Plato maintains love should always seek to make us more virtuous. Love should be an aid to virtue and therefore, we should love someone better than ourselves. Loving someone whose virtue, supercedes our own allows us to rise above our common behavior, thereby increasing our self-respect and our capacity to love. This is certainly true for Ilsa. Ilsa's admiration for the noble Victor Laszlo is the source of her love for him. From the time she was young, Ilsa has attached herself to the person who best embodies the principles she wishes to live by. Ilsa attempts to explain her story to Rick:

> It's about a girl who had just come to Paris from her home in Oslo. At the house of some friends she met a man about whom she'd heard her whole life, a very great and courageous man. He opened up for her a whole beautiful world full of knowledge and thoughts and ideals. Everything she knew or ever became was because of him. And she looked up to him and worshipped him with a feeling she supposed was love.

Second, we learn that love can also be an educator; love teaches both Ilsa and Rick about virtue. Love is the basis of redemption for Rick, and he, in turn, forces Ilsa to face the fact that she has other loyalties and attachments that she should not abandon. Ilsa's love for Rick—as well as her love for Laszlo—makes her unable to ignore her duties, much as she wants to indulge her love. Thus, Ilsa's parting from Rick strengthens their attachment, because it demonstrates to each the virtues present in the other. At the airport, Ilsa looses Rick but recaptures the sense of Rick's nobility, what attracted her to him in the first place. However, their separation also demonstrates the irreconcilable tensions and tragedy that haunts human existence. Ilsa's tragic choice illustrates the dilemmas that face human beings throughout life. We must sometimes choose between loyalty and love, virtue and desire, morality and self-indulgence. In *Casablanca*, it is Ilsa above all who demonstrates the constrained nature of the human condition, and her choices (or lack thereof) are brought into sharper focus by the harsh realities of war.

Casablanca is a place that lends itself to changing identities and allegiances. People go to Casablanca to escape war, but it is difficult to escape. War confronts people with experiences that are not typical in everyday life. The neutral zone of Casablanca is not truly neutral—it is a place of transition between despair and hope, the despair of war-torn France and the hope of peaceful and free America. In Casablanca, suspended between two worlds, people seem unable to indulge the "better angels" of their natures. They are forced to make decisions that they would not even consider making in ordinary life. For instance, Richard, principled, trusting, and charming, transforms himself into the cynical, self-centered Rick. It is almost as though Richard has taken on a new personality along with his changed name. It is instructive that whenever Ilsa wants to appeal to Rick's better nature, she calls him Richard. This is something that is even noted by Rick, a tacit acknowledgment that he is a different person from the Richard that she knew in Paris. Indeed, one can intuit that there is an importance to Ilsa's use of the name. Ilsa is appealing, not only to the memories of Paris, but also to the qualities of the person that she used to know then—the person who fought for the underdog and whose motto was not: "I stick my neck out for nobody." The question is: does Ilsa, too, take on a different personality in Casablanca, one that compels her to make decisions that she would not have otherwise made? Why does she decide to stay with Rick in Casablanca when she could easily have made that decision in Paris? What has changed since then?

Although Ilsa is essential to the plot of *Casablanca*, her character is so underdeveloped that it is hard to answer this question. Almost everything that we know about Ilsa pertains to her relationship with Victor and Rick—there is little that we know of her apart from how she reacts to these two men. What did she do before she met Laszlo? What was her life like in the interval between leaving Paris and arriving in Rick's Café Américain in Casablanca? These questions go unanswered. The paucity of information about her has a dual impact: because her life seems to lack independent action it makes her separation from Rick appear more tragic than Rick's ultimate separation from her, and it justifies her sudden rebellion against her chosen path of duty—to stay with Victor Laszlo. But is her decision to leave Victor really condemnable? Victor Laszlo is unquestionably the most admired and upright person in *Casablanca*. He is noble, selfless, and heroic, and as Rick notes the world knows it. We cheer at his bravery and wit in orchestrating the singing of the "Marseillaise" (an accomplishment of Herculean proportions in the United States after the divisions over the war in Iraq). Yet, while we champion his cause, everyone watching the movie is hoping he will get dumped. It is only the enigmatic character of Ilsa that allows the audience to hold these contradictory thoughts together.

The underdeveloped nature of Ilsa's character works in her favor in a number of ways. First, the viewers know that she is a principled soul—she has already sacrificed love once when she refused to leave Paris with Rick. Already, therefore, the sympathies of the audience lie with the virtuous, torn, and heroic Ilsa. Second, the audience knows nothing of her struggles between leaving Paris and arriving in Casablanca as well as nothing of her life after she leaves Casablanca. Since this part of the story is indeterminate, it is left to the imagination— and sympathy—of the viewers. Third, Ilsa obviously cares for Victor and is torn between the two men. She did not count on seeing Rick in Casablanca. She thought that she would never see him again. The audience can appreciate the position in which Ilsa finds herself. Although the story is particular to Ilsa the situation is universal. We all live with the problem of divided loyalties. While we may not all experience the pull of divided loyalties in love, we come across other forms of the same problem at different times in our lives. Thus, we *feel* that Ilsa has loved Rick all this time and experience her loss when she is required to leave him a second time. The indeterminacy of her life before coming to Casablanca and after leaving it make her all the more a sympathetic character.

Love, ironically, forces Rick to recognize the nature of the divided loyalties that Ilsa has to face. Love becomes a vehicle of redemption for Rick. It generates in him a desire for virtue and replaces his cynical selfishness with a desire for honor and glory through a display of bravery and patriotism. Indeed, love is the single vehicle for redemption for all the characters in the movie. Love of humanity characterizes Laszlo. Love for country and friendship (fondness) with Rick, redeems Louis Renault. But it is love for Ilsa that redeems Rick. The mere presence of Ilsa in the same town has a transformative effect on him. The effect is not a result of anything that Ilsa says or does—rather it is the emotion of love itself that changes Rick. Rick realizes that Ilsa is drawn to Victor because she admires his principles and heroic actions. Rick himself is impressed with Laszlo, though perhaps somewhat grudgingly when it comes to Ilsa. In the end Rick imitates Laszlo's virtue. This assessment of the effects of love is also seen in Plato's *Symposium*. In the *Symposium*, Phaedrus asserts that an army of lovers would be comprise the bravest soldiers since each person would be trying to impress his lover. This concept is articulated by Victor who tells Ilsa that he too is scared but would not be comfortable saying so in front of his wife. Thus, at least in the men, love seems to inspire the desire for bravery, self-sacrifice, honor, and glory.

Ilsa, on the other hand, is not rescued by love; instead love puts her virtue to the test. Yet, love also allows her to pass that test. Indeed, contrary to their first inclinations, it is Rick who finally keeps Ilsa on the path of virtue. Of all the main characters in the film, it is Ilsa who decides to indulge her feelings at the cost of loyalty—she decides to leave Victor and stay with Rick. After all, she has already sacrificed for duty—she left Rick in Paris in order to fulfill her duty to the ailing Victor. She "ran away" from Rick "once," she "can't do it again." The second time around, it is Rick who convinces her to leave him, thus demonstrating the nobility latent in his character, the noble sacrifice of Ilsa's previous actions in Paris, and Rick's own recognition and appreciation of Ilsa's choice.

Who does Ilsa really love? On one hand, it is clear that she feels a responsibility toward Victor, a loyalty engendered as much by admiration for his character, principles, and work as by her status as his wife. But admiration and concern are not love, and Ilsa claims that she mistook those sentiments for love when she first met Victor. Yet, she is obviously bound to Victor by an emotion that is more than respect and loyalty. In her own way, she loves him for who he is. On the other hand, Rick's presence in Casablanca releases passions that she felt she had put behind her. Richard is the person she loved and still loves. But this love is plagued by conflict—conflict between her love for Rick and her love for Victor.

Caught in this conundrum, Ilsa abandons the dutiful choice she had made in Paris and decides to follow her inner longings—she decides to remain with Rick. For her, love necessitates abandoning duty. It is perhaps debatable whether it is possible to *prove* that her duty is to remain with Victor, especially in our time when freedom of choice is venerated above all else; but it is ultimately a moot point since she believes it her duty to stay with him. She gives in to the very selfishness that she accuses Rick of: "With so much at stake, all you can think about is your own feelings." In a battle between duty and love, Ilsa allows love to win out. In a story of redemption, Ilsa seems to be the only exception: she is the only one who moves from virtue to selfishness. Thus, it seems to be the kind of love that thinks only of its own happiness and does not place itself within the larger perspective of virtue and dutifulness. Ilsa is not unconscious that her decision may be the wrong one. She concedes to Rick that she cannot distinguish right from wrong anymore—she is incapable of making any decisions and concedes that Rick will have to "think for both of us." She, of course has succumbed to her desire to stay with Rick—she is tired of struggling against her feelings.

Ilsa's choice to remain with Rick may have different explanations. One possibility may be that she is in a position similar to Annina Brandel who is willing to give herself to Captain Renault to obtain exit visas for her husband and herself. Ilsa might be giving herself to Rick because of she loves her husband and hopes that Rick will give Victor the exit visa. This explanation is easily dismissed because there are glaring differences between Annina and Ilsa. Annina loves her husband; she is virtually prostituting herself for the sake of her husband and their freedom. But Ilsa loves Rick and knows that he loves her. Thus, by staying with Rick, Ilsa will be staying with the man she loves—not simply sacrificing herself for her husband's safety.

Or—and this seems the most plausible and romantic explanation—she has experienced the reality of living without the person she loves and decides that she can no longer abide a passionless relationship. She made the decision to leave Rick at the train station in Paris, and she did not think that she would have to make that choice again. Now, forced to confront the same decision again, she is unable to act as she had before. Ilsa goes to Rick's apartment with the best of intentions: to get the exit visas that will allow Victor and her to escape. At first, she upbraids Rick for being so concerned only with himself. She threatens him with a pistol. Yet, she surrenders to her feelings when she realizes that she may have to kill the man she loves to help the husband she admires. In making this choice, Ilsa inspires conflicting emotions in the viewers. On the one hand, there is sympathy for star-crossed lovers, Rick and Ilsa. Yet, there is the feeling that Ilsa's previous choice—to renounce her love and stay with her husband—had a certain self-sacrifice and nobility to it that lacking in her decision to become the lover of a saloon owner. There is also sympathy for Laszlo whose trust in his wife has been amply demonstrated. Thus, Ilsa's decision, though understandable, is not without shortcomings and seems to lack the high-minded self-sacrificing quality that has characterized her earlier behavior in Paris. The identification with Ilsa's confusion and the sympathy for her choices is what gives *Casablanca* much of its universal appeal.

Yet, it is Rick, not Ilsa, who is shown to have an awareness of the constrained nature of human affairs—that human beings are not free to make whatever choices suit them. He restates Ilsa's earlier reproach to him saying, "The problems of three little people do not amount to a hill of beans in this crazy world." Rick engineers not only his own redemption but Ilsa's as well. Rick's solution demonstrates that love is strengthened when it involves virtuous people. By redeeming himself and parting from Ilsa, Rick, ironically, strengthens Ilsa's faith in him (and her love for him) and keeps their love alive. As he explains to Ilsa at the airport, their love would be embittered should they stay together. Rick forces Ilsa to adopt the right path—against the force of her emotions, but not against her will.

Rick and Ilsa's parting, though sad, is the least tragic ending to the movie possible. Rick's words at the airport reveal that he is appealing to Ilsa's inherent nobility. Rick, like the audience, is aware of the confusion in Ilsa's mind. Ilsa understands this too—her last words to Rick are "God bless you"—not upbraiding, not reluctance, not even a passive acquiescence. Indeed, there is an instant when both Rick and Laszlo wait for Ilsa to acquiesce to leave. There is a silence for a fraction of a second—and I, at least, sat breathlessly awaiting her response, conflicted about what I wanted her response to be, watching her as intently as the two men on the screen. However, Ilsa, like Rick, is aware that this is the move that will be the least harmful to their love. Thus, Ilsa, too, does understand the fact that human freedom is both illusive and elusive. The best place for a demonstration of the condition nature of freedom is Casablanca—a place that gives the illusion of freedom but where, as everyone who stays there rapidly realizes, not only freedom but also their very life may not be under their own control.

Ultimately, Ilsa's fate is the most tragic, for her future will always center on the man she is with—a man she does not passionately love. Her life is not independent of the work of Victor Laszlo. She is bound up in his struggles and his cause; there is no view of anything that is solely her own. The audience has already seen Rick live a life without Ilsa, and they can see that Rick's new life in the Free French Resistance, though without Ilsa, will be fuller than it had been in Casablanca. He will have friendship and moral purpose. Although he has suffered a great loss in his personal life, he will have both independence and a noble mission. But Ilsa has no such mission, no such independent work that will give her life meaning. The song that she loves states as much, "It's still the same old story / A fight for love or glory / A case of do or die." Yet, none of these possibilities apply to Ilsa. She gets neither love nor glory out of the choice she makes. Her life is to be bound up with that of Laszlo, Her love for him is neither ardent nor unencumbered. Though Ilsa does love him, she is also torn between him and Rick, and she is fated to live out this tension for the rest of her life. Thus, Ilsa's fate ends up looking more tragic than Rick's, Victor's, or indeed, anyone else's in *Casablanca*.

But Ilsa is not the only woman who has to wrestle with the options offered by Casablanca. A distinctive facet of Casablanca is that it places men and women on a strange plane of equality. Obviously, this is only true of the refugees—the people who come to Casablanca in order to get away from occupied Europe. The permanent residents of Casablanca retain a male hierarchy of power, a hierarchy that was characteristic in both Casablanca and America during the period when the film was made. Yet, due to the very nature of the men who run Casablanca, refugee women have greater leverage in the place than men. By compromising their principles women can get access to money and power that the male refugees cannot. In a world where money and access to power are one's passport to freedom, the gender roles among the refugees is reversed. Men cannot be protective, and women cannot afford to remain abstentious. They sell their possessions along with their virtue to acquire the necessities of life and the much-sought-after exit visas. The best example of this is in the case of Jan and Annina. While she contemplates giving herself to Renault in order to obtain their dream of getting to freedom in America, Jan is reduced to relying on pure chance—gambling in order to make the money to leave Casablanca. Yet, Annina is not immoral—for her, love dictates that she make a choice, which in less dire circumstances would be morally suspect. Casablanca does not so much force people to abandon their moral outlook as it presents difficult moral options, options that probe into the deepest complexities and principles of human life. To maintain a moral balance, those who come to Casablanca must always be on guard and vigilant. In this atmosphere we shouldn't be too hard on Ilsa. Virtue does not come easy in Casablanca.

In this atmosphere, it is telling that only one character never strays from the course of duty and righteousness—Victor Laszlo. It is not that Laszlo is never tested. Indeed, his trust in his wife is put to the test when Rick demands that he ask Ilsa why they cannot have the exit visas. Nor does Ilsa explain the relationship that she had with Rick—she demands that Laszlo trust her, and he does. His love for Ilsa does not allow doubt. Thus, whereas the other characters give in to the world around them and change their priorities to suit the situation in which they find themselves, Laszlo remains undeterred and true to the highest principles. He embodies dedication, loyalty, selflessness, and trust even in an atmosphere that leads others to violate one (or all) of these principles. Because of his purity of principle, Laszlo does not seem aware of the limitation that nature places on other human beings. He is not as human as are Rick and Ilsa. In his single-mindedness, his nobility, his dedication to his work, and his trust in his wife, Laszlo stands out as the exception rather than the rule. He seems to stand above contradiction, confusion, and tension. For him choices are easy.

Again, Ilsa's situation best demonstrates that freedom to choose can be as much a curse as a blessing. Ultimately, what option could Ilsa have made that would have made her life easier after she left Casablanca? The tragedy of Ilsa's character lies in the fact that none of her choices are perfect. There are irreconcilable tensions in her life, and none of her decisions would allow her to be completely happy. Any outcome would be tainted for her. Staying behind with Rick would lead to guilt and bitterness just as Rick describes. Leaving with him for America would have had the same, if not worse, consequences. Yet, going with Laszlo at a time when Rick demonstrates his nobility and virtue must be even harder for her. Rick has been restored to the Richard that she knew in Paris—the person she admires as well as loves, a person with principles.

There is no doubt that Rick's and Ilsa's parting makes *Casablanca* end on a sad, poignant note. But the words "We'll always have Paris" reclaim the ending from pure sorrow. Paris is made possible because of Casablanca. Love is restored because of Casablanca. Rick's love for Ilsa has been restored due to her explanation of the circumstances that made her leave him and due to her declaration of her love for him even now. Ilsa's faith in Rick and her love for him has been restored by his actions and by the fact that she no longer carries around the burden of guilt for leaving him at the train station. Thus, Casablanca is a place of redemption through love, it makes love possible, and it rejuvenates Rick and Ilsa's love for each other even as it ensures their ultimate separation.

Ultimately, then, Ilsa's character in *Casablanca* speaks of a higher tension than merely the choice between two lovers. It reflects the tensions that have haunted human beings throughout time—the tension between freedom of choice and adherence to duty and tradition, the tension between morality and virtue and the degree to which our lives are bound up with the lives of others. These tensions and questions are further complicated by the fact that *Casablanca* is placed in a setting of war, putting the issues of human behavior in a starker perspective. Ilsa Lund represents the human condition, one that must face alternatives, none of them perfect, forced to choose among those imperfect alternatives. The characters around Ilsa serve to highlight the variety of reactions to these difficult circumstances, thus making *Casablanca* a movie that encompasses human behavior in all shades. That *Casablanca* is a story of redemption shows a faith in human beings, in the human capacity for reform—in an environment that allows both the best and the worst characteristics of human beings to come to the fore. The words of George Eliot could easily be spoken by Rick and Ilsa:

> "It seems to me right sometimes that we should follow our strongest feeling; but then such feelings continually come across the ties that all our former life has made for us . . . . Love is natural, but surely pity and faithfulness and memory are natural too. And they would live in me still and punish me if I did not obey them. I should be haunted by the suffering I had caused. Our love would be poisoned."[2]

NOTES

1. All quotes from *Casablanca* can found at:
http://www.geocities.com/classicmoviescripts/script/casablanca.pdf.
2. George Eliot, *The Mill on the Floss*, found at: http://www.bartleby.com/309/613.html.

CHAPTER 8

BOGART'S HEROES:
THE CHANGING FACE OF HEROISM IN AMERICAN FILM

DAVID K. NICHOLS

DEFINING HEROISM: THE EVOLUTION OF THE BOGART CHARACTER

Humphrey Bogart's portrayal of the character Richard Blaine in *Casablanca* is a classic expression of the American ideal of heroism. The mix of cynicism and idealism and of selfishness and patriotism captures the paradox of the American conception of virtue.[1] American heroes are independent, self-confident loners, willing and able to defend their rights. But not far beneath this surface of rugged individualism is a sense of justice and a concern for others. We know from the beginning of *Casablanca* that Rick will ultimately fight the Nazis and recover his lost love. Bogart may have become an existentialist icon of the 1960s, but his existentialism was always of the tough-but-decent American variety, rather than the morally ambiguous European strain. The French may have liked his movies, but they never understood the soul of his characters. To Americans Bogart was not an antihero, but an exemplar of the most deeply held American values. For those who have difficulty understanding American's peculiar mix of realism and idealism, *Casablanca* provides more profound insight than a hundred political science texts.

Bogart's depiction of American heroism in *Casablanca*, however, represents neither the beginning nor the end of the exploration of that theme in his films. If we examine Bogart's films from the 1930s through the 1950s we will see a complex and evolving vision of heroism, in part reflecting the changing historical context of his films, but also, I will argue, developing a more sophisticated understanding of the character of heroism in a modern democratic society.

The Roaring '20s and the Depression are the breeding ground for Bogart the gangster. The gangster becomes a hero in a world where conventional values seem to have failed. By the early 1940s, however, a new possibility of heroism emerges. If society is still not clear on the meaning of the good or the noble, it is clear about the possibility of evil. The Nazis offer a fixed point for our moral compass, one that even a hard-bitten cynic is forced to recognize. By the end of the war more conventional values of friendship and love emerge, although still leavened by a healthy dose of realism. We even see the emergence of a social conscience in the 1950s, although in some films such as *Knock on Any Door* the character with a conscience may be as one-dimensional as the gangsters of the early films. In the best of the later films, however, we see an increasing self-consciousness about the question of the relationship between life and acting, a question that is crucial to an understanding of heroism and of Bogart. In *Sabrina*, *The Left Hand of God*, and Bogart's last movie, *The Harder They Fall*, we see how role playing can transform not only the audience but the also actor. We may become what we pretend to be.

GANGSTER AS HERO

The gangster movie has been one the most enduring genres in the history of film. By the time Bogart came to Hollywood George Raft, James Cagney, and Edward G. Robinson had made the gangster into a contemporary legend. Because of fear of public outrage or political censorship, the gangster almost always had to die at the end of the film as a concession to public morality, but it was clear that the appeal of the gangster film was based on the attraction to a character that shunned convention and took what he wanted from the world. The gangster as hero appealed to both the rugged individualism of the American tradition as well as to the growing cynicism about the efficacy and legitimacy of contemporary political and social institutions. The gangster was a nonconformist, a self-made man, and a rebel against established authority. The self-indulgence and hedonism of the 1920s evolved into the political and social unrest of the Depression years. The two decades that appear in so many ways to be polar opposites are linked by the common mythology of the gangster.

Bogart often joked that he got all of his early roles in films that George Raft had rejected, and in many respects these early roles may have been more suited to Raft than to the character Bogart was to develop. It is in *Petrified Forest* that Bogart redefined the Bogart gangster role.[2] Duke Mantee, the gangster, and Alan Squier (Leslie Howard), the wandering poet, highlight two sides of American individualism. In these two characters we see the epitome of the realist-idealist debate that so often animates American political thought. Some have even criticized the film for its self-conscious philosophizing about these competing views of life. Mantee is an unrepentant villain, a man who has the courage of his lack of convictions. He is, as Alan describes him, the last of the rugged individualists. He has killed at least eight men, and we believe that he is ready to kill more.

Alan is weak, a man of ideas, who at the same time disdains intellectuals. He was supported by a wife who thought he was a promising writer, but the promise was never fulfilled. Instead he wanders in search of something he cannot define, something "worth living for and dying for."[3] He finds it in a falling-down gas station in the middle of the desert, in the person of Gabrielle Maple (Bette Davis). Gabrielle is a young girl who dreams of escaping the Arizona desert for a life in France. At first Alan tells her that France is no different from the desert. For him happiness has remained always over the next horizon, but he becomes captivated by the dreams of the young Gabrielle. He sees the possibility that she may be able to find the happiness that has eluded him.

Although Gabrielle finds his ideas a little strange, she is enchanted by his discussions of poetry, art, and life. He gives her a glimpse of the world he inhabits, the romantic world of his never-ending and lonely quest. Her dreams take on a concrete reality in the person of Alan Squier. The problem is that Alan is unable to embrace real happiness. His ideals may be within sight, but they are always out of reach. He sees his destiny in the stars, and his destiny is death.

In the person of Duke Mantee, Alan finds the means to achieve his destiny. Duke appears to be Alan's alter ego. He has no illusions and no principles that would get in the way of pursuing his self-interest. He has no hope of another better world, no hope of finding a world of truth and beauty. He deals with the world as he finds it. He has no reluctance to act and to act violently. We might suspect that Alan would be repelled by Duke, but instead he sees in Duke a kindred spirit, a romantic iconoclast like himself. Alan is almost as taken by Duke as he is by Gabrielle. Duke is an anachronism, an individualist who no longer can find a place in the world, a man doomed to die.

Alan, however, is also aware of the differences between the two. Alan lacks the courage to kill anyone, even himself, but Alan knows that Duke can kill, and in this possibility he sees his salvation. Alan has a life insurance policy, the proceeds of which could finance Gabrielle's trip to France. When Gabrielle is out of the room, he asks Duke to kill him, so that Gabrielle can have her chance for happiness. He does not conceive of the possibility that she could be happy in a life together with him. We might suspect that Alan, overcome by his own weakness, would be unable to go through with his plan, but a noble death is the one thing consistent with his romantic longings. We might also hope that Duke would show some sign of decency, some recognition of their kinship, and spare Alan's life. But Alan knows something we would rather forget; Duke is a killer. Although Duke starts to leave without killing Alan, when Alan blocks the door, Duke hardly hesitates before he shoots. Alan dies in the arms of his angel, Gabrielle. A few moments later we hear over the radio a report of Duke's death in a shoot-out with the police. The two individualists have taken different roads to the same end.

It is not clear what moves Duke to kill Alan. The most obvious answer is survival. Duke would not go out of his way to kill Alan, but when Alan threatens to delay his departure Duke automatically kills in his ruthless quest for survival. It is also possible that he thinks he is doing Alan a favor. Perhaps he sees their common destiny and shoots him in tribute to their spiritual kinship. Whether or not Duke thinks of this possibility, the audience surely does. Alan is a conventional hero who dies for the sake of his beloved, but the link between Alan and Duke has been established in the mind of the audience. Therefore there is little sense of celebration in the announcement of Duke's death. A world that has no place for Alan or Duke is a smaller place.

We are left with the world of the mortgage banker and his wife, whom Duke also held captive in the gas station. The mortgage banker, like Duke, is a self-interested individual, but his selfishness exhibits nothing of nobility. When his wife suggests that he might have tried to defend them against Duke, he calls her an idiot. The wife is the more interesting and appealing of the two. She is such a romantic that she actually asks Duke to take her with him. We suspect, however, that in the final analysis she would not go. Instead she would remain with her husband. She sees herself as a martyr to her sense of obligation to others. What the audience sees is that she is willing to sacrifice her sense of self for the comfort and security her husband can provide because she is unwilling to accept the risks necessary for true independence. She and her husband are pale reflections of the romantic idealism of Alan and the rugged individualism of Duke. Alan and Duke are the symbols of the heroism that is missing in contemporary American life, a heroism we long for but cannot find.

There is one loose end that remains undeveloped in *The Petrified Forest*. Duke hides out at the gas station because he is waiting for his girlfriend, Doris (Constance Bergen), to arrive. We do not learn much about Doris in the course of the movie or about Duke's feelings for her. As Alan notes, however, she represents another link between Duke and himself. If we cannot say that both Alan and Duke die for love, we can at least say that they both die because of a woman. Gabrielle and Doris cause Alan and Duke to veer off their established paths, resulting in the death of both men. Duke may even have made a greater sacrifice than Alan. Duke could imagine a life with Doris, and, unlike Alan, Duke fights to live, even when that fight appears to be hopeless.

The role of women is an even more prominent theme in a movie made by Bogart a year after *The Petrified Forest*. Baby Face Martin, the gangster played by Bogart in *Dead End*, is the tough, smart kid who has become a success as a violent criminal. He has all the money he needs, but he is surprised to find that he is not satisfied with his life. He has even stolen enough money that he can buy a new face, but he is still not safe from the cops, because he cannot change his fingerprints. He has tried to burn them away with acid, but it seems that nothing he can do and no amount of money can cover up his identity as a criminal. Nonetheless he returns to his old neighborhood in search of a more fulfilling life.

His reason for coming home is to see his mother and an old girlfriend. Like Duke and Alan, he alters his course because of the women in his life. From the beginning we have a sense that these reunions will not turn out the way he hoped. His poverty stricken mother calls him a no good tramp and slaps him in the face when she recognizes him. She has no interest in his money and, in spite of the poverty and wretchedness of her life, has only contempt for her son's success. Her sense of moral superiority to her son is even greater than the sense of moral superiority exhibited by the wealthy inhabitants of the luxury high rise who, in the movie, look down on those who suffer in the slums beneath their terraces. It is hard to say whether the audience is to admire the mother's uncompromising principles or to feel sadness at the fact that she has lost the ability to feel even a tinge of affection for her own son. In either case by the end of the scene between Martin and his mother it is hard not to feel some compassion for the blow Martin has suffered. As his partner says, "I know what you feel. Anybody would."[5] Whatever memories of maternal love and nurture he had were destroyed forever. He can no longer take any comfort in the thought of a mother's embrace. Instead he will always remember that he had killed a guy who had looked at him the way his mother had that day.

His old girlfriend is a symbol of his unfulfilled hopes for the future. He remembers the promise that their young love had held for him and thought that now those dreams at last could be fulfilled. Instead he sees a picture of depravity without any trace of success or glory. His former young love is now a disease-ridden prostitute who has little time left. It is like another slap in the face when she suggests that there is no difference in the paths they have taken. The money and the success cannot hide the ugliness of his life. He begins to see that he has no future as well as no link to the past.

In spite of his limitations, Martin still has the possibility of becoming a hero in the eyes of the neighborhood youths. The only time in the movie when Martin appears to be enjoying himself is when he is watching the gang of neighborhood kids. After he hears them arrange a fight with another gang he goes over to the neighborhood kids and offers them some advice. They should arrive early for the fight so that the other gang will be unprepared. They should ignore the ground rules they set and come armed with milk bottles and electric bulbs. They should take out the toughest guys first—a sack full of sand and rocks is recommended for the job. Martin displays all the satisfaction of an old master passing on his craft to a group of eager young apprentices. The kids at first resist. They do not think they should break the rules to which they had agreed, but they are obviously impressed with Martin's knowledge and experience, as well as his retort that the rules are not important. "The important thing is to win; it doesn't matter how."

This scene is the fulcrum on which the movie turns. It is interrupted when Dave Connell (Joel McCrea), the decent but unsuccessful young architect who has been reduced to painting a sign for a local bar, interrupts and tells Martin to stay away from the kids. Dave is the more conventional hero of the film and the foil for Martin's villain. In spite of their differences, however, the film is at pains to point out their similarities. They were friends when they were young, and each seems to have a kind of grudging respect for the other. Dave even tells his girlfriend that Martin was "a smart and brave and decent young boy" who might have turned out differently. Even now he seems willing to put up with Martin's presence, although he knows that Martin, like Duke Mantee, has killed eight people. He does not think of turning him over to the cops initially, because as we learn in another scene the cops are themselves corrupt and use their power to keep down the underdog—for example, beating up striking workers to protect the interests of the wealthy. In this morally ambiguous world, Martin is free to walk the streets. It is only when he threatens to corrupt the young that he must be eliminated. If he is not, he will become the model of survival and success to boys of the neighborhood.

Dave cannot tolerate this outcome. When he finally threatens to go to the police, he is stabbed by Martin, dumped in the river, and left for dead. Of course he is not dead. He rises from the river and kills Martin, doing the job the police were incapable of doing. The hero wins and the villain dies, but our idea of morality remains clouded. Like Dave we are left to feel some sympathy for the Martin that might have been, the Martin that even after all his crimes was drawn back to memories of his childhood home and his hopes for a new life. In the closing scenes we see the neighborhood kids discussing the newspaper accounts of his death. The romanticized story in the paper has little resemblance to the facts known by the kids, but at least one of the kids is ready to reject his own experience in favor of the authority of the newspaper. He is ready to accept the romantic version offered by the paper rather than the truth about the squalid life and death of Baby Face Martin.

The greatest ambiguity comes, however, when Dave recognizes that he has been able to triumph over Martin's version of heroism only by himself becoming a killer. When told there is a reward for killing Martin, his response is "They pay you for it, huh?" Thus the audience is left to wonder if there is any other way out of this dead end life than the trail blazed by Martin.

FINDING VIRTUE IN AN AMORAL WORLD

In 1941 Bogart finds a new signature role; he moves from Bogart the gangster to Bogart the detective. *The Maltese Falcon* is the model of the modern detective film, and Bogart the epitome of the tough, cynical detective. It is surprising to note that in addition to *The Maltese Falcon*, Bogart made only one other actual private detective movie, *The Big Sleep* in 1946. Nonetheless, Bogart, more than any other single actor, defined the genre.

Although the move from gangster to detective is not such a large stretch for an actor, in the case of Bogart it does represent a significant refinement of his character. Like the gangster the private detective is an individualist who spends much of his time in a shady underworld. He has few illusions about life and is often at odds with the law. The private detective, however, is on the side of justice, even though he shares the gangster's ambivalence about the law. He provides an appealing middle ground between the gangster and the establishment. He has much of the gangster's romantic individualism, but without his selfish villainy. At the same time he has a sense of justice, without yielding to the conformity and hypocrisy of the establishment. In the world of the private detective, law and order is best supported by the private sector, a lone individual with no legal authority. The truly independent individual does not live by taking from others, but by a code of personal integrity.

The Maltese falcon is the unholy grail that provides the motive for the story. The falcon is supposed to be a jewel-encrusted statue of immense value with a history of mystery and danger, but by the end of the film it is revealed that the statue is a fake. We do not know if there ever was a genuine falcon, and somehow that is not important. What is important is revealed in the most famous line of the movie. When Bogart is asked about the identity of the statue; he replies, "It is the stuff that dreams are made of."[6] People are moved by dreams, but often those dreams turn out to be as empty as the Maltese falcon, or the dreams of Alan Squier or Baby Face Martin.

If the dreams of a better life are empty, what is left to guide our lives? Certainly, it is not a greedy materialism. The black bird is as much a symbol of the emptiness of that quest as the life of Duke Mantee or Baby Face Martin. The answer of the film lies in the character of Sam Spade (Bogart). Spade is neither an idealistic dreamer nor a hardened criminal. He is willing to bend the law and even argues that it sometimes helps for a private detective to cultivate the reputation for being unscrupulous. Perhaps that explains his choice of a partner, Miles Archer (Jerome Cowan).

Archer is murdered very early in the film and most of what we learn of him comes from passing comments made by Spade. Spade expresses no particular affection for Archer and says that he did not even particularly like him. Nonetheless, Spade spends most of the movie trying to figure out who murdered him. When asked about his apparent loyalty to Archer, Spade explains that Archer was his partner, and "when your partner is killed you are supposed to do something about it." It is this simple belief or commitment that drives the action and ultimately determines the outcome of the film. There are rules of behavior. It is not clear where they come from; perhaps they are based on nothing more than a personal belief, but they are nonetheless binding. Heroic individualism is thus elevated from selfish realism or romantic escapism to a commitment to personal integrity and the values that support it.

Those values have little to do with established laws or institutions. Instead they are values the individual must discover for himself. What kind of man is Sam Spade? He is obviously a man of courage, determination, and wit, and by the end of the movie we see that most of all he is a man of principle. Although he never fully trusts Brigid O'Shaughnessy (Mary Astor), he falls in love with her. His luck with women, however, seems little better than Mantee's or Martin's. Brigid turns out to be Archer's killer, and Spade is left to choose between his love for her and his commitment to do something about his partner's death. He chooses to keep his commitment to his principles, even at the expense of sending the woman he loves to be executed.

Unlike Alan Squier, Spade is able to turn his principles into action, and unlike Mantee and Martin his love of a woman does not get in the way of his survival. Spade knows that any long-term relationship with Brigid may not be healthy for him. Thus Spade's heroism is both nobler and tougher than the possibilities we saw in the earlier movies. At the end of the movie Spade is alive, though no less alone than our earlier heroes. His heroism is the lonely heroism of an individual with no lasting links to society, friends, or lovers. There appears to be no fixed point on a moral compass that can guide an individual's choice or action. His rules are his own, and there is no higher standard than his own personal integrity.

At the time *The Maltese Falcon* was being made, however, there was growing recognition of the limits of this kind of personal morality. The distance between Spade and Martin or Mantee might not be great enough for comfort. The relativism on which this morality was based, it was becoming apparent, might lead to the worst kind of intolerance and violence. As the gangster hero began to fade, a new opportunity for heroism burst on the scene. In the 1942 film *All Through the Night* Bogart plays Gloves Donahue, a gangster who turns his talents to fighting Nazis in New York.

A comedy about gangsters and Nazis, starring Bogart, may not be the most promising premise for a movie. One can see the wheels turning in the minds of studio executives. "Gangster films have been the bread and butter of the industry for years, but now we have this war thing going on, and we need to look as if we are concerned about the war effort. But Pearl Harbor was a real downer, and we need something upbeat; so let's do a comedy. Who is the most bankable star at the moment? Bogart, of course. Now Bogart is not exactly known for his slapstick comedy, but that is not important; we will just surround him with comedians like Phil Silvers, William Demarest, and Jackie Gleason." It is without a doubt that with these lofty artistic considerations in mind *All Through the Night* was conceived.

All Through the Night may not be on anyone's list of immortal Bogart movies, but perhaps it should be. The movie was a bigger box office success than *The Maltese Falcon*. More important, it makes explicit the transition between the period of the gangster film and the period of the war movie and even provides a rationale for that transition. Gloves Donahue is no Duke Mantee. He has a gang, but their major criminal activities involve gambling scams rather than murder and mayhem. They are tough guys, engaged in a feud with a rival gang, but they mainly talk about their propensity for violence. Gloves appears as a very well-adjusted gangster, who has become a success, takes good care of his mother who loves him, and is respected in the neighborhood. The problems for Gloves begin when a neighborhood baker is murdered and Gloves's mother insists that he investigate the crime. He tries to explain that this is a job for the police (he has his business to worry about), but his mother will not let the matter rest, and before long Gloves is deeply involved in the mystery. While investigating a woman who had appeared at the bakery shortly after the murder, Gloves is framed for the murder of a rival gang member. And then there are the Nazis.

We soon learn that both the baker and the woman had been forced to work for a group of Nazi sympathizers who are plotting to blow up a U.S. battleship in New York harbor. The movie culminates in a scene where Gloves and Sunshine (Gloves' sidekick played by William Demarest) have infiltrated a Nazi meeting masquerading as demolition experts from Detroit. Asked to make a report about their work, they engage in a comic double-talk routine that leaves the Nazis a little confused. This scene is without doubt the highlight of Bogart's career as a comic actor. The saboteurs are finally foiled when the rival gangs come together to break up the meeting and bring the Nazis to justice.

There is nothing subtle about the symbolism in the movie. Gloves, the gangster, is clearly the hero from beginning to end. He represents the tough, smart, unconventional American who is not averse to cutting a few corners when it comes to the law. He is also fundamentally decent and honest. He loves his mother, takes care of his friends, and never knocks off anybody who does not deserve it. And, as the opening scene of the movie demonstrates, he is not very concerned about politics. As the movie begins, Gloves's cronies are using toy soldiers to simulate battles between the Nazis and the British. They are demonstrating how their tactics in gang wars might be applied to the war in Europe. Gloves is uninterested, even when one of his pals complains that it's time that he "got his mind off the sports page and on to the front page." *Casablanca* makes the point better, but certainly not more clearly. The problem of the movie is how to get these selfish, but clever and courageous, Americans to pay attention to the problems of the world.

The answer is that they will pay attention when the problems hit closer to home, when a friend is killed, and when their family becomes alarmed. They will also reach a point where they have no choice. When Gloves is framed for the murder, his own self-interest is threatened, and he must get to the bottom of the mystery. Gloves, however, becomes engaged not just for his own safety, but for the safety of his country as well. Why does this small-time gangster become a patriot? The answer comes in a scene between Gloves and the Nazi leader. The Nazi asks why Gloves does not join their cause. He claims that Gloves has much in common with the Nazis. He takes what he wants and has little respect for democracy. Gloves is outraged. He says that he may be a crook, but he is a good American and has been a registered Democrat all of his life. When the chips are down, even American gangsters are patriots. They recognize evil when they see it and are ready to turn their talents to the fight against it.

As the gang members fight the Nazis in one of the closing scenes, Phil Silvers, one of Gloves's friends, stands to the side, and as people are tossed in his direction he says "sieg heil." If the person returns his salute he clubs him over the head, knowing that he is one of the Nazis. It is not easy to distinguish between the Nazis and the gangsters, but the movie suggests that it is possible. No true American would return a Nazi salute. If we cannot always recognize the good, we can identify evil when we see it.

HEROISM AND TRAGIC LOVE

Casablanca remains the classic Bogart movie and Rick the classic American hero. In a number of respects, however, *Casablanca* is merely a more serious version of *All Through the Night*. Rick, the owner of Rick's Café Américain in Casablanca, is not a gangster, but he is a man with a past. He cannot return to his native America for some mysterious reason. Louis Renault, the captain of police in Casablanca, says he would "like to think it was because he killed a man. It's the romantic in me." Whatever the reason, we also learn that Rick's shady past includes a period as a gun runner to the Ethiopians and fighting with the loyalists in Spain. He has profited from fights for freedom, but he was also always on the side of the underdog.[7]

Rick's repeated proclamation that "I stick my neck out for nobody" evokes the same self-centered individualism that we saw in Gloves Donahue. The main difference between Rick and Gloves is that Rick suffers from a pervasive sense of disillusionment. Rick has turned from freedom fighting to running a saloon. He is embittered because the woman he loved, Ilsa Lund, has abandoned him. Rick embodies the lost idealism of the post-World War I generation. He has had enough of noble causes. He wants to be left alone to play chess, drink with his friend Louis, and have brief romantic flings with women like Yvonne, who sings in his club.

The problem in the movie for Rick, however, is the same as the problem for Gloves: how can these self-centered individuals be awakened to their patriotic duty? For Gloves it is enough for him to see the evil Nazis in New York. We are even reminded of Gloves and his gang when Major Strasser, the Nazi commander in Casablanca, asks Rick if he can imagine the Germans in New York. Rick responds, "There are certain sections of New York I wouldn't recommend you try to invade." Unlike Gloves, from the beginning of the movie Rick is aware of the evil of the Nazis, but either he believes that ultimately the Nazis are no match for Gloves and his buddies, or he is simply so detached from his country and from any other human being that he does not care about the Nazis. As he says to Major Strasser, he is apolitical, or, as Louis describes him, "a citizen of the world." His disillusionment has led him to withdraw from any attachments, personal or political.

The only thing that can penetrate the armor he has put around himself is the appearance of Ilsa in Casablanca. At first his reaction is to become more embittered and withdrawn. He is pained so much by the encounter that his friend Sam, the piano player, suggests that they drive all night, get drunk, and stay away until she is gone. He knows how much Rick has been hurt by Ilsa, and he does not believe that Rick can take another encounter. But Rick must see Ilsa again, and eventually he learns of her own personal struggle. As a young girl Ilsa had met Victor Laszlo, a Czech freedom fighter. She was so moved by his ideals that she agreed to become his wife. When she had met Rick in Paris and fallen in love with him she believed that Laszlo had been murdered by the Nazis; but on the day she was to leave Paris with Rick, she learned that Laszlo was alive. She abandoned Rick to go to her husband and to help him fight for the ideals in which they both believe. Ilsa is also shaken by her reunion with Rick years later in Casablanca. Although she still believes in Laszlo's goals and feels an enormous personal duty to him, she can no longer deny her love for Rick. Together Rick and Ilsa recover the love they had shared in Paris.

When Rick's eyes are no longer clouded by his disillusionment, he recovers his own sense of moral obligation. Once again the Bogart character will give up the woman he loves, but this time the fault lies not with the woman. Ilsa Lund is not the dangerous murderer played by Mary Astor in *The Maltese Falcon*. She is as noble as Rick, but Rick sees that that nobility is a threat to their long-term happiness. As he tells Ilsa, if she is not on that plane with Laszlo she will regret it for the rest of her life, and so, we suspect, would Rick. Rick knows that they are all in a fight now, and in the midst of that fight the lives of two people do not amount to much. Rick, Ilsa, and Laszlo must do the right thing. Even the corrupt Captain Renault must join the fight against the Nazis. When confronted with obvious evil, it is time for people to choose sides.

It is the nobility of Rick's sacrifice that ultimately allows him to reclaim Ilsa's heart. As he says, they had lost their love in Paris, but now they have found it again. Love does not mean possession; if it did, their love would be lost forever. Their love is grounded in a common vision, a common set of principles. It is possible because of a belief in the fundamental goodness of the other. That is what is recovered in Casablanca. It is what Rick and Ilsa will have to hold onto in the fight ahead.

Is it enough? Is it merely the ultimate symbol of the romantic love that is too perfect to exist? Is it the case that the love between Rick and Ilsa, just like the emerging friendship between Rick and Louis, is only possible in the context of a desperate fight against an evil enemy? Is heroism defined by our enemies rather than by ourselves? When the war is over will Ilsa desert Laszlo for Rick? Will Louis become Rick's partner in a bar? Will life be more than an evening's entertainment played out at the tables of Rick's Café? The hero of *Casablanca* may not return to the cynicism and ennui of the prewar period, but what will take its place once peace is restored? At the same time we may wonder about the lesson in romance offered by the picture. Is romantic love always doomed to fail? Is it its very failure that makes it romantic? Or to put the question another way, can Bogart ever get the girl?

Although *Casablanca* is said to be the film in which Bogart establishes himself as a romantic leading man, the movie ends with Rick walking off toward the horizon with Louis, not Ilsa. The end of the movie marks the beginning of a beautiful friendship. Does the possibility of this friendship mark a transformation in the isolated individualism of the Bogart character?

Dead Reckoning, released in 1947, explores the character of heroism in the postwar world as well as the meaning of friendship. It should be seen not only in light of *Casablanca*, but also in light of *The Maltese Falcon*, produced before the war. Although the Bogart character, Rip Murdock, starts out in uniform, *Dead Reckoning* is more like a detective story than a war story. Rip must find who murdered his friend and fellow soldier Johnny Drake (William Prince), and he must also discover the truth about a murder that Johnny was involved in before the war. In the *Maltese Falcon* Sam Spade is moved to find the murderer of his partner because of his commitment to a personal code, not because he likes Archer; but in *Dead Reckoning* Rip Murdoch is moved by friendship. A change has taken place in the kind of relationship possible for the Bogart character.

Dead Reckoning is also the film that presents the most explicit defense of heroism of any of Bogart's films. The movie begins with Rip and Johnny being ordered from an army hospital in France, carried on a top-priority flight to New York, then headed for Washington on the train that has been held awaiting their arrival. Rip, growing more curious about their mysterious trip, searches the papers of the officer who has been assigned to them and discovers that they are being taken to Washington to meet with the president so that Johnny can receive a Congressional Medal of Honor. Rip is also to be decorated for his heroism in combat. When photographers arrive at the train to take their pictures for the evening papers, Johnny runs away. Rip knows that he is in trouble and goes in search of him.

He trails Johnny to a small southern town on the Gulf coast. There he finds that before the war Johnny was involved with a married woman, Coral Chandler (Lizabeth Scott) and had been accused of the murder of her husband. Johnny had escaped and joined the army under an assumed name. Rip quickly learns that Johnny has been murdered the day Rip arrived in town. Not only does Rip want to avenge his friend's death, he wants even more desperately to clear Johnny's name so that he can still receive the Congressional Medal of Honor. Rip knows that Johnny was a hero in combat, and he knows that Johnny was not the kind of man who could have committed cold-blooded murder. By defending Johnny's good name, Rip is defending Johnny's integrity and with it the possibility of true heroism.

Rip is also taking what he has learned of Johnny in the war and using it to reinterpret events that took place in the prewar period. Johnny and his girlfriend Coral, had been mixed up with some shady characters, especially the gangster Martinelli (Morris Carnovsky). It would be easy to assume that there were no good guys in this morally ambiguous prewar world, but Rip knows that is not the case, because he knows Johnny's character. Johnny was not just another partner, like Archer was to Spade; he has been Rip's friend, and Rip knows he was deserving of that friendship.

The movie also reinterprets the myth of the gangster. Martinelli is no romantic hero. He is not responding to a corrupt social system—he is responsible for the corruption. He is as unambiguously evil as the Nazis Rip and Johnny fought and defeated in the war. Rip has some ties to the shady prewar underworld, but he had not been a gangster in the prewar period. Instead he was an honest businessman who ran a fleet of taxi cabs. He has no qualms about bending the law to his purposes, but there is also no reason to believe that Rip would ever turn to a life of crime. He will fight the outright gangsters just as he fought the Nazis, because he knows they are every bit as dangerous. In the climatic shoot-out, Rip has even borrowed some of the weapons of war to defeat this domestic foe. The war is over, but the fight between good and evil continues. We can still identify bad guys and at least remember the friendship of a noble hero. An ideal of heroism can still animate action in the postwar world.

That possibility of heroism still comes at a great price. Rip can certainly take more comfort in the memory of Johnny than could Sam Spade in the memory of Archer, but the difference between Brigid O'Shaughnessy and Coral Chandler, whom Rip himself falls for in the course of investigating Johnny's

murder, is hard to see. Both Brigid and Coral exhibit the kind of tough independence and the sense of mystery that make them so attractive to a man like
Sam or Rip. But they are ultimately corrupt. Each is a murderer, and neither
would hesitate for a minute to kill the man who loves her. In some ways, as
Coral says, "it is a blue, sick world."[8] Romantic love is doomed to be as big a
disappointment as the idea of the gangster hero. Both are the product of a dangerous imagination that carries us beyond conventional boundaries in search of a
dream. At the end of *Dead Reckoning* our tough and cynical hero has found the
possibility of justice and friendship in contemporary society, although love and
happiness have remained elusive.

HEROISM AND LOVE IN A LIBERAL SOCIETY

In *To Have and Have Not*, released two years before *Dead Reckoning*, Bogart
does find what promises to be a lasting love. *To Have and Have Not* probably
owes as much to *Casablanca* as it does to the Ernest Hemingway novel on
which it is based. As the *New York Times* review claimed, "*To Have and Have
Not* is *Casablanca* moved west into the somewhat less-hectic Caribbean but
along the same basic parallel. And, although there are surface alterations in
some of the characters you will meet here, they are substantially the same people
as in that other geopolitical romance."[4] Bogart plays Harry Morgan, a professional fisherman living in French Martinique shortly after the fall of France.
Unlike Rick, Harry does not appear to be running away from his past. We learn
of no lost love or mysterious crime. But in most respects Harry and Rick share
the same competence, cynicism, and fundamental decency.

There is also a piano player, Crickett (Hoagy Carmichael), Captain Renard
and his henchmen, representatives of the Vichy government, and a Gaullist freedom fighter and his wife, Paul and Helen De Bursac, who are smuggled onto the
island by a reluctant Harry, and seek Harry's protection as Paul recovers from a
gunshot wound. There are, however, some important additions or variations on
the characters from *Casablanca*. An American girl named Marie (Lauren Bacall) arrives in Martinique trying to return to the United States from Trinidad.
She is short of funds and takes a job working with Crickett as a nightclub singer.
In a reversal of the plot from *Casablanca*, it is this night club singer rather than
the wife of the freedom fighter who sparks Harry's romantic interest. There is
also Harry's sidekick and friend, an old drunk named Eddie (Walter Brennan).
Eddie claims to take care of Harry, but it is obvious that it is Harry who takes
care of Eddie.

Eddie and Marie represent a significant shift in focus between *Casablanca*
and *To Have and Have Not*. The climax of the film centers, not on the freedom
fighter and his wife, but on the need to rescue Eddie. Captain Renard is searching for Paul De Bursac and believes that Harry knows where to find him. He is
eager to learn of Harry's involvement with the Gaullists and takes Eddie into
custody. Renard knows that he can torture Eddie by withholding alcohol from
him. Harry, who is preparing to leave the island with Eddie and Marie, must first

rescue Eddie. This is necessary to protect the Gaullist underground, but it is even more important to save his friend. The political and the personal are not in conflict, but friendship clearly plays a more prominent role in Harry's heroism than it does in the case of Rick. It would be a tough call if Harry had to choose between the freedom fighters and his friend.

This distinction is even more obvious in his relationship with Marie. Rick's love for Ilsa has an abstract quality to it, especially in their ultimate separation. Harry calls Marie "Slim," a nickname that seems too down to earth for a character like Ilsa. Harry and Slim are cut from the same cloth. From their first meeting they are more than a match for each other's wit, and we see that they are moral equals as well. Harry cannot turn his back on the injured Paul De Bursac, just as Slim cannot return to America, leaving Harry in Martinique. They are tough and cynical, but very much in love. They are more in love with each other than they are with any cause. It is their romance, rather than the romance of a noble fight, that drives the picture. By 1945 the need to awaken patriotic resolve seems less urgent. It is instead the personal story to which the audience is drawn.

With the end of the war the lives of two people begin to take on renewed significance. If *Casablanca* demonstrates the need to recognize and fight the reality of evil, *To Have and Have Not* reminds us of the desire to find the good in concrete form. By some standards Rick is the nobler hero, because he is willing to give up the woman he loves in the name of an ideal or principle; but Harry may be the more American hero, in that he is not content with an abstract ideal. He wants to know that Slim is only a whistle away, and certainly not in the arms of another man, no matter how noble his cause. At the end of *To Have and Have Not* Harry, Slim, and Eddie leave Martinique, taking Paul and Helen DeBursac with them to rescue a resistance leader from Devil's Island. It may take a while for Harry, Slim, and Eddie to make it back to America, but the audience has little doubt that they will stick together. If this threesome does not remind us of the Cleavers or the Nelsons, they are nonetheless unmistakably our own. The fact that we know that in real life Bogart and Bacall find happiness together provides a serendipitous reinforcement for the message of the movie. Lasting love of a real woman has replaced futile romanticism in the portrait of the hero.

The romantic comedy *Sabrina*, released in 1954, explores the question of whether either heroism or true love can survive in the more prosaic setting of 1950s America. The plot of *Sabrina* sounds more like the worst kind of sentimental romanticism than either the noble love story of Rick and Ilsa or the more earthy love of Harry and Slim. There are, however, some remarkable parallels between the plot of *Sabrina* and the plot of *Casablanca*. If *To Have and Have Not* is *Casablanca* transported to the Caribbean, then *Sabrina* may be *Casablanca* transported to the peacetime commercial republic of 1950s America.

Bogart plays Linus Larrabee, the chief executive officer of Larrabee Industries, an international corporation that reaches into every aspect of the world economy. Linus, the eldest son of the Larrabee family, lives for nothing but business. Cynically calculating and driven by ambition, he is the rugged individualist perched at the top of corporate America. At first sight he appears to be the modern embodiment of the robber baron. He has even arranged a marriage for his younger brother, David (William Holden), in order to promote a corporate merger. But just as the cynical Rick has a more noble side, we soon learn that Linus is not simply a greedy businessman. He explains that Larrabee Industries performs a noble function. It provides jobs, goods, and services that make possible a better life for millions of people. Without his Machiavellian machinations there would be no Larrabee Industries and no "homes, hospitals, baseball diamonds, and movies on a Saturday night"[9] for people who are now stuck in poverty. Cynicism and nobility are merged in the character of Linus, just as they are in the character of Rick. Rick may be the man you want to fight Nazis, but Linus is the man who makes a better world once a pax Americana has been established.

In the world of Nazis, Rick's cynicism may best be tempered by Laszlo's commitment to political principles. We need to find a way to encourage Rick to become more serious about the problems of the world or, as Sunshine tells Gloves in *All Through the Night*, "to turn from the sports page to the front page."[10] The problem with Linus, however, is that he needs to lighten up. The work he is doing is important, but the Nazis are not going to conquer the world if he takes a day off. All causes do not require the same degree of dedication. In place of the political idealist, Victor Laszlo, in *Sabrina* we find Linus's brother, David, the idle playboy.

David's character bears little resemblance to the noble Laszlo. Laszlo is dedicated to a cause, and David is dedicated to nothing other than his own enjoyment. But we must remember that the world has changed. David represents the romantic alternative in the world of corporate America. He has all the money he will ever need. He cannot imagine that Larrabee Industries will collapse without him, so why should he not enjoy the fruits of his wealth? Work provides the means to an end. It provides the resources to enjoy life. It is not an end in itself. David is in search of the pleasures that transcend the necessities of life. If work is the means, the end must be play. So David drives a sports car, goes to parties, and chases women. He is the antithesis of his bachelor, workaholic brother who rides to work each day in the back of his chauffeur-driven limousine at the designated speed of thirty-five miles per hour.

And then there is the woman, the chauffeur's daughter, Sabrina (Audrey Hepburn). Sabrina begins the film as a romantic adolescent with a crush on David Larrabee. She is not attracted to the world of books and ideas that the young Ilsa finds so fascinating; instead she is attracted to the elegant world of the Larrabees' parties and the fairy tale dream that the chauffeur's daughter can capture the heart of the dashing young David Larrabee. If Ilsa is committed to a world of ideals, Sabrina is entranced by the world of fantasy. The young Sabrina is to Ilsa what Danielle Steele is to Jane Austen.

The young Sabrina is sent to Paris for an education, an education ostensibly in cooking, but which predictably becomes an education in life. She returns home a few years later having "learned how to live—to be in the world and of the world." But if the young Sabrina is a pale reflection of Ilsa, then the older Sabrina is a sanitized version of the worldly Slim. She can now imitate the life-style of the rich and famous Larrabees and even conduct a sophisticated seduc-tion of David; but at heart she remains an innocent young girl pursuing an ado-lescent's dream.

David, of course, cannot resist the charms of the sophisticated Sabrina, and the plot of the movie revolves around Linus's response to this romance. Linus and his father are appalled to discover that David's infatuation threatens his im-pending marriage and the business merger it was intended to cement. David per-forms no other useful function. The least he could do is to marry an attractive heiress for the good of the company. Linus treats the problem as he would any other hitch in a business deal. He comes up with a strategy to overcome the ob-stacle. First he tricks David into sitting on two champagne glasses, thereby inca-pacitating him for a few weeks. Second, he decides to woo Sabrina himself in order to wean her affections from David and prepare the way for her eventual return to Paris. As Linus tells his father, the problem is "dissolving itself into a straight export deal." David will then do his duty and marry the heiress. Al-though Linus's father fears that Linus has no idea how to seduce a woman, Linus uses every resource at his disposal in his campaign for Sabrina's love.

It is not surprising to find that what begins as a business deal ends up as a love match. Linus not only succeeds in his seduction of Sabrina, but is himself seduced by her charms. This is in part made possible by the fact that in the course of their courtship Sabrina learns a new lesson about appearances and reality. She learns that the man who on the surface seemed austere and forbid-ding is in fact lovable, a fact that had been beyond the imagination of the dreams of an adolescent. Sabrina will never become a self-sacrificing idealist like Ilsa or a tough wisecracking adventuress like Slim, but she has become serious enough to see Linus's virtues and tough enough to recognize her own self-worth. She sees that the ambitious Linus has sacrificed himself to his work. He has become so engrossed in calculating for success, he has lost sight of personal happiness. Sabrina knows that she helps him to correct this defect, at the same time that he offers her a more realistic and in some ways more noble dream.

The last scene of Sabrina is a replay of *Casablanca*. Linus has succeeded in his plot. He has won her heart and sent her on board an ocean liner bound for France, promising that he will join her. She will find a letter and a check when she reaches the ship and will sail away to France heartbroken. With the obstacle of Sabrina removed, David will marry his fiancée, and the merger will be con-summated. But Linus has been changed by his experience with Sabrina, and he cannot force David into an arranged marriage. As the families are meeting in the Larrabee Industries boardroom, Linus abruptly calls off the deal and tells David to join Sabrina in Paris. Linus thus imitates the self-sacrificing Rick, arranging for David to have the woman they both love.

Sabrina, however, has one final plot twist. David refuses Linus's offer hav-ing decided that his fiancée is the right woman for him. Like Shakespeare's Prince Hal in *Henry V*, David abandons his frivolous past in order to assume his responsibilities as a husband and captain of industry. He has also arranged for a tugboat from Larrabee shipping to take Linus out to meet Sabrina on the Paris-bound ship. Unlike Rick, Linus is united with the woman he loves.

Where is the heroism in this contemporary fairytale? Perhaps we find the kind of heroism that is appropriate for a society that is as secure and affluent as our own. There is nobility to Linus's combination of duty and ambition. Unlike the businessman of *The Petrified Forest*, he lacks neither imagination nor a sense of responsibility to others. The commercial republic is not the corrupt and decaying system many had thought it to be. It had once again been shown to offer the possibility of individual success and social improvement. But it is also a world that can breed complacency and perhaps a world where people may take themselves too seriously. Although the commercial republic can create a secure and comfortable life, we can never achieve complete mastery over the world or even over our own lives. For a man like Linus in a world like ours, the most courageous act may be to recognize the limits of our ambition. Linus Larrabee is part of a long line of American heroes going back at least to Huckleberry Finn, heroes courageous enough to give up the security of the world of work for uncharted waters of the world of leisure.

Lest this seem the most romanticized version of heroism imaginable, it is important to remember that the ultimate message of the film is one of moderation. Just as the Linus who is all work must learn to play, David the playboy must learn to accept responsibility and develop some personal ambition. The most difficult, and therefore most courageous, act for most individuals is to recognize their own shortcomings and seek to overcome them.

David and Linus may appear to be pale reflections of Duke Mantee and Alan Squier or Rick Blaine and Victor Laszlo. David and Linus have no evil enemies to defeat. The do not have to risk their lives. Their situation seems neither to require nor to provide the opportunity for true heroism. But if the defining characteristics of heroism are the courage to face death and the imagination to appreciate the possibilities of life or action, then perhaps heroism remains necessary and possible in the world of the Larrabees.

If we look more closely at the lives of Linus and David at the beginning of the film we see that each is engaged in an effort to deny his own limitations or, to put it more precisely, to deny death, and in doing so each misses an important part of life. Linus appears to believe that by immersing himself in work he can create a world of absolute security. All obstacles can be met and overcome. If he stopped for a moment, he might have to recognize that ultimately his efforts would be futile. There will always be work left to do, and in the end he will have to stop because he will die. David seeks security in a world of play. If he can eat, drink, and be merry, he may be able to forget that tomorrow he will die. Linus's ambition and David's playfulness each have an element of nobility in them, but by themselves they are primarily a form of escape, an escape from recognition of their own limitations. When Linus learns to stop working and David learns to take responsibility, each is really learning to face mortality. It takes a certain kind of courage to face death at the barrel of a gun, but it takes another, perhaps more subtle, form of courage to face mortality in a world where success and affluence are the norm. It takes a certain type of imagination to see the possibilities of life in a dangerous or barren world, but it may require even more effort to imagine that things can be much better or much worse than they are from the perspective of a relatively secure and comfortable world.

Heroism is more difficult to define in the absence of the threat of an obvious evil, but it is no less necessary. As Aristotle reminds us, courage is the foundation for all of the other virtues. Moderation, justice, magnanimity, and even the intellectual virtues depend upon our ability to look beyond our instinct for self-preservation to a more elevated understanding of ourselves and our possibilities. In contemporary American life, we do not often face immediate threats to our survival, but we are routinely faced with choices that allows us to define who we are. We can choose whether to do what we have always done, to do what is most comfortable, or we can be willing to trade our sense of security for the possibility of enlarging our sense of self. Without such courage, life may lose its meaning, and if a time comes when our survival is threatened, it may be too late to develop habits of courage necessary to respond to such a threat.

THE ACTOR AS HERO

Sabrina also addresses a theme that recurs in a number of Bogart's later movies: the relationship between acting and life. We learn in *Sabrina* that acting is not just a technique that can be used to manipulate or deceive an audience, it can have an effect on the character of the both the audience and the actor. Linus's act inadvertently reveals something of his true self to Sabrina, something that had previously remained hidden. More important, it transforms Linus. He becomes what he pretends to be, a lover.

In *The Left Hand of God* Bogart plays James Carmody, an American flyer shot down in World War II China. He is rescued by a Chinese warlord and forced to become his military advisor. For a time Carmody accepts his assigned role, and acts as the warlord's second in command. When the warlord kills a priest during a raid on a village, Carmody can no longer continue in this role, and he escapes from the camp disguised in the clothes of the priest. He goes to the village where the priest was to have been assigned and assumes his identity. What begins as a convenient disguise becomes a kind of reality. Bogart carries out the functions of the village priest and is successful, if sometimes unconventional, in the performance of his duties. Although there is some initial awkwardness in this new role, he grows into it.

There are limits to the masquerade, however. Carmody and an American nurse in the village are increasingly attracted to one another. Carmody forces himself to stay in character, but it becomes more and more difficult. The nurse finds herself flirting with the "priest" and is overwhelmed by guilt. Carmody decides to seek the advice of a real clergyman in a nearby village, but in his absence the warlord appears at the village seeking to retrieve the deserter. Carmody's masquerade has placed the village in danger, but Carmody manages to avert the danger by persuading the warlord to gamble on a roll of the dice. The villagers are surprised by the priest's ploy, but are pleased with the outcome. Carmody wins his bet, and the warlord leaves the village and Carmody in peace.

A representative of the Bishop arrives at the village and decides that Carmody must go to the Bishop and seek penance for his impersonation of the priest, but he concludes that the masquerade need not be revealed to villagers. Carmody has in fact been a good priest. Carmody is not permitted to explain the situation to the American nurse before his departure, but after Carmody leaves the Bishop's representative tells her the truth, and we have no doubt that she will follow Carmody.

The assumption of a role can be a means of survival, as it was for Carmody in the warlord's camp. It can be a needed means of escape, as it was when Carmody fled the warlord. It can help us to learn to be something we never thought we could be, as Carmody finds it within himself to become, at least for a time, a good priest. But finally our ability to transform ourselves has limits. If we fail to recognize this fact, then we will expose ourselves and others to great danger, and we will never be able to find the good that is appropriate to us.

In Bogart's last movie, *The Harder They Fall*, we see the fullest presentation of the dangers of a world where acting plays too large a part. Eddie Willis (Bogart) is a respected sports columnist, who finds himself out of work when his newspaper folds. The only job he can find is on the rewrite desk or as a low level reporter for another paper, but he wants more than that. He has repeatedly been offered work by Nick Benko (Rod Steiger), a successful and corrupt boxing promoter, but has always turned down the offers. With no good prospects in sight, however, he finally goes to work for Nick promoting an unknown boxer from South America, Toro Moreno (Mike Lane). Moreno is a muscle-bound giant who looks indestructible, but in reality has a "glass jaw and a powder-puff punch."[11] None of this matters to Benko, who sees in Moreno the image of a boxer that can be sold to the public. It is Eddie's job to polish that image and make the sale.

Initially Eddie objects that there are limits to what an image maker can do. When Toro steps into the ring, it will become obvious that he is a fraud. Nick is not worried, however, because he and his henchmen will arrange for Toro's opponents to take a dive. Eddie is dubious that this can work for long, but he underestimates Benko's persuasiveness. Between Benko's bribes and threats and Eddie's skill with the media, Toro is made into a contender for the heavyweight crown. Eddie is so successful an image maker that even Moreno himself comes to believe that he is a champion. Of course, as Eddie reminds Benko, Moreno still cannot fight.

What Eddie cannot see is the fact that he is as unsuited to the role he is playing as is Moreno. There is a reason he had resisted Benko's offers for over eight years. He knows that Benko is contemptible. The problem is that he has contempt for himself when he loses his job. He is no longer the man he thought he was. He does not want to return to kind of job he did twenty years ago. To do so would be demeaning. When his wife questions his decision to go to work for

Benko, he argues that selling a boxer is no different from selling soap. He will do whatever is necessary to make some real money, because in spite of what people say, "If you do not have it, everyone thinks you are a bum." Eddie's wife disagrees and eventually leaves him when she sees the kind of man he is becoming.

Eddie, however, still believes that he is better than Benko. He thinks that he can actually help to protect the fighters whom Benko exploits. He forces a group of promoters to pay their fighters an additional thousand dollars to take a dive. They will make some real money for their efforts, and they will have the pleasure of remembering that "they once made a thousand dollars for a night's work." Even after a former champ dies in the ring with Moreno, Eddie still believes he can find a way to do some good while making money for himself. When Moreno wants to quit boxing because he thinks he has killed a man, Eddie explains that he was not responsible for the death. The ex-champ had gone into the ring with severe injuries. Eddie humiliates Moreno by having his fifty-three-year-old sparring partner knock him down, thereby demonstrating to Moreno that he could not hurt anyone. If he will just go into the ring this one last time, stay away from the champ for a few rounds, and then go down and stay down, he will be able to return home to South America with a great deal of money. Eddie and Moreno will both get what they want from the corrupt system if they just continue to play their parts.

When Moreno asks Eddie what the people will think of him if he lets them see that he cannot fight, Eddie responds: "Why should you care about what a bloodthirsty mob of people who pay to see a man beaten to death think?" But Moreno does care and cannot just go down. He puts up a brave fight, but takes the worst beating imaginable. Lying on a stretcher waiting to be taken to the hospital, he asks Eddie if he will bring his money to the hospital. Eddie still has hope that he can have it both ways.

Eddie goes to Benko for the money, and Benko immediately gives Eddie his share of the take, $26,000. When Eddie asks for Moreno's share, he finds that Benko has tricked Moreno into signing away most of his interest in the profits and has padded the expense accounts to take care of the rest. The gate receipts are over a million dollars, but Moreno's share for taking the worst beating Eddie has ever witnessed is $49.07. In addition Benko has sold Moreno's contract to another promoter, who has arranged for Moreno to return to the site of all of his former victories and be beaten by the local fighters.

Eddie now sees the price he and Moreno must pay for their bargain with Benko. He takes Moreno from the hospital and puts him on a plane for South America. When Moreno asks for his money, Eddie cannot bear the thought of telling him the truth. He cannot tell him that he has suffered so much for nothing and that he must return home humiliated. Instead he gives him the $26,000 he has received from Benko. Moreno is more than satisfied.

Eddie is not sure what he will do, but he gets back together with his wife. The movie ends with a scene in their apartment, where Benko confronts Eddie and demands that he produce Moreno. Benko tries to intimidate Eddie, but

Eddie explains that he can no longer be bribed or scared by Benko. It is now Benko who has reason to fear, because Eddie now knows all of his tricks and is going to reveal them to the public. Benko leaves, and Eddie sits down to the typewriter and writes the first line of his story. It says: "Boxing must be outlawed in the United States even if it takes an Act of Congress to do it."

Bogart who started out in the movies as a gangster plays his last scene as a writer using his skills to persuade Congress to pass a law to ban professional boxing. Of course we have learned from the movie that even the skills of a writer or an actor can be a powerful weapon for evil, but art also offers to most of us our best chance to spark our heroic imagination. Bogart is one of the least likely actors to choose to exemplify the sentiment that the pen is mightier than the sword, but in one sense his whole career offered the possibility that we could find heroism in art rather than in violence. Through hard work and dedication to his craft, Bogart was able to create a character that could face the myriad of possibilities that life had to offer and maintain his identity. That identity is so strong that we hardly notice as he moves from gangster to detective to war hero to business tycoon to crusading reporter. We hardly notice as that character learns how the talent for destruction or dissolution can be transformed into a creative talent, a talent that opens up new possibilities.

We also learn something about the character of American individualism. Just as Eddie had tried to convince Moreno that a bloodthirsty mob of boxing fans was not worthy of consideration, by the end of *The Harder They Fall* Eddie no longer cares what people think about his bank account or social status. He knows that people who would care about such things are not worthy of consideration. But this does not mean he has no concern for what others think. He cares deeply that people understand about the brutality and corruption of boxing, and he will do his best to change their opinions on the subject. He will use his skill as a writer to reveal the truth rather than to create a false image. When he recovers his own integrity he also turns to others to join in his fight. The community is necessary to achieve his new ambition. Heroism and law are even reconciled in the last words of Bogart's career. The audience is still realistic enough to doubt whether Eddie's crusade will be successful. There will always be limits to the power of words to reveal the truth and the willingness of people to act on that knowledge. Heroism must always be tempered by a recognition of the gap between reality and imagination. If we knew we would always succeed, there would be nothing heroic in our actions.

CONCLUSION

Bogart did not make *Casablanca* or any of his other films alone. He wrote little of his actual dialogue. He had no grand plan for his career, and although he was known for his battles with Jack Warner over script selection, the extent to which Bogart's choice of scripts contributed to his success is not clear. Much of his success may be traced to the ability of others to create films that capitalized on the character he played so well. If this sounds like faint praise for Bogart, we might wish to reconsider the degree of skill involved in creating such a character. Like Bottom in *A Midsummer Night's Dream*, we tend to think that a skillful actor is one who plays all the roles, one who literally loses himself in a character. But such an actor adds nothing that is distinctly his own to his parts, for the very quality that would make them his own would to some extent limit the roles that he would be suited to play.

We do not criticize Shakespeare for always writing like Shakespeare, because we recognize that a great artist does not simply create; he also creates an identity. If there is a vitality and versatility to Shakespeare's art, there is also an integrity that makes it his own. In the contemporary intellectual context we tend to elevate the Dionysian spirit of creativity, but we can never forget the Apollonian animus of art, the quality that renders it intelligible and self-conscious of its status as art. Art may help us to escape ourselves, it may help us to transcend our limits, it may dissolve the boundaries that separate us from the infinite possibilities of existence, but it does so through an act of definition. No matter how evocative of the infinite, art is a definite thing. That thing may seem as small as a mustard seed in comparison to the world of possibilities it opens to us, but without that core identity it is nothing.

The art of acting is no exception. An actor who only plays himself would be a bore, but an actor who cannot define a role as his own lacks one aspect of the actor's art. In creating a Shakespeare play or a Woody Allen movie, the artist creates something that did not exist before, but he also creates something that is his own, some thing that cannot be every thing. The great artist recognizes and makes the most out of his limitations. He sees that it is only in the tension between his limitations and his possibilities that great art can be created.

The purpose of this paper is not to compare Bogart with Shakespeare or even with the great film directors. Their arts are different and in some respects incomparable. It would be like comparing Shakespeare with Beethoven or Aristotle or Michael Jordan. Neither the art nor the artist can be all things. I also do not intend to argue that Bogart is the only possible model for a great film actor. There is a virtue in range and versatility, but it is not the only virtue. The creation of an identity, such as Bogart achieved, requires a special kind of talent and provides a special kind of insight.

Bogart's films demonstrate how we may maintain our integrity in the face of changing circumstances, and, more important, they show how our character may grow over time. We have traced Bogart's roles from the gangster whose integrity was defined by little more than his rejection of conventional values, to the detective who defined himself by a personal code of conduct, to the cynic who becomes a patriot, to the friend who defends the integrity of his friend, to the rugged individualist who can love and care for others, to the tycoon who understands the nobility of work and learns the virtue of play, to the soldier who plays a priest and learns something about himself from the role, and finally to the publicity agent who sees the need for law to counteract the most cynical and brutal forms of manipulation. His characters develop a more complex understanding of themselves and there connection with others. Bogart's characters do not exhaust the possibilities that are open to us, but they have helped to define who we are as Americans, or at least who we think, at our best, we can be.

NOTES

1. An early review of the film captured the essence of the character, explaining that: "Mr. Bogart is, as usual, the cool, cynical, efficient and super-wise guy who operates his business strictly for profit but has a core of sentiment and idealism inside"(*New York Times*, November 27, 1942, 27:1).

2. Bogart originated the role of Duke Mantee on Broadway, but when it came time to make the film the studio wanted someone else. Leslie Howard was set to reprise his stage role as the idealistic dreamer in the film version. Howard was the big-name bankable star, Bogart, until this time, only a bit player in the movies. It would have remained thus if Howard had not fought to get the part for Bogart. When Edward G. Robinson was cast in the role, Howard threatened to withdraw from the project if Bogart was not signed. Bogart had received his big break in the movies. Many years later, when Howard was dead and largely forgotten, Bogart named his daughter in honor of him.

3. All quotes from *The Petrified Forest* are transcribed from *The Petrified Forest* (1936), (Warner Home Video, 1997).

4. *New York Times*, October 12, 1944, 24:1.

5. All quotes from *Dead End* are transcribed from *Dead End* (1937), (MGM/UA Studios, 2000).

6. All quotes from *The Maltese Falcon* are transcribed from *The Maltese Falcon* (1941), (MGM/UA Studios, 1991).

7. All quotes from *Casablanca* can found at:
http://www.geocities.com/classicmoviescripts/script/casablanca.pdf

8. All quotes from *Dead Reckoning* are transcribed from *Dead Reckoning* (1947), (Columbia/Tristar Studios, 1992).

9. All quotes from *Sabrina* are transcribed from *Sabrina* (1954), (Paramount Home Video, 2001).

10. All quotes from *All Through the Night* are transcribed from *All Through the Night* (1941), (Warner Home Video, 1992).

11. All quotes from *The Harder They Fall* are transcribed *The Harder They Fall* (1956), (Columbia/Tristar Studios, 1992).

CHAPTER 9

MICHAEL CURTIZ:
THE MYSTERY-MAN DIRECTOR OF *CASABLANCA*

PAUL PETERSON

Despite directing *Casablanca* and a host of other classic and near-classic films, Michael Curtiz is a largely ignored figure in the history of American film. Curtiz, for the most part, seems to be seen as a highly competent director operating within the confines of the studio system that prevailed in Hollywood until the 1950s. Yet, other directors, such as Frank Capra, John Ford, Howard Hawks, and Alfred Hitchcock, who also operated within that system, are recognized as giants in the history of film direction and as precursors, if not actual practitioners, of the *auteur* theory of film direction. [1]

CURTIZ'S EUROPEAN CAREER

Curtiz was a prolific director who worked successfully in a wide-range of genres. He began directing in his native Hungary in 1912 while in his early twenties. From 1912 through 1919, he directed at least 53 films. It has been estimated that Curtiz directed twenty-five percent of Hungarian films during this period. He also starred as a performer in some of these films. In 1919, Curtiz moved to Austria where he would direct at least twenty-four films until signing his contract with Warner Brothers in 1926. Curtiz advocate Sidney Rosenzweig, in summarizing Curtiz's European career, notes: "Curtiz learned his craft from some of the great European pioneers, at some of the best-equipped European studios, and from his own long, intense experience." According to Rosenzweig, Curtiz "understood every phase of the industry. He was used to molding new talent and working with sympathetic technical assistants. He knew that filmmaking was a team effort, but he also firmly believed that that the director was the captain of the team, and he carried that belief with him to America." [2] Curtiz may or may not have had all of these beliefs when he came to America, but he certainly exhibited all of this during his American career. The one caveat in this assessment is that while Curtiz may have "firmly believed" that the director was the captain of the team, it is questionable how much the studio system allowed him to act on this belief. Although it is certainly clear that Curtiz had more freedom and leeway within the studio system than did most other directors of the era.

Curtiz's 1924 Austrian film, *Die Slavenkonigin,* literally translated for British release as *The Slave Queen,* but shown in America under the title *Moon of Israel,* caught the eye of Jack Warner of Warner Brothers Studio. *Moon of Israel* was something of an Austrian version of Cecil B. DeMille's *The Ten Commandments.* According to Rosenzweig, Warner saw in this Curtiz production the kind of spectacle that could match DeMille. Warner would later state that when he saw *Moon of Israel,* he was "laid in the aisles by Curtiz's camera work. . .[by] shots and angles that were pure genius." In Rosenzweig's view, "*Moon of Israel* indicates that Curtiz also brought to America his own highly developed visual style and thematic interests." As is often said of Curtiz, this style is heavily influenced by German Expressionism, featuring high crane shots and the unusual camera angles that so impressed Warner. In addition, "*Moon of Israel*'s plot and structure show Curtiz's fondness for romantic melodrama, for setting a small personal love story against events of vast historical importance, for driving his characters to crises and forcing them to make moral decisions."[3] Rosenzweig suggests that these thematic elements characterize Curtiz's Hollywood career. While they might not account for all of that career, they are certainly to be found in abundance in *Casablanca.*

CURTIZ'S EARLY WARNER BROTHERS FILMS

Harry Warner had envisioned a Warner Brothers' biblical epic based on *The Old Testament*'s flood account and Noah's Ark. He saw in *Moon of Israel,* the perfect director for this DeMille-like project. After talking with Harry Warner, Curtiz was evidently under the impression that he would be immediately directing *Noah's Ark.* The *Noah's Ark* project, however, would not come until 1928. Upon arriving at Warner Brothers in 1926, Curtiz was assigned to direct a mediocre film titled *The Third Degree,* which, as suggested by its title, deals with third degree interrogation tactics used on occasion by the police. *The Third Degree* would not be worthy of any contemporary interest other than the fact that it was Curtiz's first American film, and in it he demonstrated some of the qualities that would characterize his entire American career. That this is the case should come to us as no surprise. As we have seen, Curtiz was hardly a neophyte behind the camera when he arrived in America. He was hired by Warner Brothers precisely because of the distinguished career he had enjoyed in Hungary and Austria.

Curtiz worked tirelessly on *The Third Degree,* engaging in extensive personal research into American legal procedure. He spent ten days shadowing the Los Angeles County Sheriff, and he lived in prison. Curtiz "collaborated with scriptwriter C. Graham Baker to make numerous changes, both to the original play and to Baker's screenplay." This intimate involvement with the screen-writer is particularly worthy of note. It is consistent with Rosenzweig's view that Curtiz saw the director as "captain of a team," and it is an involvement that Curtiz would often have with his screenwriters, including the multitude of writers involved in *Casablanca*. *Third Degree* cameraman Hal Mohr would later indicate that "he had never had to work so hard on a film, and that Curtiz was incessantly prowling around the set seeking new camera angles." *The Third Degree* met with, at best, mixed reviews upon its release early in 1927. Curtiz's beloved creative camera angles came in for particular criticism, and he "did not forge the clumsily structured script into a balanced, coherent drama." Despite the criticism, Curtiz "had achieved enough with routine material to convince Jack Warner that he was no run-of-the-mill director," and he was rewarded with a raise.[4]

Through 1927 and early 1928, Curtiz would direct three other films with no value beyond *The Third Degree*. Curtiz biographer James C. Robertson writes of these films: "In each case Curtiz strove valiantly, but unsuccessfully to revitalize unconvincing scripts through spectacular camera work and strong central performances, the most noteworthy features of all three." In other words, the director and the performances he elicited from his lead actors vastly exceeded the quality of the material with which he was forced to work. "Spectacular camera work and strong central performances" would characterize not only *Casablanca* fourteen years later, but virtually the entire body of Curtiz's work. But these three films were not without value to Curtiz's career. Robertson adds: "[T]hese films, all just over one hour long, contributed to Curtiz's Hollywood career in that they familiarized him with Warners' methods and brought him into contact with technicians like cameramen Hal Mohr and Barney McGill."[5]

After slogging his way through these four mediocrities, Curtiz was finally given the opportunity to direct *Noah's Ark*, the film which he thought he had been brought to Warner Brothers to direct. Robertson describes *Noah's Ark* as "Warners' most ambitious and longest project thus far. For prestige reasons all the production stops were pulled out." It was certainly the most expensive film that Warner Brothers had yet produced, coming in at a bit over one million dollars. Robertson asserts that "*Noah's Ark*'s cinematic merit remain uncontestable." Robertson also maintains that "it was Curtiz's first Warner's large box-office hit." However, the figures that Robertson supplies bring that claim into question. He notes that *Noah's Ark* made only a small domestic profit (and he seems to mean box office receipts rather than profit), "but in Europe takings were more than 900,000 dollars, moving the total profit to more than 1,250,000 dollars." If the numbers Robertson is giving us are receipts rather than profit, then the receipts would have barely covered the production costs of the film. If the figures are, indeed profit beyond the production costs, then that profit figure would be impressive indeed.[6]

Noah's Ark is somewhat reminiscent of D. W. Griffith's *Intolerance*. It cuts back and forth between the story of the flood and Noah's ark and a contemporary, anti-war story related to World War I. Its artistic merit is difficult to judge because so much of the original film has been lost. It was premiered at 135 minutes, but that was cut by thirty minutes for its general release. The film was rediscovered in the 1950s, but this was in a 75 minute form with severe re-editing. But even this shortened, re-edited version garnered favorable reviews thirty years after it had been made. In Curtiz lore, *Noah's Ark* is most famous for a special effect that went awry. An enormous tank containing 500,000 tons of water was erected over a large Babylonian set. The water was released on the set where hundred of extras and stuntmen were left to their own devices to make their way through this torrent of water while fifteen cameramen filmed their reaction. Robertson tells us that "Curtiz badly underestimated the technical problems of releasing so much water in one scene, the water went out of control, and many player injuries occurred." Nevertheless, Robertson informs us in his next sentence, "However, the outcome is one of the most spectacular incidents in film history."[7]

The *Noah Ark*'s incident is symbolic of one of the recurring complaints about Curtiz. He is thought by many to have been at best indifferent to the physical (and psychological) well-being of those under his direction. The literature on Curtiz abounds with examples or, at least, claims of verbal and physical cruelty. Errol Flynn, Bette Davis, and Olivia de Havilland all held Curtiz in low regard, at least in terms of his treatment of them as well as others on the set. Curtiz directed Flynn in twelve films, including four of his signature films. Flynn despised Curtiz. He writes in his autobiography: "The direction of *Captain Blood* was assigned to Michael Curtiz. I was to spend five miserable years with him, making *Robin Hood*, *Charge of the Light Brigade*, and many other films. In each case he tried to make all scenes so realistic that my skin didn't seem to matter to him. Nothing delighted him more than real bloodshed."[8]

Flynn also attributes to Curtiz a death on the set of *They Died With Their Boots On*, a bio-pic of General Custer that was originally assigned to Curtiz. Bill Meade, a young friend of Flynn playing a member of Custer's 7th Cavalry, was killed in a freak accident following a fall from his horse. Flynn's own account of this accident mitigates his attribution of it to Curtiz, but Flynn points to an overworked cast as the primary cause of the accident.[9] Flynn biographer Jeffrey Meyers takes an even more negative view of Curtiz than did Flynn (at least in print): "The crude, tough and tireless Curtiz, a vicious polo player, resembled Erich von Stroheim in *Grand Illusion*—tall, ramrod-straight, commanding in voice and bearing. . . .Impatient and tyrannical, Curtiz screamed at and insulted both technicians and actors, and was cordially hated by both. 'He was a beast, a real beast,' said the ladylike Olivia [de Havilland]. 'He was a tyrant, he was abusive, he was cruel. . . .He was caustic, ciritical, he was ([always]) furious.'"[10] Despite its charged nature, the Curtiz-Flynn relationship was a highly productive one. It came to an end during the shooting of *They Died With Their Boots On*. As noted, Curtiz had originally been assigned as the director of the film. After an incident in which Flynn had been informed that Curtiz had ordered tips to be taken off the swords of those who would be battling Flynn, the actor went after Curtiz. "I grabbed Mike by the throat and began strangling him. Two men tried to pry me off. They succeeded before I killed him. That was the end of our relationship. I deemed it wiser not to work with this highly artistic gentlemen who aroused my worst instincts." No discussion of Curtiz can ignore his often difficult relations with cast and crew. However, there is another side to his relationship with actors that we will consider later.

Following *Noah's Ark*, Curtiz's career at Warner Brothers took off in many directions, some of them seemingly contradictory. Over the next eleven years, from 1929 through 1939, Curtiz would direct an astounding 54 films. This would be over half of his entire output for Warner Brothers during his 26-year tenure at the studio. Curtiz gained a reputation as one who worked quickly and well. His films usually came in on time and reasonably close to the tight budgets assigned. In addition to his heavy workload, Curtiz on more than one occasion would do uncredited work in directing additional scenes for other films. We might think that such a workload would come at the cost of quality, that these were films that were simply being cranked out. But during this same period, Curtiz was becoming the leading director of "A" films at Warner Brothers. From 1929 through 1931, Curtiz directed fifteen films, including *Mammy* with Al Jolson in 1929 and *The Mad Genius* with John Barrymore in 1931.

In 1932, Curtiz directed a pretty good horror film for the era, *Dr. X, The Strange Loves of Molly Louvain*, which Robertson describes as "arguably a minor masterpiece,"[11] and *Cabin in the Cotton*, notable as the film which is often said to have started Bette Davis on her road to stardom. *Cabin in the Cotton* has the famous Davis line: "I'd like to kiss you, but I just washed my hair." Both *Dr. X* and *Cabin in the Cotton* were produced by Hal Wallis, a notable observation since Wallis would later be the producer of *Casablanca*. In her book *The Making of Casablanca* (known in earlier editions as *Round Up the Usual Suspects*), which seems to be pretty much the definitive sourcebook on *Casablanca*, Aljean Harmetz gives primary credit for the final product to producer Hal Wallis while playing down the role of Curtiz. Wallis held Curtiz in high regard. In his autobiography, Wallis says of Curtiz that "my favorite director then and always was the amazing Michael Curtiz." Wallis describes Curtiz as "a superb director with an amazing command of lighting, mood, and action. He could handle any kind of picture: melodrama, comedy, Western, historical epic, or love story."[12] For Wallis, Curiz was "the best director in the business."[13] In the light of such praise and the apparently good working relationship that Curtiz and Wallis had, one might assume that these two films were the beginning of a beautiful friendship. They might have been the beginning of a beautiful friendship, but they did not lead to an extensive working relationship, or at least an extensive formal working relationship. Wallis would produce only four more Curtiz films: *The Keyhole* and *Private Detective* in 1933, *Casablanca*, and the Elvis Presley film *King Creole* (which was actually produced by Paul Nathan for Hal Wallis Productions) in 1958.

The big film for Curtiz in 1932 was the hugely successful *20,000 Years in Sing Sing*. This film is perhaps the first true signature Curtiz film in his Hollywood career. Although it seems dated today, as do many "social realism" films of an earlier era, it remains a highly regarded film.

In 1933, Curtiz directed a staggering eight films for Warner Brothers. The most notable of these are *The Mystery of the Wax Museum*, which was an even bigger box office success in Europe than it was in the United States, and *Female*, an interesting film with the under-utilized and under-appreciated Ruth Chatterton in one of her best roles. *Female* has become something of a cult classic in recent years. The following year, Curtiz's pace was relatively slow, directing "only" three films. All three are semi-classics: *Jimmy the Gent* (with James Cagney and Bette Davis), *British Agent* (with Leslie Howard), and *Black Fury* (with Paul Muni). In 1935, the best of the five films directed by Curiz was yet another signature film, *Captain Blood*. Whatever problems, Errol Flynn may have had with Curtiz, it was *Captain Blood* that made him a star. And it was Curtiz who solidified his star-standing with such subsequent films as *The Charge of the Light Brigade*, *The Adventures of Robin Hood*, *Dodge City*, and *The Sea Hawk*. *The Charge of the Light Brigade* would be the most notable film of the six directed by Curtiz in 1936, and it would become a third signature Curtiz film.

In 1937, Curtiz again would direct "only" three films, including *Kid Galahad*, the first of six films featuring Humphrey Bogart directed by Curtiz. *Kid Galahad* has a stellar cast, starring Edward G. Robinson and Bette Davis as well as featuring Bogart. The cast itself would ensure a long life for *Kid Galahad*. It is also crisply directed by Curtiz. *Kid Galahad* was one of the better boxing movies of the era, although not as good as *Body and Soul* or *Golden Boy* or the later *Champion* with Kirk Douglas. *Kid Galahad* would be remade in 1962 in an inferior version as an Elvis Presley vehicle directed by Phil Karlson.

CURTIZ HITS HIS PEAK: 1938-42

In 1938, Curtiz had a banner year, directing five films, three of which could be regarded as signature films: *The Adventures of Robin Hood*, *Four Daughters* (in which John Garfield was brought to stardom through effective direction by Curtiz), and *Angels With Dirty Faces*. In addition to these films, Curtiz also directed some additional footage in *Blackwell's Island*, a Garfield follow-up film to *Four Daughters*. This additional footage included a jailbreak sequence often regarded as the best sequence in the film. *Robin Hood* was originally assigned to William Keighley, who Flynn greatly preferred to Curtiz. Filming for *Robin Hood* began on September 27, 1937. Two months later the film was completed, behind schedule and well over budget. According to Meyers, Flynn "was shocked to hear that Jack Warner had replaced the veteran director William Keighley with the hated Curtiz. Directing Flynn and de Havilland, Curtiz used his characteristically crude techniques."[14] Hal Wallis provides an additional reason for replacing Keighley with Curtiz. As the daily rushes from *Robin Hood* were watched, Wallis thought that "the action scenes were not effective, and I had to replace the director in mid-production, an unheard-of event at that time. I felt that only Mike Curtiz could give the picture the color and scope it needed.[15] The reason we hadn't used him in the first place was because Errol had begged us not to." Color and scope is exactly what *Robin Hood* got from Curtiz. Without Curtiz, *Robin Hood* might well have been a bloated, expensive failure. It might still have been a box office hit, simply because of the star power of Flynn. However, it likely would not be the classic that it is today. Over six decades later, the Errol Flynn-Michael Curtiz *Robin Hood* remains the standard. Anyone who doubts this should ask Kevin Costner.

Although he directed finer films before and after, *Angels With Dirty Faces* was the first of three films for which Curtiz would be nominated for an Academy Award for Best Director. It is a typical Warner Brothers gangster film of the era, with a cornball ending. It remains a favorite, due largely to its outstanding cast, including Cagney, Bogart, and Pat O'Brien. It is another example of Curtiz getting the most from thin material.

Studio workhorse Curtiz would again direct five films in 1939, including another Flynn classic, *Dodge City*, based loosely on the life of Wyatt Earp, and *Daughters Courageous*, something of a sequel to *Four Daughters* from the preceding year, starring John Garfield and Claude Rains. The 1939 output would also include *The Private Lives of Elizabeth and Essex*, starring Flynn, Bette Davis, and de Havilland. One can only imagine the tension on this set given the hatred of its three leading principals for Curtiz and his disdain for them. However, *Elizabeth and Essex* remains a highly regarded film, receiving, for example, three-and-a-half stars (out of four) from Leonard Maltin. This perhaps could be considered as evidence in support of the theory of creative tension. One commentator suggests that *Dodge City* had a greater impact on the development of the Western than John Ford's *Stagecoach*.[16]

Never again would Curtiz direct as many films as he did in 1938 and 1939. He would never again direct more than three films in any single year. Partly this curtailment of activity reflected the fact that productions across all of the Hollywood studios were cut back by World War II. This curtailment also reflected the growing unionism in Hollywood. Meyers argues that Curtiz brought *Robin Hood* back under schedule and financial control through draconian means. "Driving the cast mercilessly, Curtiz completed the picture on January 14—after working continuously that day for nineteen hours, from 8:30 a.m. until 3:30 a.m."[17] *Robin Hood* is not the only Curtiz film with evidence of such work demands being placed upon cast and crew. It is difficult to imagine such working conditions in the union era.

Curtiz was clearly at the top of his craft over the next three years. From 1940 through 1942, Curtiz would make eight films. He would make three films in 1940, all of them starring his nemesis Errol Flynn: *Virginia City* (which also featured Bogart in perhaps his most ridiculous role), *The Sea Hawk* (another

Curtiz signature film), and *Santa Fe Trail* (which also featured Ronald Reagan). In 1941, Curtiz would direct another trio of films: *The Sea Wolf* (another Curtiz signature film, starring Edward G. Robinson, John Garfield, and Ida Lupino) and two films (*Dive Bomber* [starring Flynn] and *Captains of the Clouds* [starring Cagney]) serving as quasi-informational vehicles anticipating American entry into World War II.

Just as 1938 was a banner year for Curtiz, 1942 was clearly his definitive banner year. He directed only two films in 1942, *Yankee Doodle Dandy* and, of course, *Casablanca*. These two films rank with *Robin Hood* as his most enduring films and his finest work. *Yankee Doodle Dandy*, the film biography of Broadway legend George M. Cohan, featuring rousing renditions of "Over There" and "You're a Grand Old Flag," fit masterfully the full-blown Hollywood patriotic support of the war effort. Featuring the Academy Award winning Best Actor performance of James Cagney, *Yankee Doodle Dandy* was a huge commercial and artistic hit and remains one of the finest Hollywood musicals ever made. It would also garner for Curtiz a second Academy Award nomination for Best Director. *Yankee Doodle Dandy* was such a success on all levels that Hollywood would try six times to strike fire again with presumably similar projects. Curtiz would wind up directing another six show business biopics: *Night and Day* (a 1945 biography of Cole Porter starring Cary Grant), *Young Man With a Horn* (a 1949 film based very loosely on the life of jazz legend Bix Beiderbecke starring Kirk Douglas), *I'll See You in My Dreams* (a 1951 biography of songwriter Gus Kahn starring Danny Thomas and Doris Day), *The Story of Will Rogers* (a 1952 biography starring Will Rogers, Jr.), *The Best Things in Life are Free* (a 1956 film dealing with the careers of songwriters Lew Brown, Buddy de Sylva, and Ray Henderson), and *The Helen Morgan Story* (a 1957 biography of the 1920s torch singer starring Ann Blyth and Paul Newman). The last two of these films were made after Curtiz had left Warner Brothers. Several of these films had their moments. Most turned a profit at the box office. But none was in the same league with *Yankee Doodle Dandy*.

CASABLANCA

Casablanca, of course, is the crowning achievement of Curtiz's career. *Casablanca* would lead to Curtiz's third and last Academy Award nomination for best director. This time he would walk away with the prize. For all that is accomplished in *Casablanca*, Curtiz's role in its development and success is often downplayed. As noted above, Aljean Harmetz gives more of a shaping role to Hall Wallis than to anyone else. Harmetz gives Curtiz primary credit for: 1) His technical skill, particularly his camera movement. "The camera never shows off in *Casablanca*, never preens and calls attention to itself, although, as always, Curtiz carefully composed each shot." 2) "Curtiz also brought to *Casablanca* a ravenous single-mindedness." 3) And, according to Harmetz, "*Casablanca* benefited most from Curtiz's need to hurl himself on his movies, to attack them as though he were a real tiger and the camera was raw meat."[18] Certainly Curtiz did bring all of these qualities to *Casablanca*, as he brought them to all of his work. But there is more to Curtiz's role than what Harmetz suggests.

At the outset, *Casablanca* was not much different from any other Warner Brothers film of the era. It is doubtful that anyone went into it knowing that there was a potential classic in the making. Julius Epstein, one of the screenwriters assigned to *Casablanca*, said, "You must remember that nobody thought it was going to be anything."[19] *Watch On the Rhine*, a now largely forgotten film based on a Lillian Hellman Broadway hit, was considered at the time to be a hotter project than *Casablanca*.[20] *Watch On the Rhine* went into production two weeks following *Casablanca* and would finish production earlier. *Watch On the Rhine* would be nominated for the Academy Award for Best Movie, and its male lead, Paul Lukas, would win the Best Actor award over Bogart. It also won most of the critics' year-end awards as well.

Watch on the Rhine had the advantage of being adapted from a well-conceived Broadway play. *Casablanca*, on the other hand, involved considerable alterations from its source material, *Everyone Comes to Rick's*. The story of the multitude of writers involved in *Casablanca*, the rewrites taking place right up to the final shooting, and the rush to the set of daily script changes is well known. It is difficult to gauge exactly Curtiz's influence on the script of *Casablanca*. Robertson tells us : "Curtiz knew that he possessed serious deficiencies as a writer, and he preferred to influence others' scenarios, but he always read them, usually well before production started if circumstances allowed [which circumstances obviously did not allow in *Casablanca*], and engaged in research on the subject matter where appropriate."[21] Robertson also reminds us that "Curtiz kept a tight grip on the content of his films, even scenes he did not actually direct himself, and influenced the final version." Robertson even asserts that this is true of *Casablanca*.[22] Wallis himself lends credence to this view of Curtiz and his involvement in *Casablanca*, recalling how "On Sundays, Mike Curtiz and the writers came out to my farm in the San Fernando Valley, and we spread the pages [of the script] out and tried to combine them into a satisfactory draft."[23] This is certainly consistent with Rosenzweig's view that Curtiz saw filmmaking as a team effort, but that he "also firmly believed that the director was the captain of the team." As captain of the team, it would fall to Curtiz to implement and interpret the results of those Sunday sessions.

Curtiz was, as Robertson suggests, at a disadvantage when it came to scripts, at least in terms of their verbal content. He was notorious for his fractured English and malapropisms. This was true throughout his 36 years in America. One of Curtiz's malapropisms was given long life by David Niven who used it as the title of one of his collections of memoirs, *Bring On the Empty Horses*. The phrase was, according to Niven, used by Curtiz when calling for riderless horses during the filming of *The Charge of the Light Brigade*.[24] Curtiz's stepson said of him, "He spoke five languages, and I am told he spoke all of them equally badly."[25]

Curtiz's second wife was Bess Meredyth who had been a screenwriter in the silent film era. There is considerable anecdotal evidence that she was of great assistance to Curtiz in evaluating scripts and making script changes. According to Harmetz, "When a movie was in production, Curtiz telephoned Bess at least once or twice a day. 'Bogart would say, "Why do I do it this way?" and Mike would walk away and call Bess," says Francis Scheid." Julius Epstein recalls that whenever Curtiz would make criticism or suggestions during story conferences, "we knew they were Bess Meredyth's ideas and not his. . . .So it was easy to trip him up. We'd make a change and say, 'What do you think, Mike?' and he'd have to go back to Bess."[26] One suspects that this account may be embellished, but it does have the virtue of consistency with what is known about Curtiz's facility with the English language. Robertson notes that "even before their marriage he never treated any script as sacrosanct, he almost always altered scripts on the set, and when her health deteriorated in the early 1950s and she was unable to work, he continued to comment on scripts, sometimes at great length, as with *King Creole*.[27]

While it is highly unlikely that Curtiz (or his wife) created any of the numerous memorable lines associated with *Casablanca*, Curtiz's typical habits were on display during filming, and the film itself bears all of the signature marks of a Curtiz film. Harmetz cites a July 6 Wallis memorandum to Curtiz that offers a view somewhat at odds with Harmetz's own interpretation of ultimate responsibility for the shape of the film. Wallis wrote: "I am also attaching the new ending as [Howard] Koch and I have finally worked it out. *I think you will find that it incorporates all of the changes you wanted made*, and I think we have successfully licked the big scene between Ilsa and Rick at the airport by bringing Laszlo in at the finish of it."[28] Curtiz had a strong commitment to the romantic angle of the film, an angle without which it is virtually nothing. Rosenzweig writes: "The worlds of romance and politics have their metaphoric homes in film's twin cities, Paris and Casablanca." According to Rosenzweig, Koch gives credit to Curtiz for deepening "the association between Paris and romance by insisting on inserting the flashback sequence." Koch seemed to think the flashback sequence was superflous. "However, in retrospect I suspect Mike was right. Probably at this point the romantic interlude was a useful retard and relief from tension—and the viewers needed some visual proof of he ardor of the love affair to be convinced of its profound effect on Rick. At any rate, Mike exercised his directorial prerogative and the sequence was written and shot in accordance with his ideas."[29]

Curtiz by temperament and artistic commitment was no martinet carrying out the wishes of producers and studio bosses. He had a long history of being a pain to those above him in the organizational chain of command. He had his artistic vision of what a film should look like and what kind of story it should tell. That vision usually prevailed. It certainly prevailed in *Casablanca*. Part of the greatness and enduring popularity of *Casablanca* is the visual power of the film, and this is all Curtiz's doing. Rosenzweig writes that "the most obvious aspect of Curtiz's directorial signature is his expressionistic visual style, and its most obvious feature is it unusual camera angles and carefully detailed, crowded, complex comp ositions, full of mirrors and reflections, smoke and fog, and physical objects, furniture, foliage, bars, and windows that stand between the camera and the human characters and seem to surround and often entrap them." All of this characterizes what we see in *Casablanca*. When we first see Rick, it is from over his shoulder as he signs a note approving a line of credit. We see the note, we see Rick's bold signature as he signs it, but we have seen nothing yet of Rick but his back and hand.[30] And at the end, we see Rick and Louis, now classically, walking off into smoke and fog. Rosenzweig also remind us that Curtiz "favors dramatic, nonrealistic lighting (in which the light appears from sources impossible or illogical in real situations), marked by strong contrasts between masses of bright light and deep shadow." When we first see Ilsa and Laszlo, they are shot from the distance in a striking backlight that draw us to them, and Curtiz's camera unobtrusively takes us closer to them. Curtiz was also fond of tight close-ups. And the tight close-ups, particularly in the airport scene at the end are forever memorable. But this quietly spectacular cinematic display is not simply for show. "The ultimate purpose of all his visual and dramatic devices is to make us share his characters' emotions, to involve us in their struggles, external and internal."[31] And Curtiz certainly succeeds. His success has proven to be timeless. Had *Casablanca* been directed by any of Curtiz's more highly regarded (by film historians) contemporaries, say, Howard Hawks or John Ford, it is hard to imagine that the film would have the kind of visual impact that it does have. Without that visual impact, it would not be the masterpiece that it is.

Bogart biographers Sperber and Lax remind us of the importance of subtleties. They write of Curtiz: "From his days as a silent-film director he also knew when words were superfluous and how to convey character with a look, a lift of an eyebrow, a nod."[32] A powerfully revealing moment in *Casablanca* is the scene where we have the dueling songs. As the German soldiers are singing "Die Wacht am Rhein" Laszlo leads the band in Rick's Cafe in a rousing version of the "Marseillaise." But before the band follows the lead of Laszlo, the band leader looks to Rick who gives him a nod of approval. That nod tells us something of Rick's power, and it tells us volumes about the man who "stick[s] my neck out for nobody."

Another important dimension that Curtiz brought to *Casablanca* that is often overlooked is his ability to draw outstanding performances from his cast. Despite or perhaps because of his reputation as a harsh and often cruel taskmaster, Curtiz consistently gained first-rate performances. And while Errol Flynn, Olivia de Havilland, Bette Davis, and others may have despised him, many other performers thought quite highly of him. Even Flynn acknowledges that Curtiz "was a talented man, probably brilliant, but relentless in his demands." One of Flynn's complaints was that Curtiz was "making me into a stereotype." That, however, would seem to be more the function of the studio and its casting than it would be of Curtiz. Flynn complained that "Warners was making money off my dashing, slash-bang roles. And Curtiz was the director who whipped me on to such performances."[33] That last sentence, of course, is loaded, particularly in regard to the verb choice. While Flynn may have detested these roles, they are the ones for which he is best known, and Curtiz, evidently through one form of whipping or another, drew stellar performances from him. It should also be noted that Curtiz did direct Flynn in some non-swashbuckler roles, e.g. in *The Perfect Specimen* (1937) and *Four's a Crowd* (1938). Part of the problem with the Flynn-Curtiz relationship was that Flynn was often lazy and unprofessional. He did not see film as a serious art form. That put him at odds with Curtiz, who was thoroughly professional and expected no less of those who worked for him.

John Garfield came to stardom under Curtiz's direction in *Four Daughters*. Doris Day also came to stardom under Curtiz's direction, first in *Romance on the High Seas* (1947) followed by *My Dream is Yours* (1948). James Cagney won his only Academy Award for Best Actor in *Yankee Doodle Dandy*. Joan Crawford won an Academy Award for her performance in *Mildred Pierce*. Curtiz directed Elvis Presley in what many regard as his finest performance in *King Creole* (1958).

In light of his great success with actors, it is laughable to read Paul Henreid's characterization of Curtiz. In an interview with Harmetz, Henreid related: "Unfortunately, Michael Curtiz was not a director of actors; he was a director of effects. He was first rate at that, but he could not tell Bogart he should play like a crybaby. It was embarrassing, I thought, when I looked at the rushes."[34] What Henreid seems to have failed to appreciate is that what he sees as a "crybaby" is the torn romantic side of Bogart who skillfully portrays a romantic masquerading as a cynic. It is also noteworthy that Bogart's view of Curtiz was significantly different from Henreid's. While Curtiz and Bogart had, not surprisingly given their temperaments, their share of disagreements and quarrels, when Bogart renewed his contract with Warner Brothers, he gained a form of director approval. While his contract allowed for director approval, it also specified five directors who had contractual pre-approval. Curtiz was one of the five.[35] Ingrid Berman, the other major principal in *Casablanca* would never work with Curtiz again, but this is largely due to the fact that she was not under contract to Warner Brothers and was on loan for *Casablanca*. Bergman, however, come away from *Casablanca* with a quite favorable impression of Curtiz. Bergman described Curtiz as being "very sweet and nice to me." Claude Rains also thought highly of Curtiz. Rains would make eight films with Curtiz. Harmetz states that Rains credits Curtiz "with teaching him the difference between stage and film acting. As Rains puts it, Curtiz taught him 'what not to do in front of a camera.'"[36]

Just as Curtiz was arguably the best conceivable director for *Casablanca* from a strictly technical point of view, he was also symbolically the perfect director. The Casablanca of the film is populated by shadowy characters or at least those with shadowy backgrounds. Many of these characters, including most obviously Rick, have personal histories that are largely a mystery to the others around them. Michael Curtiz was also such a man. His biographer begins by telling us that "nothing definite is known about Michael Curtiz's early life except that he was born as Mihaly Kertesz in Hungary during the nineteenth century. All other supposed data ultimately derive, in one form or another, from Curtiz himself who is unreliable since he gave out different versions at different times." He appears to have left Hungary in 1919 as something of a political refugee, but in a confusion that would typify Rick in *Casablanca*, "it is uncertain whether he left to escape Communist domination of his studio or collaborated with the Communists, perhaps unwillingly, and then feared anti-Communist retribution after the Communist government fell."[37]

Harmetz notes the mostly immigrant cast of *Casablanca*, writing: "Of the seventy-five actors and actresses who had bit parts and larger roles in *Casablanca*, almost all were immigrants of one kind or another. Of the fourteen who were given screen credit, only Humphrey Bogart, Dooley Wilson, and Joy Page were born in America."[38] Curtiz was also Jewish. Harmetz observes that "Curtiz was as much an immigrant Jew as the refugees he cast in his movie." So Curtiz's personal background would give him considerable empathy for the story he was relating on film. Harmetz notes that "Curtiz brought his mother to America in 1938, but he could only get his two brothers as far as Mexico, where they spent a year waiting for visas." The fate of Curtiz's two brothers is not unlike those in *Casablanca* seeking those all-important exit visas. Although he probably would not know this until after the war, Curtiz's sister's family was imprisoned at Auschwitz. Curtiz's sister managed to survive, but not the rest of her family.[39]

CURTIZ'S CAREER AFTER *CASABLANCA*: 1943-1946

While 1942 certainly represents the apex of Curtiz's career, he would continue to have success both commercially and artistically in the aftermath of *Yankee Doodle Dandy* and *Casablanca*. In 1943 Curtiz made three films that fit into the Hollywood effort to support the war. The first of these was the amiable *This is the Army*, a musical comedy perhaps most noteworthy today as featuring Ronald Reagan and future California Senator George Murphy. Curtiz was also tapped in 1943 to direct the unfortunate *Mission to Moscow*, based on the best-selling first-person account of former United States Ambassador to the Soviet Union, Joseph Davies. According to numerous accounts, Jack Warner made this film at the urging of President Franklin Roosevelt, who thought it would explain the nature of the Soviet Union to the American public in a manner that would make the Soviet Union an acceptable ally to the American mind.[40] Both the Davies memoir and its film version were of the propaganda mold that treated the Soviet Union as a benign variant of American democracy. *Mission to Moscow* even went beyond much of the typical leftist propaganda of the era, which had the good sense to ignore Stalin's infamous show trials. Davies justified them. Although the Warners saw their production of *Mission to Moscow* in a patriotic

light, after the war it would become a prime example of Communist or Commu-
nist-inspired influence in Hollywood during the era of congressional investiga-
tions of the subject. Often overlooked in the subsequent controversy surrounding
the film, *Mission to Moscow* was largely well-received by critics and was a success at the box office. Curtiz, however, was himself stung by the criticism that
the film would shortly receive. Robertson notes that *Mission to Moscow* "ran
into such strong anti-Communism that Curtiz took it personally and vowed
never again to direct a political film." Robertson argues that Curtiz "was as good
as his word and was prompted perhaps as much by memories of Hungary as by
the *Mission to Moscow* controversy."[41] Of course, even before *Mission to Moscow*, Curtiz rarely directed overtly political films, although political and social
concerns were often found in Curtiz films. That would continue to be something
of a pattern through the rest of his career, although it is true that he never would
again direct anything as political as his World War II-era films..

The other 1943 war-supporting film directed by Curtiz was the commercially successful, but largely forgettable *Passage to Marseille*. *Passage to Marseille* is, however, of interest, if only for reasons of contrast, to anyone interested
in *Casablanca*. *Passage to Marseille* is sometimes regarded as a kind of sequel
to *Casablanca*. Warner Brothers was clearly attempting to strike gold again. Not
only is Curtiz again directing, but the cast of *Passage to Marseille* is loaded with
cast members from *Casablanca*, including Humphrey Bogart, Claude Rains,
Sydney Greenstreet, and Peter Lorre. The screenplay was written by Casey Robinson, one of many writers who had a hand in the script for *Casablanca*. In *Passage to Marseille*, Bogart gets the girl, played by Michele Morgan, who was up
for consideration as Ilsa in *Casablanca* (and who commanded a higher salary at
the time than did Ingrid Bergman). But unlike *Casablanca*, there is no tension in
the romance and it is pushed into the background of the film. *Passage to Marseille* also has a clumsy and slow-moving narrative structure that entails numerous uses of flashbacks and even flashbacks within flashbacks. The film has its
moments, mostly some good action sequences. It also has Curtiz's trademark
visual qualities. But it is certainly no *Casablanca*. While it is not the "awful"
film that Harmetz calls it, it certainly does demonstrate that "making a follow-up
to *Casablanca* required more than using most of the same cast."[42]

Following the mediocrity of his 1943 output, Curtiz returned to his more
usual high standards of excellence with *Roughly Speaking* (1944), which, in
typical Curtiz fashion, shows its two stars Rosalind Russell and Jack Carson in
top form. The following year, Curtiz directed another of his most notable works,
the film noir classic, *Mildred Pierce*, featuring Joan Crawford in an Academy
Award winning performance. In 1946, Curtiz directed the highly successful film
version of the Broadway comedy *Life With Father*.

CURTIZ'S CAREER AFTER *CASABLANCA*: 1947-61

Harmetz maintains that Curtiz's career "went downhill" after *Mildred Pierce* and *Life With Father*. Although some occasionally good work would follow, Harmetz's observation is essentially correct. She asserts that "Curtiz had worked best in the caldron of the studio system, in which a new movie bubbled up each week and no one picture mattered too much." She also asserts, less convincingly, that "Curtiz was not suited to making for himself the decisions that Hal Wallis had once made for him."[43] The notion that Curtiz was a puppet responding to decisions that Wallis "made for him" is too difficult to take seriously in view of the few films in which they actually worked together and the many superb Curtiz films not produced by Wallis. Curtiz's downfall coincided with the creation of Michael Curtiz Productions, a film unit within Warner Brothers. According to the financial arrangements between Curtiz Productions and Warner Brothers, Curtiz would put up 30 percent of production costs and receive 30% of the profits for each film produced by his company. According to Warner Brothers only one of the eleven Curtiz Production Company films made a profit.[44] In light of what is known about creative accounting in Hollywood, Harmetz takes this studio summary in a too uncritical manner.

The financial failure of Michael Curtiz Productions would lead to a bitter split in 1953 between Curtiz and Warner Brothers. Curtiz had worked exclusively with Warner Brothers since arriving in America in 1926. In his 26 years at Warners, he directed 90 films. As an independent director from 1953 until 1961, he would direct another 15 films. While Harmetz is surely correct in her view that Curtiz's career went downhill after 1947, there were still some films of note that were made, although arguably none could be included among the first rank of Curtiz films. But fitting his reputation for working with actors and being instrumental to the success of young actors, we see the post-1947 Curtiz working successfully with the young Doris Day (*My Dream is Yours, Young Man With a Horn*, and *I'll See You in My Dreams*). He worked again with Joan Crawford and Sydney Greenstreet in *Flamingo Road* (1948), helping to create another noteworthy Crawford performance. In 1950 he worked again with John Garfield in the well-regarded *Breaking Point*. That same year he also directed Burt Lancaster in *Jim Thorpe—All American*, a film that hit hard on social issues that often characterized Curtiz. In 1955, Curtiz directed his last Bogart film, *We're No Angels*, a film that has received mixed responses through the years. As noted above, he directed Elvis Presley to one of his finest performances in *King Creole. King Creole* may, indeed, be Curtiz's most notable work after 1947. But it is notable because it is an Elvis Presley film more than because it is a Curtiz film. But it is surely Curtiz's directing that has much to do with the historical reputation of this particular Presley vehicle.[45] In 1961, while dying of cancer, Curtiz would direct his last film, a serviceable John Wayne western, *The Comancheros*. While none of the films from the last fifteen years of his career can match the top tier of Curtiz's work, many of these are nevertheless worthwhile films and have given millions of moviegoers considerable enjoyment long after their first-run was concluded.

CONCLUSION

Two aspects of Curtiz's career that run throughout virtually every commentary (although these have been few in number) that has been written about him are his extraordinary efficiency and high degree of competence working within the confines of the studio system and the wide range of genres in which he worked. That second point may, in fact, be the primary reason for Curtiz's oddly forgotten status in American film history. Rosenzweig writes that "because of the large number and variety of his films, Curtiz has generally been viewed as a studio work-horse, competent in many genres, willing to do whatever was asked of him, but with no distinct style or theme."[46] We associate John Ford with Westerns, but Curtiz made first-rate Westerns, too (*Dodge City, Virginia City*).

Curtiz may best be compared to one of his contemporaries, Fred Zinnemann (*High Noon, From Here to Eternity, Oklahoma!,* and *A Man for All Seasons*) or the more current Norman Jewison (*The Cincinnati Kid, In the Heat of the Night, Fiddler on the Roof, Jesus Christ Superstar*) as a director who does not receive the public or critical acclaim that his body of work deserves. In the cases of Zinnemann and Jewison, as well as with Curtiz, the breadth of the work may serve as an obstacle to full appreciation of the directorial talent behind it.

Ultimately the difference between Curtiz and Ford, or Curtiz and Hitchcock, is that few would debate that *Casablanca* is Curtiz's finest work, but there are many different opinions as to which is Ford's greatest work or which is Hitchcock's. What Curtiz does have in common with Ford and Hitchcock is that there is a large body of extremely impressive work to watch and enjoy. *Casablanca*, although the most enduring and the best of his work, is, at the same time, more typical of Curtiz's work than it is atypical. What makes *Casablanca* a great film? It does have a great cast, but so do many mediocre films. Curtiz himself would direct just such a film the very year after *Casablanca*. It has now-legendary dialogue. But it is also a visually lovely and powerful film. *Casablanca* is awash with all of the strengths of Curtiz's direction, strengths that we see in many other Curtiz films. It is a great film in large part due to those strengths.

NOTES

1. It is telling that there are very few scholarly accounts of the work of Curtiz. There are only two book-length assessments: Sidney Rosenzweig, *Casablanca and Other Major Films of Michael Curtiz* (Ann Arbor: UMI Research Press, 1982) and James C. Robertson, *The Casablanca Man: The Cinema of Michael Curtiz* (London: Routledge, 1993). Both of these books make an effort to present Curtiz as an auteur. However, to do this, both authors would have to stretch the meaning of auteur in a manner that one would think few film historians or critics would accept.

2. Rosenzweig, *Casablanca and Other Major Films,* 6.

3. Rosenzweig, *Casablanca and Other Major Films,* 6.

4. Robertson, *Casablanca Man,* 12-13.

5. Robertson, *Casablanca Man,* 14.

6. Robertson, *Casablanca Man*, 16.

7. Robertson, *Casablanca Man*, 16.

8. Errol Flynn, *My Wicked, Wicked Ways: The Autobiography of Errol Flynn* (New York: First Cooper Square Press, 2003), 202.

9. Flynn, *My Wicked, Wicked Ways* 213.

10. Jeffrey Meyers, *Inherited Risk: Errol and Sean Flynn in Hollywood and Vietnam* (New York: Simon & Schuster, 2002), 125. Curiously, Meyers is also the author of *Bogart: A Life in Hollywood* (New York: Houghton Mifflin Company, 1997) in which he bypasses such characterizations of Curtiz with the exception of a passing reference to Curtiz "often berat[ing] and bull[ying] his actors" (138).

11. Robertson, *Casablanca Man*, 24. Leonard Maltin does not agree, describing it as a "typically fast paced Warner Bros. yarn, though more unpleasant than most" (Leonard Maltin, *1999 Movie and Video Guide* (New York: Signet Books, 1999),

12. Hal B. Wallis and Charles Higham, *Starmaker: The Autobiography of Hal Wallis* (New York: Macmillan Publishing Company, 1980), 24-25.

13. Wallis and Higham, *Starmaker*, 150.

14. Meyers, *Inherited Risk*, 146.

15. Wallis and Higham, *Starmaker*, 54.

16. D. Morse, "*Dodge City* and the Development of the Western," in *Monogram* (1975, No. 6), 34-9.

17. Meyers, *Inherited Risk*, 146.

18. Aljean Harmetz, *The Making of Casablanca: Bogart, Bergman, and World War II* (New York: Hyperion, 2002), 182-84. *The Making of Casablanca* is an updated version of an earlier work titled *Round Up the Usual Suspects*, published in 1992.

19. As quoted in A. M. Sperber and Eric Lax, *Bogart* (New York: William Morrow and Company, 1997), 187.

20. Harmetz, *Round Up the Usual Suspects*, 5 and 102.

21. Robertson, *Casablanca Man*, 138.

22. Robertson, *Casablanca Man*, 139.

23. Wallis and Higham, *Starmaker*, 88.

24. David Niven, *Bring On the Empty Horses* (New York: G. P. Putnam's Sons, 1975), 119.

25. Harmetz, *The Making of Casablanca*, 123.

26. Harmetz, *The Making of Casablanca*, 123.

27. Robertson, *Casablanca Man*, 139.

28. As quoted in Harmetz, *The Making of Casablanca*, 233. Emphasis added.

29. Rosenzweig, *Casablanca and Other Major Films*, 86-87.

30. Rosenzweig, *Casablanca and Other Major Films*, 157.

31. Rosenzweig, *Casablanca and Other Major Films*, 159.

32. Sperber and Lax, *Bogart*, 203.

33. Flynn, *My Wicked, Wicked Ways*, 296.

34. Harmetz, *The Making of Casablanca*, 97.

35. Harmetz, *The Making of Casablanca*, 190.

36. Harmetz, *The Making of Casablanca*, 190-91

37. Robertson, *Casablanca Man*, 5-6.

38. Harmetz, *The Making of Casablanca*, 12. Harmetz also writes: "Wallis and Curtiz did not feel under pressure with the smaller roles. American actors might be in short supply, but Hitler had make sure that Hollywood was full of German, Austrian, Hungarian, Polish, and French actors whose whose accents and mannerisms seemed interchangeable to the studio casting directors" (154).

39. Harmetz, *The Making of Casablanca*, 185. In light of this background, it is a bit shocking to read Howard Koch's statement that "On *Casablanca*, Mike was a little bit over his

head politically and socially" (Harmetz, *The Making of Casablanca*, 185). If anything, Curtiz would seem to have been right in his element in this environment.

40. See, for example, Howard Koch, *As Time Goes By* (New York: Harcourt Brace Jovanovich, 1979), 101-2.

41. Robertson, *Casablanca Man*, 149.

42. Harmetz, *The Making of Casablanca*, 303. Sperber and Lax, 220.

43. Harmetz, *The Making of Casablanca*, 191.

44. Harmetz, *The Making of Casablanca*, 191.

45. Presley biographer Peter Guralnick makes this interesting observation about Presley's performance in the 1961 film *Wild in the Country*: "He is flat, he blurts out his lines, there is an almost total absence of timing, conviction, commitment, tone. If you doubt your eyes, contrast this with his performance in *King Creole*, full of jauntiness, assurance, an ease and melodiousness of nuanced approach. Here, just two and one-half years later, there is no pulse, no beat between the lines, there is simply the sense of a young man running, in many cases racing through his lines." (Guralnick, *Careless Love: The Unmaking of Elvis Presley* (Boston: Little, Brown, and Company, 1999), 87.

46. Rosenzweig, *Casablanca and Other Major Films*, xxx. This, as indicated in note 1 above, is a view that Rosenzweig does not share.

CHAPTER 10

ON THE ARGUMENT OF *CASABLANCA* AND THE MEANING OF THE THIRD RICK

KENNETH DE LUCA

After the narrator sets the stage, *Casablanca* is set in motion by an APB (all points bulletin) calling for the arrest of "all suspicious characters" in response to the murder of two German couriers. A short time later, we are inside Rick's Café Américain—where everyone appears to be a suspicious character. One man laments as he looks into oblivion that he shall never get out of Casablanca. An unescorted woman sits opposite a merchant, who examines her diamonds, which she apparently has come to Rick's to sell. Although the woman is unsatisfied with the merchant's first offer, after being informed that in Casablanca "diamonds are a drug on the market—everyone sells diamonds," she despondently accepts. Two men speak guardedly and then clam up when men speaking German get too close. At another table, a man receives instructions for boarding a boat and is told to bring fifteen thousand francs "in cash; remember, *in cash*." For all we know any or all of the above may have committed or participated in the murder of the German couriers. All are typical of Rick's clientele, and for two reasons. First, they intensely hunger for something. They either want desperately to leave Casablanca or are greedy to profit from others wanting to leave. Some are thieves; others displaced freedom fighters. None are neutral; therefore, all are to be suspected. Second, all are also "characters," that is, all are distinctive. They all have behavioral idiosyncrasies rooted either in culture, race, class, or personality.[1] And, so at Rick's everyone is both a suspicious *character* and a character (i.e., an individual) who is suspicious. All, that is, except for Rick himself. It is not that Rick is not a character. He is in fact *the* character of both the film and the city of the film—Casablanca. People come to Rick's in part to see and associate with Rick.[2] While Rick epitomizes character, he is not a suspicious character, because Rick is neutral and therefore not to be suspected.[3] *Casablanca*'s mission is to turn Rick into a suspicious character. The film, in fact, ends right about the time Rick becomes suspicious or, in other words, a partisan. The film's burden, however, is more complicated. Since partisans are a dime a dozen, or are in some sense mere parts, and Rick is *the* individual—that is, a whole—the film must turn Rick into, or back into, a partisan, without making him forfeit his individuality. For if it does this, Rick may as well have fought on the other side. This double problem and how the film solves it is the focus of this essay.[4]

After the APB, policemen on foot and in automobiles appear like lightning in town. The speed and efficiency of their movement suggest they have done this before and are good at it. Evidently, a bit of the Reich has rubbed off on the French, as is also suggested by the indiscriminate manner in which "suspects" are arrested. Casablanca may be part of unoccupied France, but France is no longer what it was. In any case, before the usual suspects can bat an eye or get away, they are herded into the back of a police wagon. One encounter, in particular, the film calls to our attention. A man attempting to avoid the notice of the police is nevertheless approached by two officers who ask for his papers, which at first the man claims not to have. After he realizes he is then going to be arrested, he complies. However, just as the officers learn his papers are invalid, he flees—only getting a short distance before he is gunned down in front of a large poster of Henri-Philippe Pétain, next to whose image reads (in French): "I keep our promises for us and for others."[5]

One might say that Pétain's proclamation is meant to affirm the principles of 1789. The promises are the universal rights of man and are therefore to be kept for citizens of France proper as well as for the non-French inhabitants of France's colonies. In light of its place in the film and Pétain's then role in French political life, however, Pétain's proclamation is to be read in a different light. Under Pétain, France reconciles itself with Nazi rule, is divided into occupied and unoccupied territories, and has its seat of government moved to Vichy. Pétain more or less refounds France, replacing the '89 slogan with his own: "work, family, and fatherland." Since work, family, and fatherland may exist with or without political life, one could say that Pétain works not to refound, but rather to unfound France. Although on the façade of the Palais de Justice—as the film points out—is a plaque that reads "Liberty, Equality, Fraternity," the current French regime sacrifices all three on the altar of expediency. In maintaining the shell of its former self, France does not even deserve to be regarded as neutral, as this very scene suggests. For the man shot by the police is revealed (by leaflets he is carrying) to be part of the Resistance. The police of unoccupied, liberty-loving France have just shot a defender of liberty. And, as a review of the scene makes clear, had the police not done so, the freedom fighter would have run right into the poster of Pétain. If the police had misfired, Pétain would have made the arrest himself. Pétain, indeed, keeps promises with others as he does for those in France.[6]

Almost immediately after the freedom fighter is shot, a German airplane is shown in a long descent to the airport. The plane is carrying an officer of the Reich, Major Strasser. That his arrival almost immediately follows the murder of the couriers and the APB testifies further to the Reich's efficiency and power.[7] When Strasser steps to the tarmac, he is greeted like royalty by a subordinate officer and by Captain Renault (the French prefect of police). As Strasser, Renault, and the other German officer walk away from the plane, Renault says that Casablanca recently has been a trifle warm. In response, Strasser boasts that "we Germans must get used to all climates, from Russia to the Sahara." Strasser's boast reminds us of Pétain's boast. Like the principles of '89, to which Pétain's proclamation alludes, the Reich too holds the potential to cross the globe; but unlike the principles of '89, which support the individual, the Reich regards the individual as clay for it to mold. By means of force, the Reich would impose itself on countries of various climates, requiring both the conquerors and the conquered to adapt. The Reich in some ways is as hard on its own citizens as it is on others. Strasser, then, wonders aloud whether Renault was referring, not to the climate, but to the murdered German couriers, and so he asks Renault what has been done. Although Renault knows that his men are to arrest the murderer that very night—as he will say in a moment—he first informs Strasser that he has greatly intensified the apprehension of suspects. Renault does this because he surmises that this will impress Strasser.[8] Although the French strain of universalism has succumbed to a German strain, it seems that the French strain has produced a human character as adaptable to different political conditions as Strasser imagines the men of the Reich will be to the world's different climates. Renault wears the Reich's values like he wears his uniform. Both are for show. As prefect of police, he uses his own power, others' desire for freedom, and the present international crisis to score sexual conquests. As the film suggests, even his self-understanding is a façade. According to him, he, not the Reich, is the master of his destiny.[9] Renault is a lost man.[10] His character represents the hollow remains of an exhausted revolution. In its success, it spanned the globe and was planted in a great variety of lands. But its success sowed the seeds of its failure. In coming into contact with a variety of customs, the French—as depicted by Renault—learned not to take too seriously their own customs, among which are the very principles underlying French universalism.[11] This weakened attachment is evident in the fact that liberty, equality, and fraternity have been replaced by "caviar," "Veuve Clicquot '26," and "beautiful women."[12] Fiery patriotism has been replaced by an appreciation for the high life. It is as if the Revolution never happened, and we are back in the Versailles of the Sun King. French patriots have become the new courtier class of a barbaric imperial force.

From the airport, the film abruptly shifts to the front of Rick's. This transition was prepared by Renault's telling Strasser that the arrest of the murderer of the German couriers is to occur at Rick's and by Strasser's admission to having heard not only of Rick but of his café. Later, we discover that Strasser has a complete dossier on Rick: he knows Rick's full name, his place of birth, the color of his eyes, and that Rick has fought against Fascists all over the world, including the Nazi's, and that he is not permitted back in the United States. Rick, then, is not only an enemy of Fascists in practice, but in spirit. For Rick is a man apart. He rejects the corporatism for which the Reich stands and corporatism everywhere. He cannot even work within the country in which he was born and with which he shares a common enemy. And, yet, as the name of Rick's café—Rick's Café Américain—suggests, Rick stands for more than just individualism. Rick stands for America. Uncannily, Rick is both the ultimate individual and the representative of a country. It is therefore fitting that as we enter Rick's pouring from its doors is the song "It Had to be You," which is about the uncanny charm of a particular beloved in some lover's eyes. Like the beloved of this song and the country for which Rick stands, Rick's faults are precisely what make him beautiful. Rick, like America, takes a vice—let us call it selfishness— and transforms it into a virtue. Rick is the beauty mark of America; he is an alluring imperfection.

Although inside Rick's we first encounter several examples of desperation, the atmosphere of Rick's is festive. Despite the fact that war is afoot, the viewer cannot help wishing he were there. As Rick will say, he wants everyone to have a good time. Sam's second song, "Knock on Wood," summarizes the mission of Rick's Café. The song is about the human ability to laugh through and even at one's sorrows as it attempts to facilitate this very thing for the sorrowful many listening to it. The contrast, therefore, between Rick's and the Reich could not be more extreme. The Reich spreads pain; Rick's spreads pleasure.[13] The Reich forces the private to yield to the public; Rick's forces politics, or the public, to yield to the private.[14] The Reich imposes hierarchy and impinges upon the world's various cultures;[15] Rick's provides equality[16] and permits freedom of cultural expression.[17] Even Rick's staff is multiethnic, and one sings in a foreign tongue. All this would be unremarkable if not for the name of Rick's club. Rick's Café Américain is a microcosm of America—it is a blank slate, a casa blanca, if you will, which receives its content from elsewhere. Its virtue is its neutrality, for in lacking an overbearing content of its own, it does not resist what others have to offer. As it will turn out, Rick's Café not only reflects America, but its owner. Rick, like his café, is a casa blanca within whom good and evil each enjoy a place at the table. Rick's Café is Rick's extension.[18]

Although Rick's name is above the door (and on the roof) of his café, Rick at first is nowhere to be found. It is some time before we are given an audience with him. Before we do, we learn from a waiter, Carl, that Rick never drinks with customers. A woman of obvious means who had wanted his company, and is therefore disappointed to hear this, wonders aloud "what makes saloonkeepers so snobbish?" A man nearby interjects—hoping it will cause Rick to make an exception—that he ran the second biggest banking house in Amsterdam. Carl tells him it would not make a difference—the owner of Amsterdam's biggest house is their pastry chef. Thus, the film suggests—with the above and by putting distance between Rick and others (that is, his patrons and us)—that the old hierarchy has been replaced by another. Bank directors are now pastry chefs, and Rick—the man who we are about to learn was once a solitary fighter against injustice and who is now without a country—is universally revered.[19] The outcast is now king. When we finally meet Rick, we are allowed to see only his hands as he is asked to authorize a marker, which Rick does by signing "OK Rick." His first deed of the film is stamping money with his Americanish signature and putting it into circulation. His second is allowing and disallowing entry to his gambling parlor. After bouncing a customer, another, Ugarte, who we sense frequents Rick's Café, asks for an audience with him. Despite Rick's demurral, Ugarte follows him to his table. While Rick contemplates his next move in a game of chess against an absent opponent (is he playing against himself?), Ugarte pathetically (and comically) attempts to make conversation with him. He is desperate to win Rick's respect, while in word and deed Rick projects indifference. It is clear that Ugarte appears before Rick as a supplicant. What he comes in search of is Rick's recognition. Although he will ask Rick to safeguard letters of transit for him, his reason for singling out Rick for this task is odd—he says it is because Rick despises him so much.[20] In any case, that Ugarte is able to show Rick something that not even Rick has ever seen before is at least part of the reason he solicits Rick's help, and when Rick figures out that to obtain the letters Ugarte had to kill or participate in the killing of the German couriers, Ugarte grins with satisfaction. Even Rick has to be impressed with this! A little later, when Renault's men have Ugarte cornered, he begs Rick to help him. That he thinks Rick can bail him out of an impossible situation is the measure of Rick's mystique. What is it about Rick?[21]

The beginning of an answer to this question is supplied by Ugarte. During their talk, Ugarte comments ironically on the murder of the German couriers. Rick says he considers them lucky: before they were anonymous clerks; "today they are the honored dead." In response, Ugarte, with admiration, calls Rick a cynic. Cynicism seems to fit Rick like a glove.[22] It accounts for his aloofness, for as a cynic he would not deem others worthy of attention. It accounts for his unpredictability, for as a cynic he would not accept principle as a reason to act, and therefore it would be difficult to understand why he acts.[23] And, it accounts for his neutrality, for as a cynic he would not judge any cause worth his support. Among these effects, neutrality seems to be the one the film stresses most. Rick's call to arms is "I stick my neck out for nobody."[24] In our first encounter with Rick, he is playing a game of chess. Rather than participate in the struggle between freedom and tyranny, which has great significance for the whole world, he plays a game that makes a game out of this struggle. You win when you take your opponent's king. Later, Rick makes a game of the Resistance's need to get Laszlo to America where he may rejoin the partisans of freedom. Rather than help Laszlo and his cause, at first Rick uses Laszlo's and the world's plight to give himself a betting interest, and—despite his bet[25]—exhibits pleasure at Laszlo's misfortune.[26] The world and its suffering are just a game to him. It merits fascination, but not participation.[27] Rick has a fling with a beautiful woman, Yvonne, that progresses far enough for her to fall in love with him, but can never progress far enough for him to fall in love with her, because in giving no weight to transcendent ideals, Rick cannot even take love seriously. When

Yvonne asks Rick where he was last night and whether she will see him tonight, he responds that last night was so long ago he can't remember it, and that he never plans as far ahead as tonight. Thus, Rick has no past and no future. He just is. In not being determined by the past or future, in not submitting to the partisan ideals of the moment, or to the temptation to enrich himself by exploiting others' desperation, Rick remains a man totally himself. Unlike others who have become either partisans[28] or feverish profiteers (like Renault, Ugarte, and Ferrari[29]), Rick is not a creature of his environment. Rick, therefore, is in a sense free and beyond time. The man who does not believe in transcendent ideals has become a transcendent ideal. And so he is adored. And he owes it all to the Reich. Where would he be without it?

Such is the state of Rick as Victor Laszlo and Ilsa Lund enter. Their appearance has an immediate effect. For the first time "As Time Goes By" is played at Rick's Café. Since Rick had asked Sam not to play it, his doing so causes Rick to angrily storm across the café floor to inquire why his decree is disobeyed. To Rick's everybody comes, pickpockets and Nazi criminals alike, but this song was long ago banished from the realm. Evidently, Rick is neutral with respect to everything except this song. Rick wants to know how it got back in, and in doing so learns of Ilsa's presence and that the song was her request. That the song Rick wants to hear least is the song Ilsa wants to hear most shows how far they are apart. For Rick, their war, not that between the Reich and the free world, is the one to which he is committed.

In the next scene, (after hours) Rick drinks at a table with Sam playing music in the background, and demands Sam play "As Time Goes By," in order to prove that he too has the power to recall the days this song evidently brings to mind, and which quickly fill Rick's head and the screen once the song begins. As we see, in Paris Rick was in love with Ilsa and thought Ilsa was in love with him. We also learn that Rick was marked for arrest by the Gestapo, evidently for his anti-Fascist enterprising. So, as the film has been suggesting, Rick was not always neutral. He was, in fact, a romantic—a partisan of noble causes, or of the beautiful. His affair with Ilsa was in keeping with this romanticism. Rick gave himself to noble causes throwing caution to the wind, and in the same manner is willing to marry a woman he had only just met and whom the film emphasizes he knew little about and who knew little about him. Ilsa, as opposed to the political causes his enterprises had been dedicated to, offered much more than an abstract reward, however.[30] In Ilsa the romantic life, perhaps for the first time, offered him the experience of complete happiness. One might say that Ilsa constituted the reward of a romantic life well lived. Rick's being rejected by Ilsa—whose face launched Rick's every desire—therefore scars him for life. He can no longer be himself.[31] How could he ever live by the light of his heart again or take seriously human concerns, given the deceitfulness of human beings and his own apparent failure to diagnose this deceitfulness? How could he take seriously a future commitment when the most important one he ever made proved to be a fraud? Moreover, what could live up to what he thought he had?

Right about the time Rick's reminiscence ends, Ilsa enters the café. She has come to explain to Rick what she left unexplained in Paris—the breaking off of their romance. But Rick's hatred makes any explanation impossible, as Ilsa later suggests at an open-air market stall called "Au Roi de la Lingerie." Rick's hatred is made evident to Ilsa through various slurs: that Ilsa is a base opportunist ("Maybe [an ending] will come to you as you go along"; "Someday you'll lie to Laszlo"[32]) and a slut ("Who was it you left me for? What is it Laszlo? Or were there others in between? Or aren't you the kind that tells?"). In order to get around this, Ilsa tells Rick a story. The story is supposed to cause Rick to look away from her (and his hatred) long enough for him to see why she left, but it doesn't work. Rick seems to hate the way he loves, uncompromisingly. After Rick makes an indecorous innuendo (that Ilsa is a slut), Ilsa cannot bear it and leaves. Since she is still in love with Rick and is, in part, sustained in her bland marriage to Laszlo by the memories of their brief time in Paris, she can bear neither Rick's exhibition of hatred nor his soiling of those memories. The next day (when Rick is sober), he entreats her (at the lingerie stand) to explain why she left him, and after she refuses, he offers his own explanation: she must have left him because she thought she could not tolerate a life on the run with a noble rebel like Rick;[33] it wasn't that she did not love him. Had Rick's explanation prevailed, Rick's soul, or heart, might have been restored. Her leaving him would not be proof of his undesirability but instead would serve as a lesson that the life of a freedom fighter is incompatible with the life of a lover. When, however, Ilsa (in response) reveals to Rick that she was married to Laszlo even while Rick and she were in love in Paris, Rick's explanation and his heart have nothing on which to stand. Now, it must appear to Rick that Ilsa dispensed with him, unfeelingly and unscrupulously, because he lost a nobility contest with Laszlo. Ilsa judged Rick's heart inferior to Laszlo's, and therefore she discarded him as if he meant nothing. This explains why after Ilsa's disclosure Rick goes to war with both Laszlo and Ilsa and by extension the free world.[34] He will bring down Laszlo and let the free world die to make her pay for what she did.[35] The man who was once all heart goes to war over his heart the way the Reich goes to war for the heartland (i.e., to win back land that is rightly hers). Rick and the Reich have in common the belief that their cause is worth any price. At this point, one cannot help but wonder whether there is anything to the fact that the words *Rick* and *Reich* have the same root[36] and that the first name of Rick's German nemesis is Hein*rich* (my emphasis). In any case, Rick's private war on behalf of his heart has made him a valuable asset to his onetime heartfelt enemy.[37] Is this an accident of the plot or does it reveal a commonality between the Reich and Rick—this quintessential American?

Just as Ilsa's disclosure seems destined to result in Rick's continued corruption,[38] so Rick's exhibition of hatred seems destined to further Ilsa's disillusionment. As the film makes obvious, Ilsa is still in love with Rick and is not in love with Victor. In her first act of the film she requests a song that helps bring to mind Paris, while her story (referred to above) describes a young woman being moved by the stirring words and profound insights of a political idealist, whom the woman had worshipped and who had served as a guiding light in everyway, but who was only able to generate in the woman "a feeling she *supposed* was love."[39] The love she feels for Victor is more political than erotic. It is born of an abstraction and sustained by an abstraction, as opposed to the love affair she had with Rick, which was not based on knowledge, but feeling.[40] With Victor, thoughts or principles are everything. Victor's most important principle is that the free world must resist the Reich. It follows that the Reich must attempt to kill Victor and that Ilsa must worship Victor for his principled struggle.[41] Rick's thoughts, by contrast, are not even worth a franc. Ilsa's love for Victor is more voluntary, like the cause she supports. Ilsa's love for Rick is more the product of seduction. Ilsa loves Victor because of what she knows, or because of her belief in and devotion to their cause. Ilsa is in love with Rick because of what she wants to know or because of something she cannot express but wants to experience. Rick and Ilsa's derailed love affair left in place a memory that seemed to supplement her marriage to Laszlo; but now that Rick's hatred is manifest, what power does this memory continue to wield? As Ilsa suggests, it would have been better for all had they never come to Casablanca.

After Ilsa tells Rick that she was married to Victor even while they were in Paris, Ilsa hopes to have no further contact with Rick so as to leave intact the good memories she had of Rick. This is all she can do, since Rick's hatred makes it impossible for her to explain the reason for her leaving him in Paris. Destiny, however, will not let matters stand thus, for Ilsa learns (from Ferrari at the Blue Parrot) that Rick holds the letters of transit she and Victor need to escape from Casablanca. And since Rick makes plain that he will not let them have the letters because of Ilsa, she has no choice but to see Rick again and expose herself to his attempts to hurt her. The rehabilitation of the world depends on her ability to rehabilitate Rick. This she will attempt in another after-hours talk in Rick's office. Preceding this confrontation, however, *Casablanca* supplies two scenes that must be understood if we are to understand the outcome of this confrontation and of the film as a whole.

In the first, the Bulgarian refugee Annina Brandel (at the suggestion of Renault) sits down at Rick's table to ask for help. Her request falls into two parts: in the first part, Annina asks Rick to vouch for Renault; in the second part, Annina wants Rick to vouch for her. In the first part, although Annina's questions, and Rick's answers, are part of a series of events that may culminate in her having coerced sex with Renault and although—as Rick notes— Annina is "underage," Rick has no difficulty listening to the woman's account. In the second part, however, when Annina asks Rick to ease her doubts about herself, Rick does have difficulty, as we see:

ANNINA: [In a manner evocative of sympathy] Monsieur [Rick], you are a man. If someone loved you very much so that your happiness was the only thing that she

wanted in the world [Rick turns away and begins to grimace], and she did a bad
thing to make certain of it, could you forgive her? . . .
RICK: [Interrupting. Still, looking away, that is, inwardly] Nobody ever loved me
that much.
ANNINA: And he never knew, and the girl kept this bad thing locked in her heart,
that would be alright, wouldn't it?

The film makes clear that Annina's hypothetical question induces Rick to reflect
on his own life, not hers, on Ilsa's betrayal and the pain it caused him, not
whether Annina should prostitute herself for the prospect of a good life in Ame r-
ica—as opposed to living a hellish life in Bulgaria where "the devil has the people by the throat." Rick, under the spell induced by Annina's question, advises
her to go back to Bulgaria. His tone indicates that his advice is influenced by the
memories the woman's question stirs. Her question, then, succeeds too well. It
makes so vivid the worst day of his life—Ilsa's betrayal—that he cannot but
advise the woman not to betray her husband. Moments later, after Annina confesses that "if Jan should find out" he would never understand, Rick brusquely
cuts her off, wishes her well, and walks off. When the woman came to Rick's
table, Rick playfully invited her to share a drink with him, but, as we see, his
mood grew irritable. Rick soured not because he is disgusted that the world
places this estimable woman in an awful situation, but because her fidelity to her
husband reminds him of Ilsa's infidelity to him and of his awful situation. The
sting of this memory helps explain, in the next scene, Rick's callous treatment of
Ilsa: he tells Ilsa that he'll ask Sam to play "As Time Goes By" for her, adding
sarcastically, "I believe that's your favorite tune." Annina's account reopens
Rick's wound and induces Rick to issue one of his own. The woman's account
not only solicits from Rick his worst, but his best. After needling Ilsa, Rick fixes
the outcome of the roulette table enabling Jan to "win" the money the couple
needs to begin a new life in America. Rick's charity prevents the woman from
sacrificing her virtue and from cheating on her husband and, perhaps, from doing to Jan what Ilsa did to him. Rick cheats so the woman doesn't have to. When
one compares Rick's willingness to assist the Bulgarian couple, whom the free
world does not know and would not miss, an act that costs him "a couple of
thousand francs," with his refusal (made evident just a few moments later) to
assist Ilsa and Victor, whom the free world knows and needs, an act that could
earn Rick at least 200,000 francs, it will become clear that Rick has become the
archangel of Aphrodite. As Rick says—in response to Renault's accusation that
he is a "rank sentimentalist"—"put it down as a gesture to love."[42]

In the second scene, which occurs a little after the first, Laszlo leads Rick's
band and most of his clientele in the playing of the "Marseillaise" in response to
the German officer corps' singing "Die Wacht am Rhein." The scene is dripping
with patriotism. Even Yvonne, the turncoat of sorts,[43] sings the "Marseillaise"
passionately. In effect, Laszlo eliminates the neutrality of Ricks Café. Laszlo's
boundless patriotism fills the room and most of Rick's clientele. And in the
midst of it, the camera supplies a close-up of Ilsa's face which glows with love

for her husband. It is as if at that moment Laszlo embodies the cause of freedom. He is the idea of justice brought down to earth, and she is its most fervent disciple.

The first scene is emblematic of Rick. The second, of Ilsa. And, when Ilsa enters Rick's office to get from him the letters of transit, the archangel of Aphrodite squares off against the somewhat wavering disciple of Athena.

Ilsa's effort to change Rick's mind falls into four parts. First, Ilsa appeals to their common political cause, but—since it is his cause no longer, this fails. Then, Ilsa appeals to their former love and suggests she is now willing to reveal why she left him, but—since Rick considers her an opportunist ("you'll say anything now to get what you want"), this also fails. Next, Ilsa scolds him for being abhorrently selfish, a weakling, and a coward, but—since Rick has accepted, provisionally perhaps, a nihilistic worldview, this has no effect on him whatsoever. And, last, Ilsa appeals to Rick's admiration for Laszlo, but—since Rick will not subordinate himself to any man (i.e., Rick will die in Casablanca, so shouldn't Laszlo?), this fails too. Realizing that it is impossible to persuade a man who is motivated not only not to help her but to hurt her and who claims not to believe in anything except himself, Ilsa threatens to shoot Rick unless he gives her the letters of transit. Rick responds by encouraging her to pull the trigger. He tells her that if she believes in her cause, she must shoot him. He even takes a step toward her to improve her chances and tells her that she would be doing him a favor by killing him. This is a moment tailor-made by Rick. Rick wants confirmation of his importance to Ilsa, but he cannot trust what she says. So Rick conducts an experiment. On one side of the balance, Rick has Ilsa put his life; on the other, everything else—Victor, her life, their cause, and the freedom of mankind; and then Rick forces Ilsa to decide which side weighs more upon her heart. When Ilsa cannot pull the trigger, and instead melts into his arms, Rick has his answer.

In a sense, so do we. When Rick appears to have Ilsa's love again, eros conquers justice (at least for the time being), and it is a conquest regarding which the film wholly approves. For the film adorns Rick and Ilsa's kiss in romantic music. For a moment we even hear their ballad "As Time Goes By." As they kiss, we are moved not by Ilsa's commitment to political freedom, but by Rick and Ilsa's love for one another. Given what is now taking place on the screen, it appears that *Casablanca* is set in the midst of a cosmic struggle between freedom and tyranny not in order to make us partisans of freedom, but to make us partisans of love.[44] The freedom of the world is but a chip the lover places on the roulette table of life in order to win verification of true love. The political desperation of the world manifests the romantic's commitment to love. After their passionate embrace, the ensuing conversation adds flame to the fire of their rekindled love. Rick learns why Ilsa left him in the manner she did. On the one hand, she was married to Victor, and Victor needed him. On the other hand, she was looking out for Rick. Her duplicity—like the prospective duplicity of the Bulgarian woman—was for his benefit and so much more. A few moments ago, Rick had reason to envy Jan Brandel. Now, Rick need envy no one. A woman, whose beauty of form is only surpassed by her beauty of soul, is in love with him. When Rick asks Ilsa what's to happen next, she confesses that she does not have the strength to run out on Rick again, but insists that she help Victor escape, so that he can proceed with his life's work, while they can be together.

As in Paris, Ilsa's duplicity has in mind to protect two men and a movement. And, although here, in running out on Victor instead of Rick, she will be violating her wedding vow in addition to betraying and hurting Victor, there is justice in her decision. Her marriage to Victor, as Ilsa suggested with her story, was the product of a youthful indiscretion. She was swayed not by love but by idealism and the direction that Laszlo gave her while she was young and full of doubt. In addition, their marriage is unknown to all, and so Ilsa's divorcing Victor for Rick will not bring Victor dishonor—which is important, since Victor is motivated by honor. Also, precisely so as not to give the impression they are married, and also because of Victor's work, Ilsa's and Victor's lives are not well interwoven, so a divorce will not necessitate that either restructure their lives.[45] Their marriage, like Victor's work, is an abstraction, which the film stresses by never portraying them in a moment of passion. Their bloodless marriage seems partly the result of Victor's psychic anatomy. Victor is a man who measures himself not by what and whom he needs, but by what and who need him. As he says, he is at the head of a movement. And, had he never said it, you could guess it just by watching him walk. He is a pillar of stone, unwavering and above the crowd. He does not need to be completed by another; he is already complete. So when Ilsa tries to drive home a point, Victor says, "You don't even have to say it. I would believe." Without Ilsa, Rick becomes a cynical shadow of his former self. Without Ilsa, so Ilsa suggests, Victor would not miss a step. As Ilsa states, "whatever I'd say, you would carry on." Victor, in fact, admits as much when he asks Rick to take Ilsa to America. Although this is an act of heroic self-sacrifice, it not only reflects his belief in his own self-sufficiency but the lower priority he gives to love in relation to justice. Back in Paris, Rick, when faced with a similar situation, planned to get married to Ilsa despite his underground work. His love for Ilsa simply meant too much to him for him to contemplate life without her. The solution that is arrived at in Rick's office would seem to leave everyone happy: Rick and Ilsa have one another, and Laszlo will have his cause. Nevertheless, Ilsa has her doubts, for she confesses to Rick that she is confused and entreats Rick to do what is right for all involved. And, perhaps to Ilsa's regret, Rick does.[46]

After Ilsa's explanation puts the past to rest, there is still the problem of the future. As Rick says, "it's still a story without an ending." In the end, Rick supplies the missing ending in more than one sense of that word. Rick crafts a solution that takes into account small details and large, the needs of the one and of the many. In the words of Renault, after Rick issues him a command, "You think of everything, don't you?" To Casablanca, he bestows Rick's Café Americain, and assures its continued existence by selling it to the corrupt Ferrari, whose lack of scruples will assure that no official will go unbribed in the interest of keeping it open. The good time that Rick's Café provides is a sanctuary from the dreary world the Reich wishes to create which leaves no room for chance, or for the spontaneity that makes life charming. Rick's survives to remind the captives of the Reich why freedom is worth fighting for.

To Ferrari, he sells Rick's.

To his former employees, he gives secure employment, and boosts Sam's take of the profits.

To his friend Renault, he gives the continued right to win at roulette. And when his plan goes slightly out of whack because of Renault's alerting Strasser, Rick lays the groundwork for Renault's rehabilitation. For in slipping up, Rick is forced to kill Strasser, which obliges Renault to choose between supporting Rick or a Nazi for whom he has contempt. When Renault takes the predictable course, and sides with the man he admires, he dumps the Vichy water he is about to drink, and is symbolically rebaptized in the ideals of the Resistance, a struggle for human rights based on the principles of the French Revolution.

To Victor he gives Ilsa, so as to maintain the wholeness of his life, which will enable him to continue his work with maximum effectiveness. Victor is more dependent than he realizes. Here, of course, he does not fully realize his dependence on Rick. Earlier, at Rick's Café, he is similarly blind. Victor's stirring exhibition of patriotism and leadership is dependent on Rick's assent, which Victor either does not see or fails to acknowledge, even after his exhibition results in Rick's being closed. Rick sees that the loss of Ilsa would have been more disabling to Victor and his cause than either Ilsa or Victor appreciates. Victor's flaw is embedded in his name. He loves victory and what it brings—honor. Honor requires one to be honored, but is threatened by the acknowledgement of such dependence; for to act out of a desire for popularity would not be honorable. Rather than acknowledge this dependence, Victor clings to abstractions, like destiny, and supposes that he could live without Ilsa. Knowing more about love and the human soul than Victor, Rick sees that human happiness requires more than abstractions. Rick protects Victor from himself.

To America, where it is December 1941 and everyone is asleep—neutral—Rick gives Victor and Ilsa. There they will do for America what they did for Casablanca; for in America "the ceiling is unlimited." Just as they impregnated Casablanca—the white house of the Algerian desert—with idealism, so they will impregnate the white house (i.e., the blank slate) of America—the desert of neutrality—with idealism, and, in addition, the White House of Washington D.C., the seat of government. Victor and Ilsa will remind America that the pleasures that freedom affords and the power that America has will not and should not last unless America is willing to act on principle. Without this, America risks becoming a nation of Renaults.

To the world, Rick gives an America more aware of the world's evils, for by giving America Laszlo and Ilsa, Rick hopes that America will eventually come to see its responsibility to enter the war. Of course, Japan's attack on Pearl Harbor on December 7, 1941 (and Hitler's subsequent declaration of war on America) is what actually shocked America into action, but Rick could not have foreseen the cupidity or shortsightedness of the Japanese and German govern-ments. Rick could only know, on that evening before the Japanese attack, that evil regimes exist and that Laszlo and Ilsa would eloquently warn America against them.

To Ilsa, he gives the sanctuary of America and a rechristened marriage. In preparation for Victor and Ilsa's boarding the plane, Rick commands Renault to write "Mr. and Mrs. Victor Laszlo" on the letters of transit. Rick forces their marriage into the public realm, where Victor will have to give it the respect it deserves. Moreover, in America, there will be no enemies from whom Victor must hide. So it will be easier for him to be a good husband to Ilsa. Back in La Belle Aurora—which means "the beautiful beginning"—Rick proposes that Rick and Ilsa get married in transit to Marseilles. Here, Rick gives to them in transit the marriage he once envisioned. And, by lying to Victor about the events of the previous night, Rick dispels in advance whatever doubts Laszlo may one day have regarding his wife's true affections and strengthens the foundation of their marriage.

Before Ilsa's admission of love had rehabilitated Rick, Rick professed, "I'm the only cause I'm interested in." Now he accepts responsibility (at Ilsa's re-quest) for the world and almost everyone he knows. He takes into account the cause—that is, justice—while also taking into account the happiness of friends. Rick, unlike the Reich, puts things in their place—establishes a hierarchy—without allowing things to be defined merely by their place. The hierarchy that the Reich establishes and plans to make universal puts things in their place while turning them into pure parts. The Reich does violence to the particular; Rick defends the particular.

Despite the humane comprehensiveness of Rick's ending, it abounds in problems. Since the film has been suggesting that to be in love is the greatest pleasure, does not Rick's ending do an injustice to Ilsa? Rick sacrifices her hap-piness to the war effort. Just because Rick professes omniscience about Ilsa's future opinion does not make him right. We still need to weigh what Rick says against the film as a whole and our own understanding. Were we not led to be-lieve that "the world would always welcome lovers"? Rick's ending does not welcome her love, but forces her to accept a passionless marriage to Victor. Rick asserts that Ilsa must, for the sake of the cause, view herself and her love as part of Victor's work. Her marriage becomes a cog in the war machine. Does this not put Ilsa in a position similar, albeit remotely, to the Bulgarian woman? Now Ilsa will be forced to sleep with a man she really does not love for the greater good. The rationale Rick uses—that Ilsa is a part of Victor's work—to support this sacrifice is fascism writ small, and since it comes in a battle with fascism itself, one might excuse it. But what is Ilsa supposed to do after the war is over? Rick's ending eliminates the conflict that overwhelmed Ilsa in Rick's office not by reconciling her two sides, but rather by forcing one side of her to give way to the other.

Ilsa's rehabilitation of Rick succeeds too well. Before, he was the only cause he would fight for. He would not allow a universal principle or cause to assign him a role. After, he accepts the cause as a universal and allows it to assign him the role of demiurge. And as demiurge he assigns roles to others. Before, one might say, he was the ultimate defender of particularity. After, Rick is a committed teleologist. In his rehabilitated state, he articulates a worldview that contradicts the content of the film, "the problems of three people do not amount to a hill of beans." The film implies that the problems of three people, two in particular, and one especially so, do indeed amount to a hill of beans. Does this not explain the enduring popularity of the film? People love *Casablanca*, because they care about the characters the film depicts, and they care because the film uses every cinematic trick in the book to produce this result. *Casablanca* is propaganda American style. In glorifying particular people, *Casablanca* stands in stark contrast to the Reich, for whom human life—that is, the particular person—is cheap and not worthy of consideration. *Casablanca* glorifies the individual and individuality; the Reich tramples on both. It would assign a place to all people and for a 1000 years. For millions this place will be a grave.

While Rick's ending finds a place for everyone, it does not seem to have a place for him. For, despite the fact that he had it in his power—and the plot would have allowed for this result—to return to America in order to formally join the war effort, he instead remains a free agent. Rick does not become just another partisan. He tells Ilsa at the airport, "What I've got to do you can't be any part of." Rick says nothing about joining a resistance movement or taking orders. Rather, he suggests that he already knows what to do. The issue is not in what he will take part, but rather that Ilsa can take no part in it. Rick is really a part of nothing. In the final scene, he walks into the mist, God knows where. We shall never see him again, and few if any people will know what he did. For all we know, and all he cares, he will die in an unmarked grave. It seems that in getting back Paris, Rick's heart was made whole precisely so that he could give it away. In the mist of the underground effort against tyranny toward which he walks lies neither money nor glory nor love.[47] None of these goods explains why there are things that "[he's] got to do." So why does he do them? What's in it for him?

I think that the fact that it is impossible to say explains what is most alluring about Rick. He does the right thing for the feeling of doing the right thing. In giving back Ilsa, Rick gives up ever asking what's in it for him. This is the meaning, I think, of his speech to Ilsa, which, on the surface, is an elongated version of what Ilsa said to Rick the previous night. Then, Ilsa criticized Rick for being selfish. Here, he says the problems of the individual do not matter. There is not much difference. The important thing is not Rick's words, but why they are said and what they reflect. Rick persuades himself to sacrifice the thing most important to him in the world for the greater good. He cannot stomach doing otherwise; but to make sense of it, Rick needs the beautiful. So he articulates a beautiful sentiment: that the world matters a great deal and, therefore, requires individuals to sacrifice on its behalf, even though the individual may never get anything for it; that the world does not care about the individual, and yet the individual must care about the world; and that we must persist, for it's a "crazy world." More interesting than the content of Rick's moral imperative is its source: Rick himself. Rick is the rogue progeny of Jefferson, for he is moral, free, and universal. He defends justice, takes no orders, and is tied to no place in particular.[48] *Casablanca* gives him (and others who embody his soul type) the recognition he deserves but will not seek because of the encumbrances that accompany its pursuit. In the film, as Rick returns to the fight, we are to imagine he carries in his heart Ilsa and Paris; outside the film, as Americans turn to the fight, his disciples carry him.

EPILOGUE

The study we have made of *Casablanca* runs into difficulty as one delves into the facts of the film's production. *Casablanca* is not the product of one searing intellect. The film had three main screenwriters.[49] Even the play on which it is based had two authors. Moreover, scenes were changed at the last minute.[50] This gives rise to an obvious question: how could a film so haphazardly made offer a coherent argument worthy of study? Although the facts of *Casablanca*'s production make clear it is not the work of a political philosopher, the facts do not prove that *Casablanca* does not convey timeless truths of political philosophy, even though strictly speaking it is not a work of political philosophy.

First, although the facts of *Casablanca*'s production may be widely known, they are not easy to interpret. For example, Hal Wallis, the film's producer, wrote *Casablanca*'s final line: "Louis, I think this is the beginning of a beautiful friendship." He selected this line in preference to an alternative he also wrote: "Luis, I might have known you'd mix your patriotism with a little petty larceny." Why did Wallis go with the first alternative rather than the second? Did he flip a coin? Did the first sound better to him? Or did Wallis intuit, or understand, that Rick, despite his self-description, was once again under the spell of the noble or beautiful and therefore saw that the first alternative fit better than the second? If it was this last reason that accounted for or contributed to Wallis's choice, then Wallis's choice was not purely his. It was governed by the film's argument. Wallis pulled the trigger, but the film's logos affected his aim. Although one might cite many instances in which the film's script was changed on the fly, this does not prove that the film lacks a substantive teaching.

Still, how does one explain away Howard Koch's view of the film, one of the film's main screenwriters? He said "I've got almost a mystical feeling about *Casablanca* . . . that it made itself somehow?"[51] Does not the fact that one of *Casablanca*'s main screenwriters cannot identify the source of the film's coherence strongly suggest that the film lacks an argument meriting serious consideration? Not necessarily, for *Casablanca* is governed to some extent by its subject matter—World War II and the ideas motivating the countries fighting it. Wars are necessarily about big questions and World War II in particular, because abstract principles inspire one side to initiate it, which forces the other side to call to mind their own principles so as to summon their absolute commitment to victory. So, it should not surprise us that *Casablanca*'s subject matter itself guides the film's makers and limits their choices. The reason *Casablanca* embodies weighty questions is because its subject matter embodies weighty questions. Its plot merits thought, because in orchestrating its development *Casablanca*'s makers, whether they knew it or not, were forced to think about what would happen when certain weighty principles collide.

For example, let us say that the film's makers, in order to appeal to moviegoers, needed to feature a conflict between Blaine and Lund. Would not the range of choices the film's makers faced be limited by the regime and political context from which each character emerged? I suppose you could have made Rick the fiery patriot and Laszlo the love-torn, cynical individualist, but given the fact that Czechoslovakia had been taken over and America was not yet at war and has individualism sown into its founding documents, this would make less sense than what *Casablanca* depicted. Another example: let us say the film's makers also wanted to portray an uneasy coexistence between Renault and his German sponsors, so as to charm audiences with Renault's mundane hypocrisy and to setup his eventual conversion. The film's makers would have needed to solve a problem: to make Renault appear to be content with the status quo without causing his eventual rejection of it to seem artificial. So the film shows Renault enjoying petty pleasures and abusing his power as a sign of his freedom and virtue, while making clear as day that he is a veritable courtier. That is, Renault lacks freedom and virtue, exactly what he thought he had. In solving this problem, the film's makers—perhaps without knowing it—were wrestling with how the principles of the French Revolution might be reconciled with the authoritarianism of the Reich. Since Renault and Strasser are, roughly speaking, products of the former and latter, respectively, the fact that their relationship duplicates on a small scale the relationship between their regimes suggests that *Casablanca*'s makers solved this problem in a way that makes sense.

In spinning out the plot of *Casablanca*, the makers of the film were forced to think politico-philosophically. For each of *Casablanca*'s main characters represents ideas or political principles, and the principles each represents are connected to the regime or the political context from which each character springs. *Casablanca*'s main characters are, as others have noticed, archetypes.[52] Although Germany, France, and America may not have been reducible to ideas, because the film features conflicts between characters from these regimes rather than featuring conflict between the regimes themselves (there are no battle scenes in *Casablanca*), in order to maintain the coherence of these characters the film simplifies these countries. In deciding what direction to take the film's plot, in creating difficulties for the characters to overcome, the film's makers were governed by the political principles these characters embody, because the situations that would most vex the film's characters and entertain audiences would be those that would expose the problematic nature of the principles these characters embody. Perhaps "the mystical feeling" to which Koch refers was generated by the ideas he sensed he and his colleagues were all grappling with as they were hashing out the course of the film.[53]

While it seems to be the case that the depth of *Casablanca* originated with the war as much as, or more than, with its makers, it would be wrong to assume that the film's depth owes nothing to its makers. Although *Casablanca* may have been the product of several minds, its makers were thoughtful and intended to inspire thought. Take, for example, a memo written by Hal Wallis to Michael Curtiz, the director, requesting that a scene be redone:

> I saw the dailies last night, and there is one thing I would like you to shoot . . . where Ilsa comes into the café and asks Rick if he has taken care of everything, and Rick says, "Everything." At that point, if you remember, I wanted Rick to look at Ilsa a moment and then kiss her so that the audience will realize later that this was his goodbye.

According to Lawrence Mark, vice president of production, Wallis's memo to Curtiz had nothing to do with economics. Rather, "It's purely about adding another layer to a scene which the audience won't realize until afterwards, if then."[54] This is interesting for two reasons. First, it indicates that in arguing that Blaine becomes political in the sense that he thinks about the good of the whole, and assigns roles to people, we read Rick the way at least Wallis conceived him. Second, it indicates that at least one of *Casablanca*'s makers designed the film as a vehicle for thought. *Casablanca* was not just, as the Epsteins were wont to call it, "slick shit."[55]

We should also not discount the extent to which the film's argument was indeed the product of one thoughtful mind—that of Murray Burnett, one of the authors of *Everybody Goes to Rick's* (later changed to *Everybody Comes to Rick's*).[56] It seems to me that the essential ingredients of the film are discretely present in the play.[57] In the play, a "mysterious café owner bets a womanizing French policeman that a heroic anti-Fascist will escape." The cynical indifference of Rick, his individualism—as we have construed it—was conceived by the playwright. Even Rick's refusal to drink with customers or sell exit visas and his cruel treatment of an ex-mistress are in the play. Moreover, "In the end the hero tricks the policeman and sends the woman away with the other man."[58] So, as in the film, Rick's stated indifference to the noble does not quite explain him. Rick is the brainchild of Burnett, as are most of the seminal details of *Casablanca*: the Bulgarian couple, the horrible choice the woman is forced to make by the policeman, their dreams of a better life in America, her plea for help from Rick, Rick's response to her, Ugarte and his conversation with Rick, Rick's standing guard over his gambling parlor, Strasser's standing guard over the Reich by denying the anti-Fascist Laszlo entry into Europe, Ferrari—the leader of the black market and the owner of a rival café who would like to buy Rick's, Laszlo's anthem contest with the Germans, Sam—the piano-player friend who offers to take Rick fishing and go drinking with him until his ex-lover leaves. Analogues to every important character of the film are present in the play. Even "As Time Goes By" is in the play. The argument of *Casablanca* seems to me very much the brainchild of Murray Burnett.

In *Round Up the Usual Suspects* Aljean Harmetz seems to arrive at the opposite conclusion: "Of the four major characters in *Everybody Comes to Rick's*, only the noble Victor Laszlo remains essentially the same in the movie."[59] While I would not dispute this claim, or the assertion that *Casablanca* substantially varies from *Everybody*, or that the greatness of the film owes more to its makers than Burnett, I believe that the decisions that Koch and the Epsteins made followed the lead of the play. The Epsteins, for example, came up with the Rick-Renault relationship. They seem to have softened Renault's viciousness laying the groundwork for his friendship with Rick. Although the play places Rick and Renault in a hostile relationship it lays the groundwork for the Epsteins' modification. In the play both Rick and Renault exemplify indifference to the evil of the Nazis. Whether they are friends or not, they might as well be. Another example: In the play, Renault stresses his independence from the Gestapo. The Epsteins see this as an arrogant boast and exploit it for comic material. They come up with the idea of having Renault dutifully and somewhat obsequiously leave Rick's office upon being summoned by Strasser just as he boasts to Rick how independent he is. Here too the Epsteins exploit an idea already present in the play. Another example: Although the play has Ferrari attempt to buy Rick's Café, it does not have him attempt to buy Sam. Koch adds this so as to allow Rick to make known that he does "not buy or sell human beings."[60] The Epsteins, in turn, add Ferrari's response, "That's too bad. That's Casablanca's leading commodity." All this is wonderful, but as Harmetz admits, the play features "a city where everything is bought and sold," and the owner of Rick's does not sell exit visas.[61] So, the Rick of the play—in a city in which "everything can be bought and sold"—implicitly eschews trading in human flesh. Once again, the film makes explicit a point the play implies but chose not to express. Lastly, in the play, Rick is "a self-pitying married lawyer who has cheated on his wife."[62] Moreover, after his love affair in Paris ends and the Germans take Paris, he remains in Paris for a month hoping he will run into his ex-lover.[63] Whether the play's alternative would have made for great cinema is unclear; however, it seems to me that the alternative that the film decides on is faithful to the ideas of the play. As the play has it, Rick, a servant of the law, pursues love despite the fact that the world is crumbling around him and that he is unlikely to find let alone change the mind of the woman he loves. This seems to correspond with what Rick says in the film, that his "insides were kicked out" after Ilsa left him. Moreover, while the play does not give Rick a bawdy set of freedom fighting credentials, again one might say that Rick's political idealism is suggested by his profession.

While the facts of the film's production are interesting, they neither confirm nor disprove our assumption that *Casablanca* is a film worthy of thought. The thoughtfulness or thoughtlessness of this film, as with any film or text, is conveyed by the work itself. A close study of it, I believe, reveals its strengths and limitations and how seriously it should be taken.

NOTES

1. It was therefore a stroke of brilliance or perhaps good luck that the makers of the film selected actors such as Peter Lorre, Humphrey Bogart, Sydney Greenstreet, and Ingrid Bergman. All speak in their own characteristic way and are good at portraying idiosyncrasy.

2. LASZLO: "One hears a great deal about Rick in Casablanca." All quotes from *Casablanca* can found at:http://www.geocities.com/classicmoviescripts/script/casablanca.pdf.

3. The film makes a point of disclosing not only Rick's unwillingness to participate in the Casablanca underground, but also the Casablanca underworld. RENAULT [in Rick's office]: "There are many exit visas sold in this café, but we know that you've never sold one."

4. For a summary of the various ways that *Casablanca* has been interpreted see Aljean Harmetz, *Round Up the Usual Suspects: The Making of Casablanca* (New York: Hyperion, 1992), 347-54. For an illuminating study of the film, see Richard Corliss' analysis in Howard Koch, *Casablanca, Script, and Legend* (Woodstock: Overlook Press, 1973), 163-78.

5. Pétain's statement is difficult to translate and may be untranslatable. My translation fits the context, at least as I understand it. See Michael Palmer's comments in Chapter 2.

6. A similar point is conveyed on a pedestrian level in the scene immediately following. An English couple, evidently new to Casablanca and dining at an outdoor café, is startled by the commotion going on outside the Palais de Justice. A stranger at the next table explains what's going on and warns them to take care, because Casablanca is "full of vultures, vultures everywhere." While doing so, he picks the man's pocket. The hypocrisy of France has filtered down to its citizens and denizens. Under cover of justice, they act unjustly. Hypocrisy is one of *Casablanca*'s concerns. Note that when Ferrari evinces concern for Ugarte, Rick calls him a "fat hypocrite." Rick's comment is priceless. In pointing out Ferrari's duplicity, Rick, by contrast, is honest to the point of being rude.

7. Throughout the film the Reich is depicted as attempting to conquer chance. FERRARI: "It would take a miracle to get you [Laszlo] out of Casablanca, and the Germans have outlawed miracles." And after Strasser asks Renault what will happen to his allegiance to Vichy should "the prevailing wind" change, Renault says: "Surely the Reich doesn't admit that possibility?" As Rick and Ilsa both say "it's a crazy world." In a crazy world, anything can happen, and chance is the only law of nature. One might say, then, that the Reich is at war with nature herself.

8. Later, after Rick complains that Renault's men in looking for the letters of transit made it difficult for him to open, Renault tells him that he ordered his men to be "especially destructive," because this would impress his German sponsors.

9. Later, in Rick's office, Rick alludes to Renault's servility to the Gestapo. In response, Renault proudly asserts, while digging his hands into his gun belt, that in Casablanca he is master of his fate. In the very next moment, a subordinate barges in to inform him that Major Strasser has arrived. Rick, seeing the irony, says to Renault, "You were saying?" and then Renault immediately exits. Consider, also, that on the tarmac, Renault pretentiously greets Strasser with the following: "Unoccupied France welcomes you to Casablanca." To obscure the fact that Renault is not really his own man, Renault needs to hang on to the notion that

there is a substantive difference between occupied and unoccupied France. This and the sex he forces on desperate women support his deluded self-understanding. Consider also that in response to Strasser's suggestion that Renault is not committed to the Reich, Renault asserts that he has no conviction. He blows with the wind, as he puts it. Although Renault admits to being without an anchor, he suggests it's because he pulled it up. According to him, he is in control. In any case, the film leaves no doubt as to who is in charge of Casablanca. For example, see the scene in which Strasser orders Renault to close down Rick's. When Renault asks on what charge, Strasser says, "Find one." Renaults finds one—as he tells Rick—in the fact that gambling takes place at Rick's. And just as he does so, Rick's croupier—to Rick's chagrin—hands Renault his winnings. Although the scene is quite funny, it also further demonstrates Renault's hypocrisy. Finally, toward the end of the film, in response to Rick's entrapment scheme, Renault says, "Germany—(I mean) Vichy—would be very grateful." Of course, if there were <u>no</u> difference between occupied and unoccupied France, Strasser could arrest Laszlo on the spot.

10. Near the end of the film, in response to Rick's observation that his gun is pointed at Renault's heart, Renault asserts "that is my least vulnerable spot." Aeneas MacKenzie, after reading the play upon which *Casablanca* was based, said "that he saw 'the possibility of an excellent theme—the idea that when people lose faith in their ideals, they are beaten before they begin to fight. That was what happened to France and to Rick Blaine.'" See Harmetz, *Round Up the Usual Suspects*, 39.

11. In the scene alluded to in a footnote above, the pickpocket refers to Renault's "rounding up of liberals, refugees, and, of course, a beautiful young girl for Renault." One might say that the pickpocket is a protégé of Renault. There is in any case a parallel between them: both use principle as a disguise for self-interest. France rather than being the world's guiding light becomes a training ground for the "scum of the earth."

12. In Rick's, Renault recommends this wine to Strasser to go with the caviar they order.

13. When Strasser demands that Renault close Rick's after the singing of the "Marseillaise," Renault says, "But everybody is having such a good time." Strasser responds, "Yes, much too good a time. The place is to be closed."

14. At the bar in Rick's Café Rick breaks up a fight between Yvonne's new German beau and an anonymous Frenchman. He tells them either to keep off politics or leave. Of course, this all changes with the arrival of Victor and Ilsa.

15. In the conversation that takes place between Rick, Strasser, Renault, and another German officer, Rick is asked by both Germans whether he can imagine the Reich in Paris, London, and New York. Later, a group of German officers led by Strasser in a sense takeover Rick's by singing "Die Wacht am Rhein," which the film employs as the Reich's anthem.

16. The story of *Casablanca* was taken from a defunct play titled, *Everyone Goes to Rick's*. The title suggests that Rick's espouses equality, for all are welcome there. This line, by the way, is used by Renault at the airport in describing Rick's to Strasser.

17. The film showcases a variety of languages and culturally specific forms of address and attire.

18. Note, the other club in town is not called Ferrari's, but the Blue Parrot. The importance of Rick's to Rick is suggested by Rick when after selling his place to Ferrari he halfseriously reminds Ferrari of a debt he owes Rick's. It is as if Rick's stands for something and must live on.

19. On their way from the plane, Strasser admits to having heard of Rick's Café and of Rick. Also, as a friend of Rick's, Ilsa is offered a steep discount from a Casablanca street merchant. Regarding the emergence of a new hierarchy, we have this from Ferrari: "As leader of all illegal activities in Casablanca, I am an influential and respected man."

20. This seems to me a clever move by Ugarte. Had he made friendship the basis of his request, Rick would have turned him down just to prove he was not a friend. By putting the matter this way, Ugarte gives Rick the opportunity to accept his request without having to admit friendship. That Rick is not indifferent to Ugarte Rick suggests later that evening when

nursing the heartache brought about by Ilsa's sudden appearance. He succinctly sums up the day's events, saying "One in, one out." Ilsa fills a void Ugarte left behind.

21. Rick's mystique is also testified to by Renault who says to Ilsa that Rick is the kind of man that a woman cannot help but love. This is also supported by the title of the screenplay on which the film is based. In other words, it is not just that everybody is at Rick's, it is that everybody *goes to Rick's*. The question is, why does the title call attention to this fact?

22. Renault supposes that Rick's cynicism is a shell. Indeed, Rick is not a cynic to the core, as the end of the film makes obvious. Nevertheless, what does it mean that cynicism comes so easily to Rick or that he is so good at it, and what does his apparent cynicism have to do with his appeal?

23. Ferrari says of Rick, "A difficult customer, that Rick. One never knows what he'll do or why."

24. He says this to the patron who witnesses and comments on his refusal to help Ugarte.

25. Rick is therefore even somewhat neutral regarding his own self-interest. Consider also the scene where Rick tells Ilsa that by shooting him she would be doing him a favor.

26. After Laszlo is arrested at Rick's, Rick says, parodying a statement Laszlo has just made to Rick, "It seems that destiny has taken a hand." What's interesting about this is that Laszlo just invoked destiny to explain his own work on behalf of the Resistance and in order to persuade Rick to abandon his neutrality. Laszlo suggests that Rick's aloofness is a pretension; hovering above Rick is a destiny he cannot ignore without denying a part of himself. Laszlo uses an abstraction (destiny) to reattach abstract Rick to the world. When Laszlo is arrested, however, Rick uses Laszlo's abstraction in order to reassert his detachment. Rick sits back and watches destiny undermine Laszlo's partisan project and takes pleasure in it. This scene occurs right after Rick's *rapproachement* with Ilsa. It and the following scene, in which Rick conspires with Renault to entrap Laszlo, is part of *Casablanca*'s sting operation. Will Rick make off with Ilsa? Will Rick leave the Resistance's leader a broken man, perhaps in the same way that Ilsa once left him? His searching look, earlier in the film, of a plane departing the airport suggests he longs to leave. Or, will Rick give the letters of transit to Ilsa and Victor and sacrifice his own love on justice's behalf? Rick leaves us wondering what he will do next. He can do anything he wants. Thus, at this point Rick is abstracted also from us, and we are part of the world he seems to have in his hands. Like Renault, we are inclined to ask, "How do I know you'll keep your end of the bargain?"

27. See the scene mentioned above, where, in response to Laszlo's statement that without self-sacrifice the world will die, Rick says that this might be for the best. See also the conversation between Strasser, Renault, and Rick where, in response to Strasser's question about his nationality, Rick says that he's a drunkard, and therefore (according to Renault) a citizen of the world and neutral toward everything, including women. See also the scene in which Rick conspires with Renault to entrap Laszlo so that he can, ostensibly, live in peace with Ilsa. Renault is doubtful, because Rick has never shown interest in any woman. The ancient cynic, Diogenes, when asked about his citizenship, is said to have responded that he was *kosmopolites*.

28. On the one side, there is Strasser and the German officer corps, a member of which punches a Frenchman who objects to Yvonne's courtship with him because he is a member of the Reich. There is also the sycophantic Italian officer (Officer Tonnelli—he officiously greets Strasser at the airport), who the film suggests is obsessed with outdebating his French rival and scoring points with his superiors. On the other, there is the Resistance led by Laszlo and the numerous members of the Casablanca "movement." Rick's disassociation from this movement is indicated when Carl, right before heading off to a meeting, tries to tell Rick where he's going and is cut off by Rick.

29. See the scene where Rick rebuffs Ferrari's offer to join forces with him in establishing an underworld empire. As Rick says, "I do not buy or sell human beings." With Rick it is not the money but his independence that counts: "Suppose you run your business and *let me*

run mine" (My emphasis). Notice also that Renault thinks, erroneously, that Rick is in Renault's camp when he says that Rick has even fewer scruples than he.

30. As we see in a dialogue between Rick and Laszlo, Rick admits that the other side (the ignoble cause) would have paid better. Fighting on behalf on noble causes requires self-sacrifice.

31. As he says, "[his] insides [were] kicked out."

32. The former is said at Rick's; the latter the next day at the lingerie stand.

33. Rick's assumption is not so unreasonable in light of the fact that he does not know that Ilsa and Victor are married. Also, his explanation is consistent with his prediction that Ilsa will one day leave Laszlo. Life on the run with Laszlo will be no more tolerable to her than life on the run with Rick.

34. One of the conceits of the film is that Laszlo is indispensable. Recall that Strasser says to Laszlo that he "cannot be replaced." The survival of the free world is to be determined in Casablanca.

35. Consider the shifting significance of "As Time Goes By." First, for Rick it is a reminder of his heart's worst day and for Ilsa of her heart's best days. Second, it becomes a sign of Rick's ability to conquer his heart. Third, after Ilsa's disclosure, it as a sign of Rick's contempt both for Ilsa and their former love. What was once a reminder of their love affair Rick turns into a weapon.

36. *Rihhi* in old high German means "realm" or "powerful."

37. See the dialogue between Rick and Laszlo in his office. In an effort to get Rick to make available to him the letters of transit, he appeals to Rick's former idealism. Rick deflects this attempt by claiming he is now a saloonkeeper (that is, a businessman). Laszlo then offers to buy the letters, but Rick—in contradiction with his claim to be a saloonkeeper or businessman—says they are not for sale at any price, and for an explanation Laszlo should ask his wife. It is not that Rick is a saloonkeeper, and not an idealist, that explains his refusal to sell Laszlo the letters. It is that he is fighting on behalf of his heart. At first, he fought from his heart. Now, he fights over his heart. Seeking justice on behalf of it is now his cause. He turns his own heart into an ideal worth fighting for, and no amount of money can induce him to betray it. In any case, as the film suggests, it is not the case that Rick no longer respects Laszlo's cause. His conversation with Laszlo is cut short by Laszlo's indignation at hearing the singing of the Reich's anthem on the café floor. In response, Laszlo tries to commandeer Rick's Café's band, ordering it to play the "Marseillaise." At first the band refuses, but when Rick nods, it plays, and as a result Rick's is closed. If Rick was just a saloonkeeper he would not have broken his own rule ("no politics allowed") and risked the closing of his saloon in order to make a meaningless political point. (A pure saloonkeeper might have allowed Strasser to finish his song and then informed Strasser of his policy). So, it is not that Rick does not see the beauty in Laszlo's work. It is the fact that Rick *does* see its beauty and nevertheless is willing to see Laszlo's cause defeated that is significant. It signifies Rick's commitment to his own cause and the problematic nature of his own character.

38. See the dialogue between Ilsa and Rick in his office, later, in which Rick says, "I'm the only cause I'm interested in." If indeed Renault is right that Rick's cynicism is just a shell, the film here suggests that it may become more. His encounter with Ilsa has the potential to harden what might have been a provisional self-understanding into a philosophy of life.

39. See also the scene in their hotel room after Rick rejects Laszlo's attempt to buy the letters of transit. In response to Victor's confession that he loves Ilsa very much, all Ilsa will say is "Be careful." In this scene, Ilsa is portrayed as beset by doubts. Apparently, she wonders whether she should confess to Victor her fling with Rick so as to preempt Rick's disclosing it to Victor in an effort to hurt her.

40. In Rick's reminiscence, they make a deal to ask no questions. Their love is in part fueled by what they don't know. They make a game of it. Their mutual ignorance is supported

by Ilsa at the lingerie stand where she says that "we knew very little about each other when we were in love in Paris."

41. See Strasser's reference to Laszlo's eloquence.

42. There is no inconsistency between Rick's aforementioned cynicism and this gesture to love. There is a difference between a gesture—a token nod of the head, as it were—made on love's behalf and an act that is borne of being in love.

43. She was just seen arm in arm with a German officer. This soon results in fisticuffs between her German escort and a French soldier, who objects to Yvonne's indifference to the call of patriotism. When Rick sees Yvonne with the German, he jokes that she "has gone over to the enemy." This reflects the conflict that drives these two scenes, that between romance or eros and patriotism or justice.

44. Consider that as Rick and Ilsa make out, Laszlo risks his freedom and life at a meeting of the Casablanca underground. After the police dissolve the meeting, he narrowly escapes capture and injures himself fleeing. The film relegates Laszlo's heroic self-sacrifice to the background. Rick and Ilsa's love takes precedence over the welfare of the free world. One might also consider the globe that is on the screen in the beginning of the film, as well as the introduction. While beginning with a controversy that involves the whole world, we come to see that this controversy was merely a prelude to the happiness of two people.

45. The couple does not share a name or have children.

46. The problem is perhaps underscored by the mirror image we see of Ilsa in Rick's office as Carl climbs the stairs to take Ilsa back to her hotel. Ilsa is split in two and has been since Paris. The question is, can she be put back together or be made whole again?

47. The manner in which Rick rescues the Bulgarian couple illustrates Rick's indifference to all three. He could have just taken money out of his safe and given it to the couple. The illusion that the roulette wheel paid off to Jan, that Jan is "just a lucky guy," keeps Rick in the background—at least somewhat. He does not do it for the purpose of gaining recognition as a philanthropist. Moreover, Rick will not even accept a kiss from Annina, let alone what Renault had in mind.

48. Rick thrives everywhere; he is a citizen of the world. He is our Alcibiades. Is the film suggesting Rick is the superhero America wishes it could generate—an individual produced by the regime, who nevertheless stands outside of the regime and is dedicated to its welfare? The regime cannot contain him, but needs him to preserve itself. Thus, like Aristophanes' *Knights*, *Casablanca* would be suggesting that only a god could save democracy. Recall, again, the significance of Rick's act of charity in his gambling hall. He cheats or breaks the law so as to prevent another from cheating or breaking the law. For an alternative view of Rick, see Robert B. Ray, "The Thematic Paradigm" in *Signs of Life in the U.S.A.: Readings on Popular Culture for Writers*, ed. Sonia Maasik and Jack Solomon (Boston: St. Martins, 1997). Ray holds that Rick fits the American cinematic paradigm of the two-sided hero, part outlaw, part defender of the community.

49. Harmetz, *Round Up the Usual Suspects*, 13. *Round Up the Usual Suspects* offers a comprehensive and detailed account of *Casablanca*'s production, the circumstances within which it was made, and its cast.

50. Harmetz, *Round Up the Usual Suspects*, 10, 172. See also all of chapter 13, which shows the evolution of the film's ending, as well as Koch, *Casablanca, Script and Legend*, 9ff.

51. Quoted in Harmetz, *Round Up the Usual Suspects*, 13.

52. Harmetz, *Round Up the Usual Suspects*, 349ff.

53. According to Harmetz, a division of labor emerged between Casablanca's three main screenwriters. The Epstein twins provided comic flare; Koch provided political content. Screenwriter Casey Robinson was added to the mix later and helped develop the romantic content of the film. It is interesting that Murray Burnett claims that the idea for *Everybody* was hatched while in a "polyglot" Paris café having just returned from Vienna. The anti-Semitism that had taken over Viennese society and government horrified Burnett. He then concluded

that neutrality in the face of such obvious injustice was unconscionable. Koch, by the way, admits to having had communist leanings and was always on the far left. In light of this, one is not sure how seriously to take his claim that the film was being directed by cosmic forces. Indeed, one is not sure how seriously to take any of the many after-the-fact accounts of the origins of *Casablanca*.

54. Harmetz, *Round Up the Usual Suspects*, 29-30. Harmetz and Koch suggest that Wallis was deeply involved with *Casablanca*'s production. He was a hands-on producer.

55. In Harmetz, *Round Up the Usual Suspects*, see, for example, 43. Wallis chose the film's title, and—one suspects—much more. See 30.

56. As I understand it, *Everybody* was his idea.

57. See Harmetz, *Round Up the Usual Suspects*, 38-39. "'That first part [up to Rick's reminiscence] was very close to the play,' Epstein says. 'It was with the second half that we had trouble'" (Harmetz, *Round Up the Usual Suspects*, 46).

58. Harmetz, *Round Up the Usual Suspects*, 46.

59. Harmetz, *Round Up the Usual Suspects*, 49.

60. Harmetz, *Round Up the Usual Suspects*, 57.

61. Harmetz, *Round Up the Usual Suspects*, 38.

62. Harmetz, *Round Up the Usual Suspects*, 46.

63. Harmetz, *Round Up the Usual Suspects*, 50.

CHAPTER 11

A MOVIE SKEPTIC'S THOUGHTS ON *CASABLANCA*

LEON HAROLD CRAIG

I feel somewhat out of place as contributor to this volume, for I am fairly sure that the other contributors, and a majority of the likely readers, have a higher opinion of movies as an art form than do I. By this, I do not mean to deny their very considerable significance in a democratic culture—a different matter entirely about which I shall have more to say later. But unless there really are Muses who impart their wisdom to human beings, the profundity of movies will never be greater than that of the people who craft them. Therein for me is the root of the problem. And it naturally follows, of course, that this prejudice of mine regarding the inherent quality of movies would carry over to learned commentaries and interpretations that make much of them, to say nothing of theories and theoretical approaches to the study of the cinema. Not that I often read this sort of thing; but when I do, such efforts usually strike me as wasted ingenuity, being disproportionate to the intrinsic importance of the subject examined. That distinguished universities actually offer degrees in film studies I find slightly comical (though no more so than several other studies programs).

This said, I must in fairness add that I am equally sure that the other contributors, and doubtless many readers, have a more ample basis for their judgment about movies, both in general and with respect to particular films, than I do. Not the least of reasons that my watching the Academy Awards would be pointless is that it would be a rare year in which I would have seen more than one of the movies for which awards were being considered. I will eventually see some of them, but not presented in the format for which they were primarily intended. I am aware that seeing a movie on my family's TV is a significantly different experience than seeing it in a properly equipped public theatre as a member of a large audience of mainly strangers. But that difference, so far as I can tell, affects mainly its entertainment value—I've seen *Master and Commander* on both big and small screens and, for sheer thrilling entertainment, "there's just no comparison," as we say. I enjoy a good movie; but on an intellectual level, I really can't take any of them all that seriously. And this goes for

Casablanca, one of my very favorites, which I believe I have seen somewhere between fifty and a hundred times (I know I wore out a couple of VHS copies of it before acquiring it on DVD). And while the several interesting, well-crafted essays that make up the rest of this volume have enhanced the film's savor for me and prompted me to reflect more systematically on why the movie pleases me they have not materially affected my view of its 'philosophical' significance.

Partly as a consequence of the DVD explosion, with the various discussions about the making of the movie that are now typically included in the extra features the DVD version offers, I've come to the conclusion that movies too are like sausages. Too often respect for a movie that not only entertained me but impressed me as having some intellectual depth was greatly diminished by listening to the director's (or whoever's) account of how the movie was made. Ironically, one of the better illustrations of this takes its title (but so far as I can see, nothing else) from *Casablanca*. The first time I watched *The Usual Suspects* I was so intrigued that I immediately watched it again. I still found it intriguing, and thought provoking, as well as technically very slick. Excellent cinematography, interesting characters skillfully acted, intelligent dialogue, and, what is most important (as any competent Aristotelian knows), a strong plot, . . . or so it seemed, though I wasn't quite sure how I was to understand what really happened in the movie. I soon viewed it a third time and then made the mistake of choosing to hear the director and writer discuss their creation. They provide a lengthy, quite detailed narrative of how the whole was pieced together; and like most of these behind-the-scenes accounts, one is treated to amusing and bemusing anecdotes, as well as provided insights into modern techniques of moviemaking. But more to the point here, they made it painfully obvious that—far from having a coherent story with a clear, carefully considered thesis—these guys were to a considerable extent just winging it (as were the actors in some scenes). I learned, for example, that the dramatic opening scene of that movie was written years before there was any story for it to introduce: the writer simply thought it would make an effective scene. As a consequence of these and other unplanned twists and turns in the course of actually filming the movie, much of the final result was serendipitous. But what was most disconcerting was how creators' narrative on their film ends: they address the question that obviously puzzled viewers besides me—"What really happened?" "What is the reality here?"—such that everything we are shown adds up, makes sense, is coherent. From the tangle of their ambiguous responses emerges the powerful suspicion that these two talents haven't a clue themselves: they just strew intriguing possibilities all over the place, never having worked out the coherent synoptic perspective one has to presume exists for rational analysis of a film (or a novel, or dramatic poem, or other such piece of music) to be worth undertaking. Worth undertaking, that is, for the purpose of learning something worth knowing from the work being analyzed.

There is no such doubt about the portrayed slice of reality in *Casablanca*. That it is so totally, perfectly, beautifully coherent is doubtless intrinsic to why it remains so enjoyable, an established classic of cinema whereas, *The Usual Sus-*

pects is destined (this suspect suspects) to be soon forgotten. And yet, the two films were not altogether unlike in their making. A lot of serendipity and just winging it also contributed to *Casablanca*, as is exemplified by what is now commonly known about its last scene—puckishly acknowledged to us in Rick's ironic line: "But it's still a story without an ending," for that was so at the time his speaking it was captured on celluloid. Thus the apparent integrity of the film would seem to present something of a mystery. But, for that matter, so too does its perennial appeal, its charm—the latter mystery only further compounded by the plausibility of Umberto Eco's (in)famous assessment that, viewed critically, *Casablanca* is a mediocre film, banal, a hotch potch of clichés, a comic strip. How then do we explain the fact that it is nonetheless such a resounding success, almost universally regarded as a classic, and amongst the top ten (typically amongst the top three) of all reputable rankings of films?

James F. Pontuso's discussion of how stereotypes figure in the story may indirectly throw some light on the question. Any person who really does find all stereotyping offensive (and doubtless there are many today who think they do, given the relentless propagandizing we've all been subjected to) is not apt to enjoy *Casablanca*, since its ensemble of characters is made up almost entirely of stereotypes. Such a person, then, cannot recognize that this is precisely the means of showing a kind of multiculturalism in action, one of the film's special virtues. *Everyone Goes to Rick's* was the title of the original play on which the movie was based; that Rick's nightclub is the American melting pot writ small is intrinsic to the film's message. But whatever our abstract view about the morality of stereotyping, in our everyday lives most of us feel right at home with it, and for good reason. There is often considerable truth embedded in our stereotypes (about kids, cops, women, men, bureaucrats, bartenders, whatever—including the characteristics typical of people shaped by this rather than that culture). They are, after all, simply a kind of generalization, and generally speaking, generalizations facilitate human living; in their total absence, our behavior would remain perpetually childlike, indeed, infantile. *Casablanca*'s invocation of stereotypes for the most part simply plays on its audience's antecedent familiarity with those types; if in subtle ways it attempts to refine or even reform certain of them (as Pontuso shows that it does), the fact remains that the film relies on what Plato calls imitation and of a rather superficial sort.

Plato's dialogues, and his *Republic* in particular, have long provided me my intellectual architecture for both living and understanding life. Doubtless, my modest regard for movies derives in goodly measure from that fact. As with everything else of consequence, his analysis of dramatic art, so far as I understand it, seems essentially correct to me. As he presents it in his *Republic*, Plato has his own dramatic character, Socrates, criticize dramatic poetry from two distinct perspectives. His first critique is embedded in the thought experiment he leads his young partners to undertake: that of making "a city in logos" (i.e., in rational speech), on the assumption that the form of justice would be writ large therein—understanding the truth about justice being the ostensible goal of the entire portrayed conversation. Accordingly, the ground of this first critique is primarily moral and political. Regardless of what is strictly true or false, what does one want the citizens of one's regime —and especially its rulers—to believe is true about the most important matters (such as the relation of the divine to the human and about death and about virtue and its relation to happiness). Having analyzed what must and must not be said (the part of the critique bearing directly on the logos component of dramatic art), Socrates turns next to dramatic form: what should and should not be realistically portrayed, as opposed to merely narrated (which allows for appropriate moral comment)? This is followed by a consideration of the proper musical accompaniment for poetry: what melodic modes and rhythms engender moderate and courageous dispositions in young souls. The upshot of this first critique is that the most entertaining kinds of dramatic art must be banished from a good polity if, that is, nurturing and maintaining virtue in the citizenry—not that of providing pleasure—is one's foremost concern. Socrates has in mind an underlying danger here, and I shall return to consider its special pertinence to movies.

Socrates' second critique of poetry is focused on its intellectual adequacy. It comes late in the dialogue, almost at its end, after the ostensible goal of the discussion has been achieved: the form of justice in both a city and a man has been discerned, and it has been shown to be desirable for its own sake, being essential to true happiness. This second critique—the one fresh start in the dialogue that is not prompted by one the other interlocutors but is solely on Socrates' own initiative—is such as could be undertaken only in light of a proper understanding of philosophy, or love of wisdom.[1] A proper understanding of philosophy requires, first, a clarification of what it is to love something, and (second) what would count as true knowledge, or wisdom. This Socrates was obliged to provide by way of explaining what he meant in suggesting that their city in logos, to be at its best, would need rulers who were at once philosophers and kings. This second examination of poetry, comparing it with philosophy as a source of knowledge, is accompanied by Socrates' admission that there is "some ancient quarrel between philosophy and poetry."[2]

Translated in terms of the principal contributors to today's popular culture, Socrates' criticism amounts to this: that the poets (makers) of our movies and TV shows, as well as of our novels and plays, are essentially imitators of the appearance of reality, and as such are several steps removed from genuine knowers of that which they portray. There are, to be sure, rare exceptions to this dismissive critique of dramatic art as a source of knowledge and understanding (Shakespeare comes to mind[3]), but I know of no movie makers who qualify— who are, that is, sufficiently philosophical themselves as to provide spectacles worthy of intensive analysis and sustained contemplation. Moreover, the primary appeal of dramatic art is not to the intellect, but to the lower, irrational parts of the soul, to the desires and the emotions, thereby strengthening them simply by providing occasions for their exercise—an indulgence we mistakenly presume is harmless, without lasting psychic consequences. This is the surface of the criticism Plato has his Socrates expressly articulate in this latter consideration of poetry.

However, when the two critiques are integrated with the account of human nature the dialogue presents—which includes a most careful acknowledgment of the tyrannical longings at the base of the human soul—one confronts the deeper, more dangerous moral, hence political, problem drama presents, namely, that vice is inherently more interesting than is virtue (a truth exploited to the full in *The Usual Suspects*).[4] In order to make a virtuous character appealing, the dramatist must provide some vicious opposition for him to overcome. And if the hero's victory is to be fully satisfying, the villain must be formidable: intelligent, resolute, strong, courageous, facile, perhaps even witty and charming. In short, for a villain to be worthy of a hero's best efforts, he must be powerful. For purposes of moral education, this is hardly the way one would prefer vice be portrayed, since for many people, especially many young men, the attractions and attractiveness of power per se is greater than that of power encumbered with ordinary morality. Thus, to make a powerful hero more attractive for emulation than a powerful villain, he to some extent must also be a law unto himself, scorning some if not most of the niceties of conventional morality—which, from the perspective of maintaining decent political life, is not really the sort of thing that needs encouraging.

Returning now to *Casablanca*, does it not prove Plato right almost too perfectly? Begin with the last of my platonic criticisms. As Peter Augustine Lawler rightly notes, Laszlo is the film's "most perfectly admirable character"—dispassionately assessed, that is. But as he goes on to observe, "Critics have found Laszlo's idealistic devotion rather repulsive"—this despite "the intention of the film, which is to present him as a great *man*."[5] I doubt that the typical naïve viewer of *Casablanca* finds anything about Laszlo to be downright repulsive, but probably most people—and what is especially pertinent, most women—do not find him lovable (whether for his stoicism, his passionate idealism, or whatever). For that reason alone, few men wish to be like him. Our sympathies are all with Rick, whose basic goodness is liberally spiced with several roguish qualities (to call them nothing worse). And is this not the formula for engaging cinematic heroes generally: not paragons of virtue, but complex, all-too-human mixtures of virtue and vice? Thus, I find Paul A. Cantor's contention that Rick is cast in the mould of a Byronic hero entirely convincing, and the popular appeal of that model goes a long way toward explaining the appeal of *Casablanca*. A rake and a ramblin' man is naturally a lot more interesting as a dramatic figure than is a sober, law-abiding, tax-paying father working a routine job to support his wife and four kids. But the dubiety of the Byronic hero as a moral exemplar is precisely the problem, according to Plato's teaching. Even the thoroughly corrupt Captain Renault has a beguiling charm that is inseparable from his cynical amorality—as a dramatic character, that is, for we probably would not find him all that charming in real life (as the police chief of our own community, for example). But does he not make cynical amorality in the abstract seem rather cool? We naturally accede, rather too readily for moral health, to the proposition that "he's just like any other man only more so"—"a true democrat," at least "when it comes to women." And my kind of conservationist:

"How extravagant you are, throwing away women like that. Someday they may be scarce."[6]

However, it is with respect to the principal villain of the piece, Major Strasser, that the film manages a dramatic trick. For though Strasser is (as Lawler notes) the very embodiment of evil in the film, he is not himself a formidable villain for the hero to defeat—indeed, quite the contrary: he comes about as close to a Snidely Whiplash-type caricature as a serious film dares. But, of course, the sinister Strasser, along with Colonel Heinze and the other uniformed Germans, is merely a symbol for the real evil Rick opposes and outwits: Nazi Germany, formidable villainy writ enormous. Thus, while the political perspective of *Casablanca* is every bit as unsubtle as almost everything else that came out of Hollywood in those days, who could object to it? And compared with most of what comes out of Hollywood these days (which is typically just as ham fisted), they are infinitely preferable.

This points to the other platonic criticisms of dramatic art: its appealing primarily to the passions and its superficiality. Whereas, what the poet (maker) offers is a mere imitation of the mere appearance of reality, we are apt to be beguiled into regarding it as a source of knowledge and understanding—and the more realistically it creates the appearance, the more readily do we fall for it, as if we were actual eye- and ear-witnesses of the events portrayed. And this is most emphatically the case if it fits with what we already believe (or wish to believe), that being for the most part what determines our emotional reactions. On this basis, one may explain both the banality and the appeal of *Casablanca*. Indeed, Lawler puts it in a nutshell: "we can hardly say that the film challenges the American viewer much." The film is in virtually every respect a ratification of things we Americans want to believe about ourselves, about our supposed rugged individualism, about an underlying patriotism and commitment to what we know is right, about our tolerance for human diversity, about the superiority of our ingenuity and practicality (Americans know, or can figure out, how to get the job done), that America's fundamental principles of liberty and equality are universal, that accordingly America is the land of promise. The strength of character we admire in Rick is American strength of American character, and its all the more admirable and American for his not flaunting it. So what if brown-eyed "Richard Blaine, American" for some "vague" reason "cannot return to his country." We're all pretty sure that whatever the real reason, it actually does him credit. It's certainly not because he absconded with the church funds; and if it's because he ran off with some senator's wife, it would only prove that American women prefer the kind of real man who would run guns to Ethiopia and kill any man who tried to stop him. Rick's egalitarianism is of a discriminating sort, for he treats people in accord with their natural deserts, not their conventional status. And we see that, despite his professed indifference to everyone else's fate, he is respected and trusted throughout Casablancan society, from its top crime lord to its street vendors. The establishment he runs, like the America it is named after, is pluralistic, a haven of freedom, where all kinds of people (including even nonviolent petty criminals, such as the pickpocket) can pursue their own happiness as best they can, gambling for large stakes or small.

Casablanca is a virtual paradigm for stylized, romanticized fantasy, ratifying the natural appeal of self-sufficiency, including moral self-sufficiency, while at the same time validating the distinctly modern valuation of romantic love. It exploits in its necessarily modest way something of the intuitive appeal of whatever makes for an enduring myth. This is no criticism in my book. That the film has no philosophical pretensions is very much to its credit. Rarely, in my experience, do movies that have such pretensions bear up under competent scrutiny—as coherent wholes, that is, however thought-provoking or insightful may be some of their parts. *Casablanca* does well what a good movie can do in the course of entertaining us: ratify our better beliefs, while gently prodding us to reform views that do not do us credit, perhaps even slightly shaming us in the privacy of each person's own conscience for preaching what we don't sufficiently practice. The decency and loyalty of Sam toward Rick, and of Rick toward Sam, the confidential cordiality of their relationship, is perhaps the best illustration of this. And its perfect ending reminds us of our natural longing for something higher than mere personal safety and comfort, ultimately for virtue and nobility.

In earlier questioning the profundity of even the best movies, I rhetorically dismissed the possibility of divine inspiration by one or another Muse. And yet, a movie such as *Casablanca* that, despite the semichaotic way it was made, turns out to have such integrity—aesthetic, moral, intellectual—begs to be explained. And invoking something akin to Muse-ical inspiration may well be required. As we know from the various testimonial and documentary accounts of its making (which Paul Cantor has so ably summarized), what became the finished story most emphatically did not guide the production team from start to finish. Various gambits would be tried, then discarded, until they got the one that seemed right. Neither the considered idea nor its acceptance or rejection was the result of any logical process—at least none that we understand or probably ever will. As a philosopher once observed, ideas come when they want to, not upon command; and similarly, the recognition of the right one when actually confronted with it just happens—it's not something one does. Given the profound mystery of the inspiration and recognition at the heart of artistic creativity, it makes as much sense to attribute it to daemonic possession as to electrical currents in the brain (much more sense, actually).

However, a further factor that may enhance the apparent quality of a particular film might be called audience inspiration. That is, some (even most) of the deeper significance and insight one attributes to the film may actually be a product of one's own interpretive efforts—ascription rather than discovery, the viewer investing it with meaning(s) that never occurred to its makers. In such a case, rather than the theatrical experience being simply the result of its makers' inspiration, it makes poets of its viewers, inspiring them to an act of creation, perhaps superior to that achieved by the film's ostensible creators. I suspect that the makers of *The Usual Suspects*, with all of its unresolved (and, per hypothesis, irresolvable) ambiguities, intended to exploit this natural human propensity to presume meaningfulness, thus to look for it, and even unwittingly to invent it where absent. They would hardly be the first, and have no chance of being the last, to do so. After all, recognition of this phenomenon with respect to poetry— that its apparent profundity, its wisdom, may be a function of its ambiguity, which allows each member of its audience to make of it what he or she will, usually something already believed to be wise—is quite ancient. In fact, Plato has his Socrates suggest that this sort of thing is more the rule than the exception.

Socrates speaks of it in the course of his rather offensive defense of himself when finally brought to trial for not believing in the Athens's gods and for corrupting its youth. Explaining how he became so unpopular with so many people, he in effect blames the Delphic Oracle. Its officiating Pythia, having pronounced that "no one was wiser" than he, he claims he was puzzled rather than flattered by the notion, because it seemed so very unlikely, ignorant as he knew himself to be.[7] Thus, he set out to investigate the matter, presuming he would have no difficulty refuting the claim by finding someone wiser. He tells of examining three groups of people that are reputed to be wise—politicians, poets, and technical specialists—finding in each case that while the individuals examined did indeed think themselves wise, discussion revealed that they did not actually know what they presumed they did. So, eventually he concluded that the Oracle was right: that in his self-conscious ignorance he was, on balance, wiser than those who believed that they had knowledge of the most important things but in fact did not. Needless to add, exposing these intellectual pretensions neither earned him the gratitude of those he examined, nor of their many admirers.

His account of examining the various kinds of poets, however, is especially pertinent here. He says that in each case he chose those works in which it seemed the poet had invested the most effort and then questioned him thoroughly on what he meant. And, ashamed though he is to have to say it, the truth is, "Almost everyone present, so to speak, would have spoken better than the poets did about the poetry that they themselves had made." Thus, he concluded that, since the poets say "many noble [or, beautiful, fine; *kala*] things," and yet "know nothing of what they speak," they make their poems then not out of wisdom, "but by some nature and while god inspired [*enthousiazontes*], like the diviners and oracle-givers."[8] Socrates does not elaborate on who "those present" were, nor on how or why what they would have to say about the poet's work was better—nor does he explain what is perhaps most intriguing: why he was ashamed to tell the truth about the poets (he confessed no shame in speaking about the ignorance of the politicians and the technical artisans). Was it simply because the poets of his and earlier days were the primary source for his fellows' conceptions of the gods and their ways (and he *is* on trial for not believing)? That he is ashamed of the basis of Greek religion?

Or is there more reason for shame? For the influence of the poets was not confined to religious matters. Then, as now, most people got much of their general view of the world and how it works, of the order of importance of things, especially their understanding of the different kinds of people and how they fare, of what is admirable and what loathsome (what today are summarily referred to as people's values) from the poetry that constituted so-called popular culture.[9] Now, if the most popular makers of popular culture—whose success doubtless has more to do with the skills and efforts they devote to their making, than to the time and labor they expend in deepening their understanding of that about which they make—are actually ignoramuses, it would be embarrassing to have to point this out, especially to the very people who rely on them for their own general understanding. Nor would it be all that surprising if certain individuals who were more experienced with real life than with writing poems (or making mov- ies) were able to interpret more intelligently a particular drama than could the dramatist who is merely imitating (with great skill) the surface of things he does not understand.

Precisely because popular culture has such widespread moral and political effects it is certainly worthy of serious attention by people capable of analyzing these effects and how they are achieved, especially of what popularly succeeds with the general populace, most especially with young people, and what the con- sequences are. The issue is not primarily that of high-brow versus low-brow— though Gresham's law seems as pertinent to culture (and journalism) as it does to finance. But, as the persistent charm of *Casablanca* proves, popular enter- tainment need not be high-brow to be morally and politically wholesome, even edifying (whereas fare aimed at a cultural elite can be, morally speaking, so much sophisticated sewage). From what I see and hear of the state of it today, Socrates' case for the intelligent censorship of pop culture (such as was in place when *Casablanca* and a host of other fine films were made) is easily confirmed. Who other than a natural fool could believe that the cumulative effect of the bulk of visual entertainment to which young people currently subject themselves (including professional sports and pseudo-sports, news, and pseudo-news, video games and internet browsing, as well as movies and television) is wholesome, shaping them into responsible citizens and decent human beings? Not even those who produce this steady diet of witty insolence, slick pornography, celebrations of hedonism, and spectacular violence are audacious enough to claim that it ac- tually improves people—that this tasty junk food for the soul is actually good for those who gourmandize on it. But like big tobacco's defense of their product, they justify how they pursue big money with hypocritical protestations that there is no conclusive proof that it does harm. In neither case are these makers apt to cease and desist because of appeals to their conscience. And they can, quite cor- rectly, cite the survival demands of the free market. Still, a polity need not be ruled by its economy; it can establish the terms upon which its makers pursue money. Everyone involved in the making of *Casablanca* was concerned with its being a commercial success.

However, whether it is practically possible to restore wholesomeness to popular culture through a moderate censorship once the taste of a democracy's populace has been corrupted is doubtful. Sadly, Rousseau may be right, that

It is useless to draw a distinction between a nation's morals and the objects of its esteem; for all this follows from the same principle and necessarily con-verges. Among all peoples of the world, not nature but opinion determines the choice of their pleasures. Reform men's opinions and their morals will be puri-fied of themselves. One always loves what is fine or what one finds to be so, but it is in this judgment that one is mistaken; hence it is this judgment that has to be regulated. Whoever judges morals judges honor, and whoever judges honor takes opinion as his law.

A people's opinions arise from its constitution; although law does not regulate morals, legislation does give rise to them; when legislation weakens, morals degenerate; but by then the Censor's judgment will fail to do what the force of laws has failed to do.

It follows that the Censorship can be useful in preserving morals, never in restoring them. Establish Censors while the laws are in their vigor; once they have lost it, all is hopeless....[10]

If Socrates was ashamed to speak the truth about what the dialectic between popular culture and people's beliefs and behavior had produced in the democ-racy of his day, what does one suppose he would think of ours now? Perhaps this also contributes to the charm *Casablanca* has for me: it carries me back to a time when ours was better. The technology of movie making was far cruder and the resources skimpier, but morally speaking, "there's just no comparison."

In sum, I view films as it turns out most of the other contributors to this volume seem to also. In teaching, I sometimes find movies a convenient source of examples and illustrations for general points I wish to make. And the better films provide me opportunities for the exercise of my own analytic powers, as I assess what the makers got right and what wrong in the slice of reality they por-trayed. Occasionally a movie may further my self-knowledge, should a particu-lar film prompt me to examine and thereby perhaps better understand a peculiar reaction it provoked, aesthetic, moral, or whatever. But as teachers about reality, I just can't take movies seriously. And so I find this volume of essays most aptly named: political philosophy *comes* to Rick's—it's not found there.

NOTES

1. Plato, *Republic*, 595a; cf., 357a, 419a, 449c.

2. Plato, *Republic*, 607b.

3. As I have argued in *Of Philosophers and Kings: Political Philosophy in Shakespeare's* Macbeth *and* King Lear (Toronto: University of Toronto Press, 2001), 251-68.

4. Plato, *Republic*, 571b-d, 572d-573c, 577a.

5. Peter Augustine Lawler, Chapter 5, 71, 73.

6. All quotes from *Casablanca* can found at: http://www.geocities.com/classicmoviescripts/script/casablanca.pdf.

7. Plato, *Apology of Socrates* 21a. Translation of the *Apology* based on that of Thomas G. West and Grace Starry West in *Four Texts on Socrates* (Ithaca: Cornell University Press, 1984).

8. Plato, *Apology of Socrates* 22b-c.

9. This term has lost most of its original meaning, which was to nurture—to cultivate—something in accordance with its nature, so as to bring that nature to it proper fulfillment—ideally, to perfect it. By that standard, there would be comparatively few societies whose way of life might plausibly be judged a culture. Today's use of the term, however, is far more democratic, essentially egalitarian. Every way of life, however it shapes people, is a culture. And it's that usage that figures in the notion of pop culture, meaning that which predominately shapes most people in a given society and—for better or worse—touches virtually everyone in our society.

10. Jean Jacques Rousseau, *Of the Social Contract*, Book 4, Chapter 7 (Of Censorship) in *The Social Contract and Other Later Political Writings*, trans. Victor Gourevitch (Cambridge: Cambridge University Press, 1997), 141.

Cast and Credits of *Casablanca*

- ❖ Director – Michael Curtiz
- ❖ Producer – Hal B. Wallis for Warner Brothers
- ❖ Screenplay – Julius Epstein, Philip Epstein, and Howard Koch (Casey Robinson's contributions were not credited), based on Murray Burnett and Joan Alison's 1940 play *Everybody Goes Rick's* changed to *Everybody Comes to Rick's*
- ❖ Cinematography – Arthur Edeson
- ❖ Music – Max Steiner, with Herman Hupfeld's 1931 "As Time Goes By"
- ❖ Editor – Owen Marks
- ❖ Costumes – Orry-Kelly

CAST:

- ❖ Humphrey Bogart – Rick Blaine
- ❖ Ingrid Bergman – Ilsa Lund
- ❖ Paul Henreid – Victor Laszlo
- ❖ Claude Rains – Captain Louis Renault
- ❖ Conrad Veidt – Major Heinrich Strasser
- ❖ Sydney Greenstreet – Signor Ferrari
- ❖ Peter Lorre – Guillermo Ugarte
- ❖ (Arthur) Dooley Wilson – Sam (the piano was played off stage by Elliot Carpenter)
- ❖ S. Z. "Cuddles" Sakall – Carl
- ❖ Madeleine LeBeau – Yvonne
- ❖ Joy Page – Annina Brandel
- ❖ Helmut Dantine – Jan Brandel
- ❖ John Qualen – Berger
- ❖ Leonid Kinskey – Sascha
- ❖ Curt Bois – the "dark European" pickpocket
- ❖ Marcel Dalio – Emil
- ❖ Corinna Mura – Andrea
- ❖ Ludwig Stössel – Mr. Leuchtag
- ❖ Ilka Grüning – Mrs. Leuchtag
- ❖ Frank Puglia – Arab street vendor in the bazaar
- ❖ Dan Seymour – Abdul, doorman at Rick's Café Américain

- ❖ Oliver Prickett (Oliver Blake) – Blue Parrot waiter
- ❖ Gregory Gay – German banker refused entry to Rick's Café Américain
- ❖ George Dee – Lieutenant Casselle
- ❖ Richard Ryen – Colonel Heinz, German consul
- ❖ Alberto Morin – Captain Tonelli

ACADEMY AWARDS:

- ❖ Winner – Best Picture, Warner Brothers
- ❖ Winner – Best Director, Michael Curtiz
- ❖ Winner – Writing (screenplay), Julius Epstein, Philip Epstein, and Howard Koch
- ❖ Nomination – Best Actor, Humphrey Bogart
- ❖ Nomination – Best Supporting Actor, Claude Rains
- ❖ Nominations – Cinematography
- ❖ Nominations – Score
- ❖ Nominations – Editing

INDEX

ABOUT THE CONTRIBUTORS

Paul A. Cantor is Clifton Waller Barrett Professor of English at the University of Virginia. He is author of several essays on popular culture and *Gilligan Unbound: Pop Culture in the Age of Globalization* (Rowman & Littlefield, 2001).

Ralph S. Hattox is William W. Elliott Professor of History at Hampden-Sydney College in Virginia. A specialist in Near Eastern and Eastern Mediterranean history, Dr. Hattox is author of *Coffee and Coffeehouses: The Medieval Origins of a Social Beverage*. He has also written several articles on Levantine diplomacy in the late Middle Ages and is currently completing work on the manuscript of a book on the same subject.

Michael Palmer is professor of political science and on the faculty of the Honors College at the University of Maine. He is author of *Love of Glory and the Common Good: Aspects of the Political Thought of Thucydides* (1992) and contributing co-editor, with Thomas L. Pangle, of *Political Philosophy and the Human Soul: Essays in Memory of Allan Bloom* (1995), both published by Rowman and Littlefield. His most recent book, a collection of his published articles and reviews from scholarly journals over two decades, together with a new chapter interpreting Machiavelli's *Prince*, is *Masters and Slaves: Revisioned Essays in Political Philosophy* (Lexington Books, 2001).

Mary P. Nichols is professor and chair of Political Science at Baylor University in Waco, Texas. She is author of numerous articles in the history of political thought, politics and literature, and politics and film. Her books include *Socrates and the Political Community: An Ancient Debate* (1987), *Citizens and Statesmen: A Study of Aristotle's Politics* (Rowman and Littlefield, 1992); and *Reconstructing Woody: Art, Love, and Life in the Films of Woody Allen* (Rowman and Littlefield, 1998).

Peter Augustine Lawler is Dana Professor of Government at Berry College. He is author or editor of nine books, including *Aliens in America: The Strange Truth about Our Souls*. He is executive editor the scholarly quarterly *Perspectives on Political Science* and a of member of the President's Council on Bioethics.

James F. Pontuso is William W. Elliott Professor of Political Science at Hampden-Sydney College in Virginia. He is author of *Václav Havel: Civic Responsibility in the Postmodern Age* (Rowman & Littlefield, 2004), *Assault on Ideology: Solzhenitsyn's Political Thought* (Lexington Books, 2004), and coauthor with Roger Barrus et al. of *The Deconstitutionalization of America: The Forgotten Frailties of Democratic Rule* (Lexington Books, 2004).

Nivedita N. Bagchi is a doctoral student in the Politics Department at the University of Virginia.

David M. Nichols associate professor at Baylor University in Waco, Texas, teaches in the Honors College and Department of Political Science. His primary fields of research and teaching are American politics, constitutional law, and American political thought. His books include *The Myth of the Modern Presidency* (1994) and *Readings in American Government* 7th ed., (2004).

Paul Peterson is professor in the Department of Politics at Coastal Carolina University in Conway, South Carolina. He is the author of numerous articles, essays, and reviews on American politics, American political thought, and popular culture.

Kenneth De Luca is visiting assistant professor in the Departments of Political Science and Western Culture at Hampden-Sydney College in Virginia. He is author of *Aristophanes' Male and Female Revolutions* (Lexington Books, 2005).

Leon Harold Craig is professor of political science at the University of Alberta, Edmonton, Canada. He is author of *The War Lover: A Study of Plato's Republic* (1994) and *Of Philosophers and Kings: Political Philosophy in Shakespeare's MACBETH and KING LEAR* (2001).